# Lasting Happiness

## A GUIDE FOR TEENS AND YOUNG ADULTS

## Dr. Doug Carnine

with Mary Opalenik and Christina Cox, M.Ed.

Lasting Happiness: A Guide for Teens and Young Adults
Dr. Doug Carnine with Mary Opalenik and Christina Cox

© 2022 Choose Kindness Foundation

Published by Choose Kindness Foundation
Eugene, Oregon

Book design and layout by Natalie Conaway
Digital chapter illustrations by Alyson Curtis | alysondesign.com

First Edition
ISBN: 978-8-9855470-0-9

Library of Congress Control Number: 2022900035

Any resources and website addresses are provided for reader convenience and were current at the time of publication Report broken links to admin@choosekindnessfoundation.info.

This book is dedicated to all those who treat themselves
and others with mindful kindness.

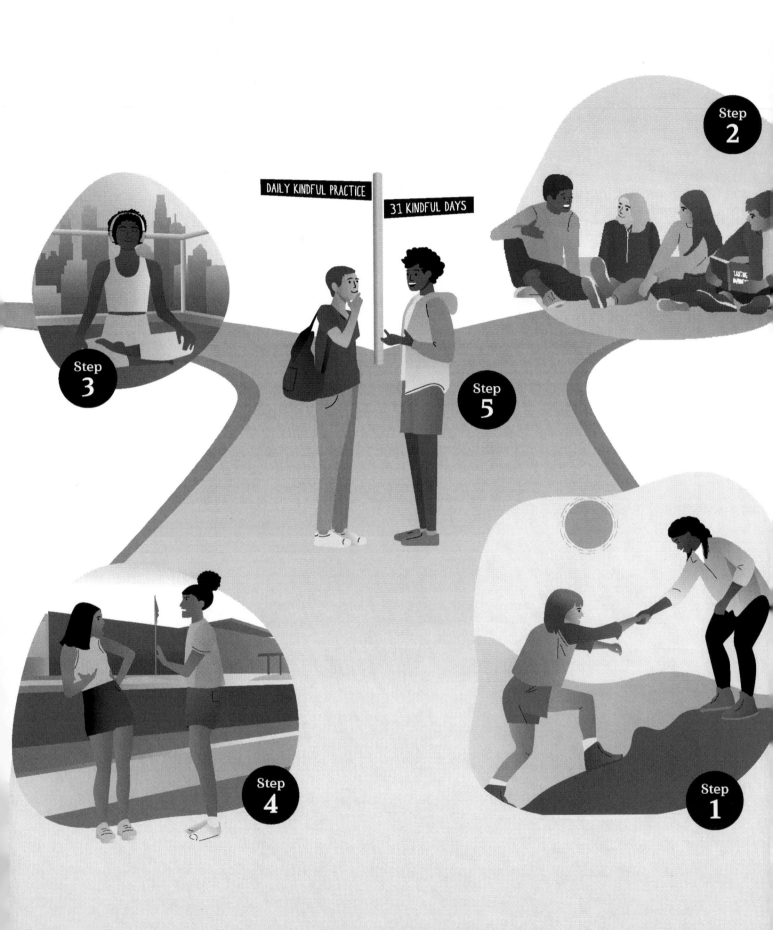

# Contents

# About the Authors

## Doug Carnine

Doug Carnine, professor emeritus at the University of Oregon and president of the Choose Kindness Foundation, spent the first 20 years of his career focused on improving the achievement of K–12 students who too often fail in school: children of poverty, limited English speakers, and students with disabilities. His scholarly works have been cited in over 5,000 books and journals from around the world. He spent the next 12 years of his career leading a campaign to increase the importance of evidence in education decision-making. This campaign involved working with business and government groups, ranging from large cities like Los Angeles to the U.S. Congress and U.S. Department of Education. He received a presidential appointment, with Senate confirmation, to the National Institute for Literacy Advisory Board and later received the Lifetime Achievement Award from the Council for Exceptional Children. For the past 12 years he has focused on mindful kindness, first coordinating the all-volunteer Spreading Kindness Campaign for Lane County, Oregon, and then launching the multimillion-dollar Choose Kindness Foundation that works with schools, businesses, prisons, and social service agencies across the United States.

Doug was fortunate to be joined in adapting his book *How Love Wins* to create *Lasting Happiness: A Guide for Teens and Young Adults* by two very talented and dedicated educators, Mary Opalenik and Christina Cox. On the next page are descriptions they wrote about why they wanted to contribute to this book.

## Mary Opalenik

As a high school teacher who has taught in both public schools in Oregon and private international schools, I've spent 40 years with young people. As rewarding as academic teaching can be, it's the community projects that brought youth into contact with their communities that mattered most. There were projects such as rebuilding a girls' school in a remote Jordanian village, setting up garbage collection and sanitation for the poor in an urban slum in India, and reading poetry to soldiers on the streets of Beirut during a time of extreme political unrest. These projects could easily be labeled kindness projects or even happiness projects because they allowed for an expression of what is the best in human nature—compassion that grows from empathy. Working with Doug Carnine to reconfigure his book originally written for adults, *How Love Wins*, for an audience of youth holds the same sense of significance for me as those community projects did—all are intended to bring joy and improve well-being. The angle is slightly different in this book in that it is a how-to book addressing the fact that happiness is a state of being in short supply in an era when youth are highly anxious, depressed, and generally seeking ways to be happy. Mindful kindness is at the heart of this book, and kindness never exists in a vacuum: It exists in relationship with others.

## Christina Cox

Having spent more than half my life in schools working as a teacher and administrator, I've experienced immense joy and a sense of accomplishment. But I've also encountered innumerable youth facing challenges—depression, anxiety, abuse—that they've become accustomed to as part of their everyday lives. When I picked up Doug's first book on kindfulness, *How Love Wins*, at a training for educators, I wasn't exactly sure what to expect. In fact, it was the excerpts from prisoner letters at the Tucker Maximum Security Unit that initially piqued my interest. As I read the letters and Doug's advice on how to weave mindful kindness into our everyday lives, it resonated with me. More importantly, I believed it could resonate with the very youth I work with, addressing common problems they routinely face. So, when Doug approached me about the possibility of collaborating on a project based on his book but focused on youth, I jumped at the opportunity to bring my areas of expertise to the table. I believe anyone—especially youth—can benefit from integrating mindful kindness into their daily lives, and this book will show you how.

# Preface

To talk about lasting happiness in the midst of COVID-19, racial tensions, and political upheaval might seem strange. Is it something that can even be achieved? However, we need to understand that there are two types of happiness. One focuses on self-gratification while the other focuses on finding purpose and meaning in our lives. This book is designed to help you develop that sense of purpose and meaning, and experience the happiness that results from it, while lessening anxiety and other negative emotions. I was inspired to write this book after learning about the widespread and deep unhappiness of today's youth. A pediatrician friend recently shared her concerns about the mental health of her young patients—kids who spend hours glued to their devices late into the night and spend their days exhausted at school. Of course, the COVID-19 pandemic and everything that has come with it—lockdowns, distance learning mixed with in-person learning, tension at home, stressed-out parents, and worries about their own and their family's safety—have only added to the pressures faced by young people today. Unfortunately, young people were under unusually high levels of stress even before the alarming events of 2020 and 2021.

I've meditated and practiced mindfulness for more than 40 years, and I know its benefits firsthand. But it wasn't until I began corresponding with a man named Roy Tester that I started to understand how mindfulness and kindness were closely intertwined. Who was this wise teacher who introduced me to the life-changing power of mindful kindness? He was a prisoner—a convicted murderer serving a life sentence for killing his parents.

Roy was, and is, an inmate at the Tucker Unit, a notoriously violent maximum-security prison in Arkansas, sometimes known as Tucker Max. I first heard from Roy because he was looking for someone to answer his questions about Buddhism. As a lay minister at the Eugene Buddhist priory, I was happy to reply. Soon we became pen pals, writing letters back and forth. While I shared teaching and advice about meditation, Roy wrote about his life in prison and the experiences that led him to commit his horrific crime.

To say that Roy had a traumatic life barely explains his life experiences. He was beaten and sexually abused by his father and his father's friends while his mother did nothing to protect him. He became addicted to drugs and left home at an early age. He got involved in a life of crime, where violence was considered normal. Then one day, while he was high on drugs, he went home, confronted his parents, and killed them. He was arrested a few days later and sentenced to life in prison without the possibility of parole.

It was in prison that Roy began to change his life. He discovered Buddhism and began practicing meditation. He found me and started asking questions about his practice. Together, we began exploring the connection between mindfulness and kindness. Roy began taking on "kindness projects"—small acts of selflessness that made life better for the people around him. With my financial support, Roy began buying food and needed supplies to lift up his fellow prisoners. On one occasion, he wrote to me about how he fixed up a pair of used tennis shoes for an older gentleman nicknamed "Old Man Cornbread":

> *He has no one, no family that cares enough to send a mere postcard. He loves to walk. The shoes the state furnishes are cheap canvas slip-ons that wear out quickly. We bought a used pair of tennis shoes for $7 and after I cleaned them up and traded a dollar for a pair of insoles, we gave them to*

*Old Man Cornbread. I thought he was going to cry. He put them on right then and it was like he was walking on air. He had a big smile all over his face and was bouncing with every step.*

Roy gradually came to recognize that practicing kindness and mindfulness would help him forgive himself for his terrible crime. He realized that, by finding this forgiveness, he would be able to help others, both inmates and guards. Finally, by doing this, he would gain some degree of happiness and peace, even within the harsh environment of Tucker Max.

Writing to Roy helped me see how the practice of mindful kindness, or *kindfulness*, could benefit everyone—not just people like me. I have had a privileged life of success, education, personal freedom, and family support. But what about those who lack opportunity, suffer terrible abuse, are rejected by society, and live with the horror of their own crimes? Truly, I realized, if Roy could change his life with mindful kindness, so could anyone.

Through Roy, I met other prisoners and began working with them as well. I wrote to men facing many tough situations, including a brain tumor, a prison gang attack, family betrayal, medical abuse, and harsh punishments for minor rule violations. I was amazed by the way each man in his own way overcame these setbacks through mindfulness and the practice of kindness. These men came from different faith traditions, such as Buddhism, Christianity, Islam, and no religion at all. Over time, I came to see these men not only as fellow human beings and students, but also as peers and teachers. Corresponding with these prisoners showed me how the practice of mindful kindness can bring light, transformation, and a sense of purpose even in the darkest of places.

I wrote about my experience working with these prisoners and shared excerpts from our letters in my book, *Saint Badass: Personal Transcendence in Tucker Max Hell*. I followed this up with *How Love Wins*, a how-to book about developing mindful kindness that could be used by prisoners and privileged people alike. This book, *Lasting Happiness*, comes in response to the deep and widespread mental health challenges faced by young people today. With this book, I hope to offer a path away from harmful and painful habits and point the way to the kind habits needed for a happy, meaningful, and healthy life.

Doug Carnine
Eugene, Oregon
June 1, 2021

## A NOTE ABOUT CONTENT

Chapters in this book sometimes mention difficult subjects. If you find yourself emotionally activated by any content or exercise in this book, it may help to process these feelings with someone. Please seek support from your support network or community, such as a counselor, therapist, peer support, pastor, or trusted friend or mentor.

# Acknowledgments

Over a 15-year period, many individuals have made invaluable contributions to the development of this book, the third in a series. The first book was *Saint Badass: Personal Transformation in Tucker Max Hell.* The second book was *How Love Wins.* These are my acknowledgments for *Lasting Happiness.* I am grateful to my wife, Linda, who has supported me in too many ways to list (as have my daughters, Leah and Berkley). Jerry Silbert has been a colleague on many projects for over 45 years and made general and specific suggestions on the four earlier versions of this book.

Because this is an us-help book, it is very important that it does provide help. For that reason we first created a field-test version to use with a variety of youth from around the country. This field-test version provided extensive feedback that allowed us to create this 2022 version you are now reading. For the field-test version, I would like to thank Ashly Cupit for editing, design, and production and Terrie Chrones for the illustrations.

For this 2022 version I would like to thank the Ancora Publishing team: Matt Sprick, CEO; Sara Ferris, lead editor; and Natalie Conaway, lead designer. Illustrations are by Alyson Curtis.

I would like to thank the following people for their contributions and feedback on this book:

Teenagers: Walker Sheidow, the leadership students in Rhiannon Boettcher's high school class, Finnian Wolf, Victor Dossin, Maren Amberg, Payton Cox, and Shaylen Gallagher

Young adults: Alison Pfaff, Taylor VanRysselberghe, Elliot G. Boodhan, Saralyn Collins, Jory Christiansen, Isabel Solano, Molly Murphy, and Haley Lavris

Professionals: Emma Avalos, Paulina Romo Villaseñor, Donna Dwiggins, Marcy Stein, Tee Garvin, Gabi Colton, Dr. Mark Kohen, Pat Fisher, Jody Bothe, River, Marty Sheehan, Phyllis Goldman, Stan Paine, Alex Granzin, Morgan Davis, Ted Adams, Dylan Hausman, and Betty Barnett

Christina Cox wants to acknowledge her husband, Travis, and her two children, Payton and Tyler.

# Introduction

The purpose of this workbook is to help teens and young adults:

- Develop a sense of purpose and meaning, and experience happiness as a result.
- Use mindfulness and meditation to break unkind habits and build kinder ones that benefit ourselves and others.
- Act with kindness by being friendly, offering help, showing appreciation, and reaching out to those in need.
- Share with others the key message about the value of mindful kindness.
- Live a happy, healthy, and meaningful life through close, healthy, and caring relationships.

The goals of this workbook are simple to understand but challenging to accomplish. Science tells us that being kind and paying attention to others builds stronger relationships. Being kind and paying attention to others even makes us happier in the long run. It is not difficult to understand that what the scientists say is important if we are to be happy. But changing how we interact with others can sometimes seem impossible. This is especially true because many teens and youth are experiencing high levels of stress, with causes ranging from lacking enough close, caring relationships to anxiety over the climate crisis. The resulting stress and depression make it even harder to break unkind habits and build new kind habits.

The truth is that everyone can learn to be mindfully kind. And with practice, treating yourself and others with mindful kindness can change your life. This workbook, *Lasting Happiness: A Guide For Teens and Young Adults*, offers such a plan. Step by step, it leads you through skills and ideas critical in changing your life for the better. Making a significant change in your life is not something to be done in an afternoon, but rather takes considerable time and effort. Making these changes is similar to building a house. We need to go through several steps, one at a time—pour a foundation, construct walls, put on a roof, install the electrical circuits and fixtures, etc.—before we can finally enjoy our new house.

Below are the steps used in this workbook. Each step teaches important skills for building happiness in your life. When you incorporate these skills into your life daily, you can reduce stress and anxiety, enjoy life more, and feel more energetic.

**Step 1: Prepare for Lasting Happiness**
*Create a foundation.*

- Chapter 1 explains the relevance of mindfulness and kindness to teenagers and young adults. Kindness is especially important in developing close, caring relationships, which are a key factor in bringing about a happy, healthy life.
- Chapter 2 presents the skills of action and character that are the building blocks for changing your life.

**Step 2: Build Kind Habits**
*Construct walls to support a house of kindness.*

- Chapter 3 gives examples and provides exercises to expand thinking about all the different ways to be kind.

- Chapter 4 guides you in how to build kind habits.

**Step 3: Train Your Mind**
*Put up a roof of mindfulness and meditation to keep out the cold unkindness and keep in the warm kindness.*

- Chapter 5 lays out practical ways to meditate and practice mindfulness in daily life.

- Chapter 6 explains what it means to be mindful. It then provides explanations and exercises to develop mindfulness practices with the senses of sight, hearing, smell, touch, and taste.

- Chapter 7 explains how mindful practices can be incorporated into daily activities, such as brushing your teeth, cleaning your clothes, eating, taking a coffee break, etc.

**Step 4: Deal with Unkind Habits**
*Install electrical circuits that conduct positive energy but prevent the flow of negative, unkind energy.*

- Chapter 8 assists you in recognizing unkind habits that hurt you and others. This type of energy blocks you from being more kind and developing close, caring relationships.

- Chapter 9 gives ways to break the unkind habits that are most damaging to a life of well-being.

- Chapter 10 focuses on several specific ways to cope with the unkind habits of others.

**Step 5: Take the Final Steps to Lasting Happiness**
*Add finishing touches that show all are welcome.*

- Chapter 11 prepares you to be resilient when hard times come, and they always do come.

- Chapter 12 explains how to make your house welcoming to others. Here you'll learn to extend the reach of your kindness to those seen as "different" because of race, language, economic status, and political or religious beliefs.

- Chapter 13 explains the importance of caring for yourself and serving others in the present moment, rather than worrying about the future or feeling bad about the past.

- Chapter 14 describes why and how to encourage others to act with mindful kindness.

- Chapter 15 offers two paths for making kindfulness a permanent part of your life.

- An afterword briefly describes the joy, contentment, and energy that come from living in a kindful manner.

Each chapter is constructed according to these principles of teaching that have been proven to be very effective in helping us learn:

- Introduce key ideas, with examples and exercises you can do on your own.

- Start with simple key ideas and build on them so you can take on more complex challenges.

- Complete exercises for each new key idea until you gain some sense of mastery in how to apply that idea in your daily life.

- Periodically go back to review earlier key ideas so they become mindfully kind habits that form a path to lasting happiness.

If you complete the exercises in this workbook, you'll end up with something as comfortable as a well-built house that you can enjoy with family and friends and feel secure in during stormy times.

# Prepare for Lasting Happiness

*Create a foundation.*

---

---

Scientific findings: 12
Real-world examples: 23
Opportunities to apply what you are learning: 19

## Teachings from the World Religions

Christianity: "Make a careful exploration of who you are and the work you have been given, and then sink yourself into that. Don't be impressed with yourself. Don't compare yourself with others. Each of you must take responsibility for doing the creative best you can with your own life." (MSG: Galatians 6:4-5)

Buddhism: "Drop by drop is the water pot filled. Likewise, the wise man, gathering it little by little, fills himself with good."

Confucianism: "It does not matter how slowly you go as long as you do not stop."

Islam: "Only those who are steadfast in patience, only those who are blessed with great righteousness, will attain to such goodness." (Quran, 41:35)

Native American: "The earth does not belong to man, man belongs to the earth. All things are connected like the blood that unites us all. Man did not weave the web of life, he is merely a strand in it. Whatever he does to the web, he does to himself." —Chief Seattle, chief of Duwamish and Suquamish tribes

Chapter 1

# Learn About Mindful Kindness—
# The Key to Lasting Happiness

*When you've seen beyond yourself,
then you may find peace of mind
is waiting there.*

The Beatles

We all experience moments of happiness and joy. It could be a sunny weekend spent with friends at the beach. Or playing with a dog in the park. These are fleeting moments—happiness sprinkled throughout the day. But what if we could extend and expand the moments of happiness until they become an enduring, long-lasting sense of well-being? This is what this chapter is about. The last two words of this chapter's title are "lasting happiness." We will learn how to develop long-lasting happiness by changing what we do, how we act, and how we think.

Researchers studied what makes people happy, not just at the moment but over their lifetime. It is not wealth, fame, popularity, success, or intelligence that gives us lasting happiness. It's close relationships. Researchers have found that **close relationships are what keep people happy throughout their lives**. In fact, they have found that close, caring, healthy relationships also protect people from life's disappointments and hardships.

Of course, lasting happiness does not mean constant happiness. Everyone has ups and downs, days when we feel happy and full, and days when we do not. The practices presented in this workbook can help prepare us for bad times as well as increase our good times.

This workbook will help you understand where true happiness comes from. Working through the exercises can help you develop the skills to find lasting happiness for yourself by learning kind habits that enable us to create and maintain close, caring, healthy relationships. You'll learn keys to happiness like being friendly, giving help, showing appreciation, and reaching out to those in serious need. In addition, you will learn to identify and weaken unkind habits that stand in the way of your happiness—habits such as lying, procrastinating, being inconsiderate, being irresponsible, blaming others, abusing drugs and alcohol, and lashing out in anger.

At this point, it is important to think about what caring, healthy relationships are. **Three types of relationships contribute to our happiness:**

1. The first type are healthy, intimate relationships with family, a partner/spouse, our closest friends, and elders. What does *intimate* or *intimacy* mean to you? The word *intimate* can mean different things in different situations. Intimacy can be emotional or physical. Having intimacy with your family, elders, and close friends means having relationships where there is a feeling of mutual caring and closeness. You feel safe to share things about yourself, and you know a lot about the other person. Physical intimacy provides a feeling of closeness through touch and occurs in all types of relationships. With a partner, it includes holding hands, hugging, kissing, and sexual contact. All human beings have a need for intimate relationships and usually spend a big part of their life seeking those relationships. When we feel a lack of intimacy in our lives, we sometimes look for it in the wrong relationships. Healthy, intimate relationships develop over time and require us to treat each other with respect and kindness.

2. The second type of relationship that contributes to our happiness are ones we experience with close acquaintances, such as friends, classmates, coworkers, neighbors, teachers, and coaches.

3. Relationships with members of a community organized around a common interest or culture are the third type that contribute to our happiness. These range from Video Game Clubs of America, to Al-Anon or Alateen, to being part of a sports team or church youth group.

Happiness is greatest when we have all three types of relationships.[1] What many people don't realize is that the foundation for all of these relationships is kindness. Four books—written by a former U.S. Surgeon

General, a psychiatrist, an investigative reporter, and a historian—have documented, from their different viewpoints, the importance of kindness in almost every aspect of our lives.*

---

**A Thank-You Note from a Reader of *Lasting Happiness***

An African American junior in high school was experiencing extreme difficulties at home and in school. Her family was homeless and living in an extremely difficult and at times violent situation. After completing half the book, she surprised her teacher with this note describing how reading the workbook and doing the exercises have been helpful. "I have been going through a lot lately in my life, and the book has really opened my eyes to see how toxic I have been to people I love and to myself . . . . With this book helping me realize that to love other people I have to love and treat myself well before I could treat my loved ones well, too, I am truly grateful for all the examples and Put into Practice exercises that I can open up about my past. Thank You."

---

## *Our Three Most Important Types of Relationships*

Do you have the three types of relationships that contribute to our happiness? Write with whom you have the relationships. (Note: Some of us may have many relationships. Some may have few.)

Intimate relationships _____

_____

Close relationships _____

_____

Community organizations _____

_____

---

* These four books are: Murthy, V. H. (2020). *Together: The Healing Power of Human Connection in a Sometimes Lonely World.* Harper Wave; Hari, J. (2018). *Lost Connections: Uncovering the Real Causes of Depression, and the Unexpected Solutions.* Bloomsbury USA; Harding, K. (2019). *The Rabbit Effect: Live Longer, Happier, and Healthier with the Groundbreaking Science of Kindness.* Atria Books; and Bergman, R. (2020). *Humankind: A Hopeful History.* Little, Brown, and Company.

# Kindness

Lasting happiness grows from extending our kindness to others. Many scientific studies have shown that being kind to others makes us happy. In one study, children younger than two expressed more happiness when they gave a treat to someone else than when they received a treat themselves. Even more interesting, the children were happier giving away their own treats—even though it reduced their own stash—than giving away treats that didn't belong to them.[2] Similar results have been found with adults around the world, and it's been shown that spending money on others gives people a bigger happiness boost than splurging on themselves.

### kindness

> The quality of being friendly, giving, and considerate. We act with kindness when we connect with others by offering help, being friendly, showing appreciation, and reaching out to those in serious need.

## — Key Idea —

Acting with kindness not only improves the quality of our relationships, but also contributes a great deal to our physical health, greater social acceptance, and prolonged feelings of happiness.* Kind actions have been shown to boost our immunity to disease. Compassion can also reduce feelings of pain, anger, and depression. Kind and compassionate acts produce positive energy and a feeling of interconnection with others.[3] Considerable research has shown a connection between happiness and physical health. One of the most remarkable research studies found that kindness is so powerful that women who are in a kind relationship heal more quickly from an experimenter-induced minor wound. Kindness can increase our sense of well-being.

Acts of kindness also lead to increased social acceptance. In a month-long research study, several hundred youths performed at least three acts of kindness per week and kept track of their actions in a journal. Another group visited three pleasant places each week and logged those visits. Both groups reported significantly increased feelings of happiness and satisfaction. But the study showed that the youths who performed acts of kindness also gained an average of 1.5 friends during the four-week period, while the "pleasant places" group didn't see the same benefit. This research shows that being kind to other people benefits the giver.[4] **By demonstrating kindness toward others, you too can have increased feelings of happiness and satisfaction. How does behaving with kindness make you feel?**

Researcher Sonja Lyubomirsky, author of *The How of Happiness*,[5] reported similar findings in young adults. She writes that people often think treating themselves to something special will make them happy. However, the results of her study led her to conclude that the opposite is often truer. When we choose instead to do something for someone else, it can result in greater feelings of happiness.[6] Those positive

---

* Yanping Li, a research scientist at the Harvard T. H. Chan School of Public Health, reported on how we benefit from kind habits we practice on ourselves: Eating a healthy diet, exercising regularly, keeping a healthy body weight, not drinking too much alcohol, and refraining from smoking added about 14 years of life expectancy for women and 12 years for men. Li, Y., Pan., A., Wang, D. D., Liu, X., Dhana, K., Franco, O. H., Kaptoge, S., Di Angelantonio, E., Stampfer, M., Willett, W. C., & Hu, F. B. (2018). Impact of healthy lifestyle factors on life expectancies in the U.S. population. *Circulation, 138*(4) :e75. Retrieved from https://pubmed.ncbi.nlm.nih.gov/29712712/

feelings come from chemicals called neurotransmitters, such as oxytocin, serotonin, and dopamine, which your brain produces as a kind of reward for giving and receiving kindness.†

# How to Use This Workbook

Throughout this workbook we'll show how kindness can improve your relationships. We'll give you exercises you can do to practice these ideas. We call these exercises *Put into Practice*. All of the Put into Practice exercises are linked to specific key ideas in the workbook. You might want to read an entire chapter, then go back and reread it and do the exercises as you go through it a second time. You can also break a chapter into shorter parts. If you try to read an entire chapter and do all of the exercises at one time, you may become overwhelmed. Take your time to find the best way for you to make your way through this workbook.

Some exercises will ask you to write about your thoughts or experiences, either at the time you are reading a chapter or later after you take action over a period of time. You will write about the activities you do over a period of time in the Journal at the back of this workbook. The workbook is designed so that you can easily keep track of exercises you have completed and exercises you are still working on. How much you will benefit from this workbook depends on how much effort you put into these Put into Practice exercises.

You will also be asked to practice your breathing, meditation, and body awareness—these are very important exercises. These skills are the building blocks for mindfulness. **In order to be truly kind, we need to be aware of our own needs and the needs of others. Mindfulness is how we can develop that awareness.**

Remember, it takes lots of effort and time to change habits, but doing so pays off. So, take the time to do the exercises that speak to you. No matter what speed you go through the workbook, you will benefit from knowing more about using mindfulness to be more kind and, as a result, feel that your life is fuller and more meaningful.

## PUT INTO **Practice**

Here is the first Put into Practice exercise: Think of a time that you received a kindness that meant a lot to you. Describe how you felt.

_____

Think of a time that you were kind in a way that deeply affected the other person. Describe how you felt.

_____

Make a list of a few people to whom you would like to show more kindness. You might include family members, friends, elders, teachers, neighbors, even a clerk at a local

---

† Even though the brain matures slowly until the mid to late 30s, the good news is that we are learning during that time. The attraction to newness and novelty, risk-taking, and peer pressure can be redirected to increase kindness in new and dramatic ways, activating more of the feel-good chemicals. These positive changes are possible because of neuroplasticity—which means the brain can change based on a person's beliefs and experiences in the world. As the brain matures, many people increase their proficiency with skills such as putting things in perspective, building self-confidence, and realizing that negative emotions do not need to be consuming. With these skills, the challenges of the 20s decline over time, and happiness increases.

convenience store. Next to each person's name describe a kindness you might show to that person. For example, you can compliment a neighbor on their garden, ask a sales clerk how their day is going, spend time learning family history with Grandma, or do a household chore without being asked.

| Person | Kind Action |
| --- | --- |
| _____ | _____ |
| _____ | _____ |
| _____ | _____ |
| _____ | _____ |

## Unanticipated Responses to Kindness

While kindness seems simple, the response to our kindness might not always be the response we anticipated. Sometimes, we may think what we are doing is kind, but the recipient of our action may be suspicious of our actions, or even resentful. The person may not be willing to receive our acts of kindness. As we learn more about mindfulness, we will be able to better understand the responses of others to our attempts at kindness and learn how to respond to others when our kindness isn't well received.

### EXAMPLE

The response was prejudice. A Latinx community leader tried to act with kindness when approached at a local market.

*I was buying apples at a local farm to dry in a food dehydrator. A lady approached me to ask what I was going to do with all the apples. I very enthusiastically gave her the explanation of how I cut and dry the apples. Then she asked me where I was from and then continued to say in a condescending tone that she was from Washington, D.C. She explained to me that it was the capital of the United States. I felt anger and did not want to continue the conversation with her. My initial desire and enthusiasm to help her turned into an aggression that she did not realize was happening.*

### EXAMPLE

The response was ridicule. One of the prisoners Doug mentors asked other prisoners to be kind with the stimulus checks they received.

*I urged them to give a small portion of it to helping someone else. You can't imagine the response. I have been called a fool, stupid, full of shit, naive, ignorant, and a few other choice words.*

### EXAMPLE

The response was violence. A teacher reported what happened to a student of color when he was working after school to help his family with expenses.

*One of our students was making deliveries and had to ask for directions. He got beat up just by asking directions from a group of white males.*

# Mindfulness: Being Mindful to Be More Kind

In a simplistic sense, our happiness depends on close, caring relationships with others, ourselves, and our communities. Close, caring relationships come primarily from having many kind habits and few unkind habits. What helps a person build kind habits and leave unkind habits behind? One powerful tool is mindfulness.

## mindfulness

For the purposes of this workbook, think of mindfulness as: Directing our attention to what we are trying to do, feel, or see (our intention) in the present moment, and learning to redirect our attention away from distracting, judgmental, or negative thoughts.

Just as kindness has many benefits, so too does mindfulness. Regarding our physical health, mindfulness can reduce stress and lower blood pressure. As for mental health, mindfulness can reduce anxiety, decrease misery caused by dwelling on the past, and reduce worry about the future. Regardless of the cause of our anxiety, misery, or worry, practicing mindfulness can help. Allowing negative emotions to overtake us and dominate our thoughts serves only to create more unhappiness and does nothing to solve our problems.

Being mindful does not mean we will never worry. Of course, worrisome thoughts and emotions will arise in our mind, as will sensations of sight, sound, touch, and smell. Thoughts, feelings, and sensations are constantly entering our minds and hearts. It's natural for the mind to notice these things. After all, the job of the eyes is to see, and the job of the nose is to smell. In the same way, the mind's job is to notice things. However, when we are practicing mindfulness, we can allow these thoughts and feelings to arise, but be able to let them pass. When we are not practicing mindfulness, they can become a launching pad for a sequence of distracting, judgmental, and possibly negative thoughts and emotions.

For example, you might be trying to finish a project (for school or for work), but when you start working on it, you begin thinking about how much you hate that teacher (or boss) who gave it to you. Maybe you start thinking about the movie you're going to see with your friends later. Or you may look out the window and notice that it's raining. This is perfectly natural. You can't be mindful all the time. However, if you are being unmindful, you might become upset as you focus on how unfair it is that you have to do this project, or you might add unhappy thoughts about the rain you see out the window: "I don't like the rain. I'll probably get wet when I go to the movies later. When I get wet, I usually catch a cold."

These added negative thoughts agitate your mind, upsetting you and causing you to pay less attention to your intention—your project. They may even distract you enough to make a critical mistake and not complete the project correctly. Of course, while worrying about catching a cold offers you no benefit at all, noticing the rain might benefit you if you remember to carry an umbrella later. This is what this workbook intends to do—equip you with the tools to weather moments of anxiety, misery, and worry.

Can you describe times when distracting thoughts kept you from accomplishing a task or caused you to make an error?

_____

_____

## Some Benefits of Mindfulness

Learning to be mindful won't be easy. It is often a struggle in the beginning, but with continued small-step practice you can turn mindfulness into a habit. Eventually, you'll be able to quickly direct your attention away from distracting thoughts and immediately focus your attention.

### EXAMPLE

An Indigenous young adult leader talks about the value of mindfulness.

*Being more mindful has helped me not hate things like the rain. As a teen, I used to feel down every time it rained. Now that I am more mindful and aware of the meaning of rain, and all things in nature, I can go out feeling joyful as the rain falls on my face and feel thankful to the sky for watering the earth for us.*

### — Key Idea —

**Leaving negative thoughts behind allows us to pay attention to the needs of those around us (and to our own genuine needs as well).** Mindfulness makes us receptive to nurturing our connections with others. Religious traditions use mindfulness-like techniques—such as prayer, chant, and meditation—as a way to transform negativity and to open people up to spiritual self-improvement.

Mindfulness does more than shift our attention away from unhappy thoughts and back to our intention. It's an essential tool in breaking unkind habits, developing kind habits, and enjoying life. In this workbook, you will learn how to use mindfulness (and later meditation) to pay less attention to your internal worries and other causes of anxiety and deal more effectively with the world around you. One of the first steps on the path to mindfulness is learning to control your breathing. Working with your breath helps to reduce stress and anxiety, calm your mind and body during a crisis or intense emotions, and think more clearly before acting.

### PUT INTO PRACTICE **Journal**

#### *Counting Your Breaths*

Find a quiet place where you will not be interrupted. As you take deep, slow breaths, start counting each breath silently as you exhale. Count five breaths, then start again at one. Your breaths should be deep and slow, but comfortable.

It sounds easy, but you will likely find that your mind wanders. Perhaps you'll notice that you're feeling a little hungry. You might start thinking about what you'd like to eat and make a mental note to stop for something to eat on the way home. Before you know it, you've lost count of your breaths. If this happens, don't worry! Thoughts arise naturally in the mind. Just go back to one and start counting again.

You can start your practice for 2 to 3 minutes daily, then gradually increase how long you count your breaths until you're up to 4 or 5 minutes. Don't get upset if your mind wanders—just bring yourself gently back to focusing on your breathing.

On page 278, write the number of minutes you devote each day to this breathing exercise for 2 weeks.

✦ ✦ ✦

*A Note on Counting Breaths:* A young adult Indigenous leader had this recommendation for counting breaths: "If you prefer a natural approach to breathing, try going outside and breathing with nature. Choose something you resonate with—the trees, the clouds, the rain, the wind. Breathe as you notice the gentle movement and energy of the living world around you."

## How Being Unmindful Gets in the Way of Kind Habits

**When we are being unmindful, we can become unkind. We are less aware of how our unkind habits are harming us and the people around us.** For example, overindulging in food or alcohol can lead to negative feelings of discouragement, anger, and frustration. Spending too much time online or engaging with social media can cause the same types of negative feelings of inadequacy, poor self-image, or depression. Being unmindful in a relationship can lead to anxiety and stress. Not being mindful about getting enough healthy food, exercise, sleep, positive engagement with others, and preparation related to employment likewise can be harmful.

Most importantly, being unmindful keeps us from developing kind habits. We can't focus on kind habits when we are engaging in unmindful practices. For example, during a conversation, if we are unmindful, we are unable to notice the positive effects produced when we are being kind. When we're being mindful, we might notice the way the person we're talking to relaxes, smiles, and leans in when our attention is on them. If instead we are being unmindful, looking at our phone rather than the person, we miss this important feedback. Being unmindful makes it much harder to learn a positive habit, like focusing on the body language and the content of what the other person says.

## PUT INTO **Practice**

Think about a time when someone you know was not being mindful of how their behaviors were affecting others. Name the person.

_____

Describe what the person did that was unmindful.

_____

Describe how the person's unmindful behavior affected others.

_____

Now describe a time you were unmindful and you hurt someone with a thoughtless remark or ignored someone when they could have used help or a kind word. I was unmindful when I hurt someone by:

_____

It made me feel _____

It made others feel _____

## These Are Hard Times

Let's be honest. Many teens and young adults are dealing with anxiety. Reading about challenges faced by youth can be depressing, so we have put the discussion of these challenges in an appendix online at https://bit.ly/LH_AppendixA. The appendix is titled "Hard Times for Teens and Young Adults." If you feel you are alone in your struggles, think again. To convince yourself that you are not alone in your experiences, you can skim through that appendix. We need to recognize the challenges we are confronting and the pain and suffering of those around us, but still, change begins with you.

## Change Begins with You

The questions in Table 1.1, Self-Assessment: How I Want to Live My Life (pp. 17–18) will help you identify aspects of your own life that you want to work on. Your answers can help you identify areas to focus on for your own personal growth.

This workbook will address all of the topics mentioned above. It is designed to help you develop habits that can lead to lasting happiness. At the end of the workbook, you'll take this survey again. After finishing the workbook, you can compare the results of the two assessments to see the ways in which you might have changed.

**TABLE 1.1**  *Self-Assessment: How I Want to Live My Life*

Next to each statement, put a check in the box under the number that applies to you.

| | Strongly Disagree 1 | Disagree 2 | Agree 3 | Strongly Agree 4 |
|---|:---:|:---:|:---:|:---:|
| ***Relationships*** | | | | |
| I want more close relationships with people who really care about me. | ☐ | ☐ | ☐ | ☐ |
| I want to be more comfortable meeting friends in person. | ☐ | ☐ | ☐ | ☐ |
| I want to be less anxious when I'm in a group with other people my age. | ☐ | ☐ | ☐ | ☐ |
| ***Mental Well-Being*** | | | | |
| I want to feel calmer. | ☐ | ☐ | ☐ | ☐ |
| I want to be better able to control my anger. | ☐ | ☐ | ☐ | ☐ |
| I want to be less distracted. | ☐ | ☐ | ☐ | ☐ |
| I wish I was not so anxious and worried about the future. | ☐ | ☐ | ☐ | ☐ |
| I want to feel less regret for the mistakes I've made. | ☐ | ☐ | ☐ | ☐ |
| I want to forgive people for how they have treated me in the past. | ☐ | ☐ | ☐ | ☐ |
| ***Mindfulness*** | | | | |
| I want to learn how to use mindfulness, meditation, and other techniques that can be used to calm my mind. | ☐ | ☐ | ☐ | ☐ |
| I want a healthy balance between work or school and the rest of my life. | ☐ | ☐ | ☐ | ☐ |
| I want to be present and listen carefully when others speak. | ☐ | ☐ | ☐ | ☐ |
| ***Kindness*** | | | | |
| I wish I had more kind habits. | ☐ | ☐ | ☐ | ☐ |
| I want to show more appreciation toward others. | ☐ | ☐ | ☐ | ☐ |
| I want to help family and friends more. | ☐ | ☐ | ☐ | ☐ |
| I want to be more friendly to family and friends by showing that I am interested in what they care about. | ☐ | ☐ | ☐ | ☐ |
| I want to interrupt other people less during conversations. | ☐ | ☐ | ☐ | ☐ |
| I want to be more patient. | ☐ | ☐ | ☐ | ☐ |
| I want to be more appreciated and respected. | ☐ | ☐ | ☐ | ☐ |

| | Strongly Disagree 1 | Disagree 2 | Agree 3 | Strongly Agree 4 |
|---|:---:|:---:|:---:|:---:|
| ***Reaching Out*** | | | | |
| I feel I would like to be more kind to those in serious need. | ☐ | ☐ | ☐ | ☐ |
| I feel I would like to be more kind to those I disagree with. | ☐ | ☐ | ☐ | ☐ |
| I want to respect and protect the natural world, including plants, animals, and more. | ☐ | ☐ | ☐ | ☐ |
| I want to make more of an effort to be kind to those who are ignored or not treated fairly by others. | ☐ | ☐ | ☐ | ☐ |
| I want to volunteer to help others facing difficult situations. | ☐ | ☐ | ☐ | ☐ |
| I want to be included in more group activities. | ☐ | ☐ | ☐ | ☐ |
| I want to move out of my comfort zone more often so I can help others. | ☐ | ☐ | ☐ | ☐ |
| ***Encouraging Others to Be Kind*** | | | | |
| I want to help others learn that close, caring relationships make you happy and that kindness is essential for close, caring relationships. | ☐ | ☐ | ☐ | ☐ |
| I want to become more comfortable talking about kindness with others. | ☐ | ☐ | ☐ | ☐ |
| I want to learn more about kindness and meditation so I can teach others about these practices. | ☐ | ☐ | ☐ | ☐ |

**kindfulness**

Acting with mindfulness and with kindness. We use mindfulness so we can accurately see how to meet our needs and the healthy needs of others. Once we can see these needs clearly, we can act with genuine kindness.

Focusing on mindful kindness can improve many aspects of our lives. How you use this workbook to create meaningful change is up to you. We all have our own unique challenges that we want to work on. Creating your own goals will help make mindful kindness important to you and create a lasting impact on your life and even the lives of those people you surround yourself with.

## Identifying Your Most Important Goals

Think about what the quote at right means. Let's say you have a whole list of habits you want to change or goals you want to meet. If you try to work on everything at the same time, how successful do you think you will be at making lasting changes? Most people will start to feel overwhelmed very quickly. You may also start to feel frustrated because you aren't making a lot of progress toward any of the goals. The disappointment and anxiety that comes along with that can make you feel like giving up.

> **"** *If you have more than three priorities, you don't have any priorities.*
>
> — Jim Collins

Real change happens in small steps. We are much more successful if we narrow our focus to a few goals at a time. Suppress the need to change a lot of your habits or improve a number of areas in your life. Focus on making a few or just one high-priority change that will result in other positive changes as well.

 PUT INTO PRACTICE **Journal**

Now let's look closer at what changes might be most important to you. Review your self-assessment responses and circle every statement you marked as a 4. These are your strongest reactions. Which ones would you like to work on as you read this workbook? Pick three that feel the most important to you and put a star next to them.

Write these three down on page 278 of the Journal in the back of the workbook so that they are easy to refer back to. As you work through this workbook, you will come back to these statements and connect what we are learning to the goals that you have identified for yourself.

## Wrapping Up

**The main purpose of this workbook is to help you live a healthier, happier life by learning mindfully kind habits that foster closer connections in your personal life and in your community as a whole.** With these habits, you can also benefit others by helping, being friendly, showing gratitude, and reaching out to those with serious needs. **A second purpose of this workbook is to prepare you for difficult times.** We all have times in our lives that are difficult. Sometimes those difficult times are caused by our own actions and sometimes by circumstances out of our control. Mindful kindness cannot prevent these difficulties, but it can soften their effects.

Seeing your actions as a simple collection of habits gives you the mindset that you can change your life. That means new, kind habits can be learned, and unkind habits can be unlearned. Changing habits takes time and effort, though. So take your time in working through the chapters in this workbook. How do you feel thus far about using this workbook?

Chapter 2

# Check Your Foundation

*It is not the beauty of a building you should look at;
it's the construction of the foundation that will stand
the test of time.*

Jim Collins

**C**hanging habits is hard and takes time and persistence. Millions of resolutions are made at the New Year, but few are carried out. In the same way a crash diet does not bring lasting change to your body, there is no fast fix to mindfulness and kindness that will put you on the path to lasting happiness. Building a solid, kindful foundation is required, along with patience.

---

**kindful**

Combining a kind and mindful state of mind.

---

Being kindful can free people from the need for distractions that can lead to overindulging in negative thinking, eating, alcohol, vaping, internet (including pornography), social media, video games, sex, or TV. Spending less time with distractions gives us more time to be kind to ourselves and others and to reap the benefits of that kindness. This book describes the value—to ourselves and to our community—of fusing kindness and mindfulness in all aspects of our lives.

## — Key Ideas —

Three major skill groups form the foundation for changing habits. These skills give us the mental, physical, and—for some—spiritual or religious resources to bring about lasting change in our lives.

- **Skills of Action:** The ability to assume the different roles we need on the path to lead a loving, healthy, and happy life. *Includes Kindful Practitioner, Diligent Detective, and Wise Warrior.*

- **Skills of Character:** The ability to develop an attitude that supports us in making change. *Includes having a Growth Mindset and being Responsible, Patient, and Humble.*

- **Skill of Diagnosis:** The ability to *determine whether the challenge we face requires us to act primarily in our mental world, our physical world, or possibly our spiritual or religious world.*

As you read about these skills, ask yourself which of them you already have and which you want to develop. In future chapters, we will learn how to apply these critical foundational skills to increase our kindness and decrease our unkindness. These three skills will be called on again and again as we work together to build the close, caring relationships that lead to lasting happiness.

# Skills of Action

### skills of action

> The ability to assume the different roles we need on the path to lead a loving, healthy, and happy life.

Kindness does not happen on its own. Being kind is a choice we make over and over throughout each day. We all have the ability and capacity to bring more kindness to our lives. But we also encounter situations and have unkind habits that may get in the way of being kind. As we work to be kind in various situations or to break an unkind habit, we may need to assume one of these three roles: Diligent Detective, Wise Warrior, or Kindful Practitioner. Sometimes you'll need to take on more than one role to change a situation or a habit.

## Diligent Detective

Taking on the role of Diligent Detective to solve problems can be an act of kindness to yourself and others. Even better, **Diligent Detectives don't waste time worrying or thinking "what if." Their skills are called into action quickly and used efficiently to observe, gather, and process information in order to come up with a plan and implement it to solve the problem.** Some types of information might be found on the internet, such as how to find college applications. Other types of information involve more complex investigations, such as how to cope with depression and anxiety. Good Detectives understand that they cannot always find the solution on their own and are willing to get help from others.

*EXAMPLE*

> A junior in high school found that she was having difficulty completing her coursework and could not find time to study for the many tests coming up. She wanted to get into a good college, but was struggling to achieve the grades she needed for her college applications. She used the skills of the Diligent Detective to realize that she was procrastinating and spending too much time watching reality television. This realization allowed her to set goals for her homework and studying. Reality TV is now a reward she uses for completing the required coursework. Her grades improved, and she was able to attend the college of her choice. The TV show became a

reward for hard work, which also allowed her to enjoy the show more because it was a reward rather than an obstacle.

*EXAMPLE*

Ed applied for a job at a call center responding to complaints about household appliances. He was sure they would ask, "How would you handle an angry customer?" He used the skills of the Diligent Detective, first by calling his friend Jackson, who works at a call center. He also searched the internet for ideas by putting in this question: "How would you handle an angry customer?" He put together the ideas from his friend and from the internet and decided to write out how he would answer that question. He called Jackson back and asked if he would role-play the interviewer. This is how they did the role-play: Jackson took the role of the interviewer and asked, "How would you handle an angry customer complaining about a dishwasher?" Ed tried the different responses he came up with, such as "I can see why you are frustrated that your new dishwasher is not going through the rinse cycle. Now that I know the problem, I will connect you with a technician to walk you through what to do to fix the problem." They role-played for about 15 minutes, after which Ed felt prepared to answer that question during his interview. But Ed also knew he had to come up with answers to five other questions he would likely be asked. He did some more work on the internet and asked Jackson if he could help him again. Within a week, Ed felt well prepared for the interview.

## PUT INTO **Practice**

Describe a problem that you might have solved better or will be able to solve better by activating your Diligent Detective.

_____

_____

# Wise Warrior

**The Wise Warrior knows when and how to stand strong in the face of significant adversity.** The Wise Warrior is careful about choosing the problems to address and, once the decision has been made to take on a problem, the Warrior does not lose focus, remaining mindful and kind under the most difficult circumstances. Wise Warriors are not aggressive, but rather employ their inner strength to accept losses, sometimes bitter ones, yet still carry on. Think about how you can find the courage to act with integrity and refrain from lashing out when you feel attacked, or the inner strength it takes to accept a bitter loss and carry on with what you need to do. **Being a Wise Warrior does not mean you are wed to a certain plan for solving a problem. The Wise Warrior is always open to information that may lead to a new path for solving the problem.**

### EXAMPLE

One teacher described how her student tapped into his inner strength, his Wise Warrior, by forming a power pose to deal with his exhausting anxiety and depression:

*I used to work with a student who often felt anxious and depressed. He learned how to do a power pose each morning. He would stand tall and reach his arms high over his head with legs outstretched. While in this strong position, he would breathe deeply, connecting with his inner power to make change. He always ended up laughing (because it was silly) and lightening his mood enough to give himself a little kick in the butt to move forward into the day with more positivity.*

### EXAMPLE FROM AN AUTHOR

Doug speaks about his mother calling upon her inner Warrior:

*My mother, Olive, had always inspired me with her kindness, but near the end of her life, I was deeply moved to witness her ability to call upon the courage of her inner Warrior. Even though she suffered from debilitating pain as she approached death, she continued to give more thought to caring for others than she did to her own discomfort. When we were growing up, our family lived in a very small and rather racist community. I was pleased and touched when a longtime African American friend, Denver, came to say goodbye and Olive referred to him as my brother, symbolically making him part of our family. That same day, she told Masha, her caregiver, "I don't know why we were meant to become such close friends at this time, but I will miss you when I'm gone. I'm going to wait for you inside Heaven's gates until you come. Then we will be together again." Masha later told me, with tears in her eyes, that it was the nicest thing anyone had ever said to her.*

The Warrior mentality is connected to willpower, which means we set our intention and make a strong effort toward it. But some people find that willpower alone is not enough to confront difficult change. A Wise Warrior is willing to seek out and accept help. Help can come from many places. It is important to seek help from a person we trust. A Wise Warrior knows that it is OK to accept the guidance of others. There are times when it is best to let the Wise Warrior give us the strength to let go of control and request and accept help from others. It takes courage to be vulnerable and accept help. For some of us, our Warrior can seek help from being in nature, through faith in God, or through a spiritual journey.

## PUT INTO **Practice**

Describe a time that you used your Wise Warrior or wish you had used your Wise Warrior to deal with a challenge. What feelings emerged during this challenge?

_____

_____

# Kindful Practitioner

The Kindful Practitioner makes efforts many times every day to act with both mindfulness and kindness. Mindfulness allows the Kindful Practitioner to become fully present and aware of the moment. **With mindfulness, we can be aware of the impact of our actions or thoughts toward ourselves and others. The awareness and capacity that mindfulness brings gives us capacity to be kind to ourselves and others, even during difficult situations. The Kindful Practitioner does not expect anything in return.**

We can often find events throughout our lives that disrupt our ability to act as a Kindful Practitioner. During these events, we can call up the Diligent Detective and the Wise Warrior to help us deal with the events that are causing us to be upset or resentful. How do you feel when you are upset or resentful? By identifying the roadblocks to kindness and examining the skills to overcome them, we can be mindful and handle the difficult situation as a Kindful Practitioner.

## EXAMPLE

Your mom calls you and says she had a difficult and frustrating day at work. She asks you to empty the dishwasher, take out the garbage, and clean five potatoes so that the kitchen is ready for her to make dinner when she gets home. As a Kindful Practitioner, you fulfill her requests and go ahead and start a load of laundry to help even more. After coming home, your mom doesn't thank you or show appreciation in other ways. You find this lack of gratitude upsetting and call on the Wise Warrior to use mindfulness to shift your attention away from your feelings of resentment for not being recognized for your efforts. In addition, you call on the Diligent Detective to help you understand the difficult job your mom has. You realize the sacrifices she makes for you and your family. Your gratitude allows your resentment to fade and you are then able to interact with your mom as a Kindful Practitioner. Has your resentment ever disappeared when you were acting with kindness? What did that feel like?

✦ ✦ ✦

Kindful Practitioners are aware of the needs of others and the earth, as well as their own needs. Learning from a Kindful Practitioner can have a lasting effect on our lives. Many of us had the good fortune to encounter Kindful Practitioners in our day-to-day lives.

## EXAMPLE

Here's how a young adult Indigenous leader learned from her mother, a Kindful Practitioner, to practice kindness toward the earth:

*Growing up, my mom taught me that wherever we walked on the beach or in the woods, we picked up any trash we saw. If we did not have a bag to put it in and haul it back, we stuffed as much of it as we could in our pockets. I didn't like getting my pockets dirty as a child, but as I grew mindful of the reasons that we did this, the discomfort disappeared. This is being mindful of the earth, and she is as deserving as any human of the same kindness.*

✦ ✦ ✦

It's important to remember that there are many people in our society who not only seldom encounter a Kindful Practitioner, but also experience extreme trauma that can shape the course of their lives for years to come. Throughout this book, we'll bring you stories From the Other Side—letters from incarcerated men who Doug has corresponded with and mentored in Buddhism, mindfulness, meditation, and kindness. The letters, telling about their amazing shifts from lives of trauma to lives of mindful kindness, are compiled in the book *Saint Badass: Personal Transcendence in Tucker Max Hell.* You read in the Preface how even individuals with traumatic backgrounds, living in the harshest of prisons, can transform themselves and learn to live a life of mindful kindness. If they can transform themselves, so can we.

### FROM THE OTHER SIDE

Tad describes how he calls upon the Kindful Practitioner when helping other prisoners:

*I find their strengths and their weaknesses. I set up situations to help build on their strengths and opportunities to weaken any weakness that hinders them. Example would be Chris. Great people person. Big heart. But he will let people walk on him, as you cautioned on the dangers of the Kindful Practitioner. So, I help him weaken that area. How? I stay on his ass. I will tell him, "Don't sell yourself short. Be courageous. But stay professional." Yes. I do this to help. But you and I both know I do it for practice too! Practice to help myself become a skillful compassionate person.*

 PUT INTO PRACTICE **Journal**

You started practicing mindful breathing in Chapter 1. In a later chapter you will learn how mindful breathing can help you break unkind habits and build kind habits. To prepare yourself to apply mindful breathing in challenging situations, continue counting your breaths daily as you've been doing. When a distracting thought arises, notice it, then let it go and return to counting. Do this for 2 to 3 minutes. After 3 days, write about the experience on page 278. Did counting your breaths cut out some of your distracting, possibly unpleasant thoughts?

Here are examples of when to use each of the three Skills of Action.

- Whenever you practice basketball, you work on improving your 3-point shots. A friend tries to show you how to take better shots, but you quickly get frustrated with him and angrily tell him to go away, so he doesn't practice with you any longer. Realizing you have to find a way to stop being so angry, you call on the role of the Diligent Detective to figure out how to manage your anger. Maybe you pride yourself on how good you are at basketball and when you feel inadequate, you feel as if you're declining in self-worth. If you investigate this, you may then learn how to cultivate your self-worth in a way that isn't tied to your basketball skills. Figuring out how to manage your anger only addresses a symptom of an underlying condition: low self-worth.

- You want to invite Alicia to hang out with you but are afraid she'll turn you down, so you don't take any action at all. Anxiety about being criticized or seen as undesirable prevents you from joining most group activities as well. You often think negative thoughts about yourself that hold you back from seeking what you want. You know what you want to do but are too afraid to try to take action. Taking the role of the Wise Warrior, you decide to overcome your fear and invite Alicia to an event.

- A friend of yours has been binge-drinking alcohol. You are worried about her because she is missing work due to drinking. You realize she needs a friend to spend time with her, so you call on the role of the Kindful Practitioner to support her by spending time with her.

You may need to apply all three Skills of Action to some problems.

*EXAMPLE*

One teenager describes how he used the three Skills of Action to deal with a problem. After an upsetting day at school, he came home and picked a fight with his brother. Then he went into his room to think about his actions:

- First, he set out to figure out what went wrong with his day that led him to pick a fight with his brother. He thought about all the events that occurred in school that upset him and what he could do to avoid those types of situations in the future. (Diligent Detective)

- He decided to ask others around him, maybe his brother or someone at school, to support him next time and help bring him back to his center. (Wise Warrior)

- He decided to make it up to his brother by doing his chores for the week, maybe even doing them without telling his brother as a surprise. (Kindful Practitioner)

You'll see the label *Personal Challenge* for activities that give you the opportunity to take practice to a deeper level. Completing these activities allows you to improve the mindful kindness skills you are learning in this book.

PERSONAL **Challenge**

Describe a current or past problem or obstacle in your own life.

_____

How did that problem or obstacle feel?

_____

Describe how you would use one or more of the three Skills of Action to find a solution to this problem or obstacle.

_____

# Skills of Character

---

**skills of character**

The ability to assume the different roles we need on the path to lead a loving, healthy, and happy life.

Our second set of foundational skills is essential to actually making meaningful change in our habits. This set includes having a growth mindset and being responsible, patient, and humble. We call these Skills of Character because they represent the ability to call up, in a difficult moment, the core values that make us who we are. Lacking a Skill of Character can explain, in part, why we are not able to succeed in building kind habits and breaking unkind habits. Skills of Character are frequently used by the Wise Warrior.

# Growth Mindset

---

**growth mindset**

Believing we can change the way we behave, think, and live.

Everyone occasionally acts in an unkind manner, whether to ourselves or to those around us. However, having unkind habits is something else entirely. That's because, with a habit, we repeat our unkind behavior over and over again. There are two different views on what makes a habit. Some people see habits as learned behaviors that we can change. Others treat habits as something fixed—a pattern that has become ingrained and is an unchangeable part of one's personality, sometimes even passed down through generations. In other words, we believe it is impossible to weaken our unkind habits and build kind habits.

**If we want to become more kind, it's vitally important that we believe that we really can change our habits; we need a growth mindset.** Think about beginning a new craft, sport, computer program, or even a new friendship. When we begin something, we are usually open to learning and can track our growth from stumbling first attempts to becoming smoother and smoother as we keep learning. For example, when learning to play a new, complex video game, we have confidence we can learn how to play and get better as we play the game more. We learn that when we have a growth mindset, we don't expect a first try to be that good, as illustrated when you start out doing poorly with a new video game. But then you start getting better and better as you practice more. The same is true with kind habits—they actually take lots of practice to make them. Likewise, unkind habits often take a lot of practice to break.

### EXAMPLE

Sixteen-year-old Sophie Robinson's diary entry illustrates a positive growth mindset during the very difficult time of the COVID-19 pandemic. Notice how she finds a hopeful alternative to feeling discouraged due to the way the virus has changed her daily life:

*Sometimes I feel like I'm trapped in my own world, that it's only my community and country struggling, but I know that it's so much more than that. This virus can make you feel so alone, unmotivated, run down, but there's still so much that we have. We need to show strength and unity. For us to succeed, we can't be tearing each other down—we need to come together.[1]*

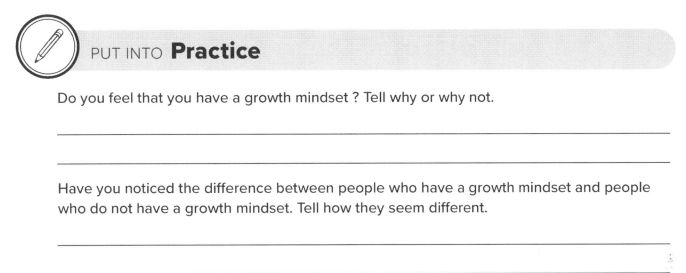

PUT INTO **Practice**

Do you feel that you have a growth mindset ? Tell why or why not.

_____

_____

Have you noticed the difference between people who have a growth mindset and people who do not have a growth mindset. Tell how they seem different.

_____

_____

# Responsible

It is not enough to believe change is possible. We have to accept the responsibility of "Getting it done!" **Being responsible includes being reliable, thoughtful (organized with good planning and attentiveness to details), having good impulse control, and acting with goal-directed behaviors. Being responsible may not be something that comes easily to us, but it is something we can grow.** An important aid that can help us be responsible is a to-do list, a list of tasks that need to be completed, typically organized in order of priority. When we think of something we need to do, we immediately add it to our to-do list and then frequently check that list with the goal of doing what we need to do in a timely manner. You might keep your list on an app or calendar on your cell phone.

When we do not feel responsible for our plans, our thoughtful, organized plans can fall apart. We may think about being kind but not follow through, or maybe we allow something else to get in the way of keeping our commitment. Even worse, we can develop unkind habits, such as being irresponsible, thoughtless, careless, and unorganized, and then blame others for our failure. **Being responsible means that if we do something wrong, we don't blame another person or event. We hold ourselves accountable for what we do and say.**

As we become adults, part of maturing is taking responsibility for our actions. We can no longer blame others for the decisions we have made. In being responsible, we accept the fact that our words and actions impact others. When we say or do something that is unkind, we must take responsibility for our words and actions.

*EXAMPLE*

A teacher describes how Joe, a student, came to take responsibility for what he thought, said, and did:

*Joe was 17 years old when fighting led to his suspension. Most of his fights included racial insults. Consequently, he was mandated to take my class on anger as an option to return to regular school. Initially, he boasted about his anger and, encouraged by his white nationalist dad, talked about minorities, especially Blacks and Jews, as being less than equal to White people.*

*In a role-play with Joe, I said, "I don't believe you're prejudiced. I think you are parroting your dad." He argued with me as I reminded him to use the steps taught in class, the first one being to take responsibility for your part of the issue. I said that I could tell he was just parroting his dad, and I could see a bigger-hearted guy underneath.*

*Joe softened and said that his dad expected him to fight; it was the culture at home to be prejudiced, and it was not an option for him to be different. He said he couldn't use the class skills at home or he would be beaten up. But Joe did take responsibility for what he did at school and began acting more like a bigger-hearted guy. For example, I remember watching him opening up to and then being kind to a Black girl in class. The class supported Joe as he made positive changes. He knew he had to tough it out at home for another year before he could live on his own. And although he engaged in a fight that led to expulsion, he made progress at a smaller school, graduated, got a job, and left home soon after.*

Joe became responsible when he realized that he was hurting other people and decided to no longer parrot what his dad said. And because he felt more responsible for others, he acted with more kindness.

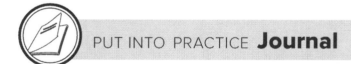

## PUT INTO PRACTICE **Journal**

For the next 3 days make a to-do list of things you need to get done. You can make the list on your phone or a piece of paper. Include the date by which the activity must be done. Check off things when you complete them. On page 279, write how you felt after completing all the activities on your list?

## Patient

**To accomplish lasting change, you must have the ability to tolerate delays, solve ongoing problems, and struggle with barriers without becoming too annoyed, anxious, or simply giving up.** Patience helps us stay the course and keep going. It's about not waiting for the problem to go away or for someone else to solve it. **Being patient is also an essential way to be kind to yourself, especially during difficult times when we need to live with our problem rather than denying it or wishing it would go away.** In contrast, the unkind habit of impatience often leads to anger, ridicule, and even violence, wrecking our attempts to change our habits. Patience, like being responsible, can be developed. Have you ever been so impatient it led to extreme unkindness? How did it make you feel to act out your impatience? What about a time you acted with patience? How did that feel?

*EXAMPLE*

Sixteen-year-old Emma has a learner's permit and gets frustrated every time her dad takes her out driving. He criticizes her, and they end up fighting by the end of each trip. As she tries to learn to be patient with her dad, the first step is to identify her emotions. After taking a few deep breaths, she might realize she is feeling sad that her dad doesn't trust her. She might also recognize she's feeling anxious about learning how to drive. Emma can then imagine the scenario differently. Maybe she even tries to take her father's perspective (she feels empathy for her father). She realizes he might also be feeling sad (his daughter is growing up) and nervous (his daughter might get in an accident). Emma realizes they are actually feeling pretty similar, which makes it easier to cope.[2]

*EXAMPLE*

A young adult explains how patience can serve as a reminder to slow down and recognize the needs of others:

*I have a hard time slowing down to other people's paces. For example, I could learn to be more patient when I'm grocery shopping with my mom. I always go in with a list, but she likes to take detours and check every aisle, which frustrates me because I hate large, crowded spaces (especially during this pandemic). Sometimes I get angry and tell her that I want to leave, but the solution could be just having a conversation about why close contact with strangers bothers me so much before we go to the grocery store.*

*EXAMPLE*

This was the second year that Raul was on his high school basketball team. He was frustrated because he was missing most of his shots during the games, and the coach was only letting him play several minutes during the games. He complained to his brother about not getting enough playing time. He thought about quitting the team. His brother, who had been on the team several years earlier, told Raul that he needed to practice his shooting more and be patient. Raul and his brother spent several hours a day practicing. Raul's brother showed him how to shoot better. Raul practiced taking almost 200 shots each day. At first, Raul showed little improvement, but gradually his shooting improved. As he shot better in practice, the coach started to give him more playing time. His patience paid off.

PUT INTO **Practice**

Is there a time when having patience could have helped you?

_____

_____

# Humble

**The final essential skill of character is humility, defined as having an accurate, realistic view of ourselves and an awareness of the needs of others.*** When we are humble, we are more able to put ourselves in others' shoes and become aware of their needs.** Think of a time you acted with humility. How did that feel? **Humility also helps us set manageable, realistic goals, which makes it more likely we will reach those goals. Setting realistic goals is helped by being able to look at ourselves clearly and accept our current strengths and weaknesses in different situations.** Studies have found that humility strengthens our relationships with others, reduces stress in competitive situations, and improves health. The opposite of humility is *arrogance*, feeling better or more entitled than others, which is a major cause of many personal and societal problems, including war.

## *EXAMPLE*

Janine had just finished the program at the community college to be a medical assistant. She had done very well in her courses and had been promised a job at the clinic where she did her internship. The last thing she had to do was pass the national accreditation exam. Janine was tired of studying and felt she would be able to easily pass the accreditation exam. She ignored the advice of her counselor and signed up for an exam that would be administered very soon. She paid the $125 registration fee. She was devastated when she received the results of the exam and saw her score was nowhere near passing. Her lack of humility in thinking she did not have to study had not only cost her the price of the registration fee, but also delayed the time when she could begin working,

PUT INTO **Practice**

Describe a situation in which you or a friend were frustrated because you did not set realistic goals for something you wanted to accomplish.

_____

_____

Tell how you felt when you were frustrated.

_____

## *Using Character Skills to Change Unkind Habits*

Our character skills help us confront and change unkind habits. Many of our unkind habits involve cravings—craving for more and more dessert, for more fun when it is time to work, for yet another video game instead of sleep, and so on. When we decide we want to diminish—if not eliminate—a craving, each character skill needs to come into play:

---

* Definition from researchers Don Davis at Georgia State University and Joshua Hook at the University of North Texas.

- With a Growth Mindset, we set the intention to not give in to the craving and accept our responsibility to not give in—for example, to the unkind habit of too much gaming. We know it is possible to change our behavior.

- We become Humble because we know there will be times we give in to our craving for more gaming. We are not perfect or a superhero.

- We stay away from gaming web sites as a way to be Responsible to increase our effort to control our craving.

- Finally, and most difficult, we are Patient and endure the struggle to fight our craving without giving in to it. We understand that changing a habit takes time. Sometimes we will give into our bad habit, but it's important to not give up. There will be times of weakness. The most important part is how we recover from the situation and continue to persevere toward our goal.

## PUT INTO **Practice**

The four Skills of Character are Growth Mindset, Responsible, Patient, and Humble. What is your strongest Skill of Character?

_____

Can you describe an experience that shows this strong skill?

_____

_____

What Skill of Character do you need to work on most?

_____

Has your weakness in this skill resulted in an unkind habit? Describe the unkind habit.

_____

_____

## Skills of Character Are Complicated

Skills of Character are not always as straightforward as they might seem. For example, what appears to be humility in the following example is actually low self-esteem leading to self-hatred.

### EXAMPLE

Here's what a young adult said about their humility actually being a mask for low self-esteem:

_I think it is important to make a clear distinction that humility and poor self-image/low self-esteem are not the same thing. For years growing up, I was always praised that I was so humble and that that was such_ *a great trait to have. In reality, I just despised who I was—a result of my intense depression. What this constant reminder to me to stay humble ultimately resulted in was a connection in my head that it was good that I hated myself. What others saw as an intense sense of humility was in reality a deeply damaging self-hating practice. It took many years, and lots of therapy, for me to realize that humility was valuing myself as I am.*

✦ ✦ ✦

This example does not show true humility. Humility means having an accurate, realistic view of ourselves and an awareness of the needs of others. When we are humble, we are more able to put ourselves in others' shoes and become aware of their needs. In this example, the young adult is not aware of the needs of others—she is focused only on herself.

Skills of Character can also be taken to the extreme, for example, being so patient with people who have borrowed money, clothes, electronics, etc., that nothing is ever returned to us. Or we might take responsibility to the extreme and become hyper-responsible, feeling we are responsible for everything around us, especially things that go wrong. Individuals with anxiety and depression often feel hyper-responsible.

All of the Skills of Character can be taken to the extreme—balance is key.

# Skills of Diagnosis

### skills of diagnosis

The ability to determine whether the challenge we face requires us to act primarily in our mental world, our physical world, or possibly, our spiritual or religious world.

Every problem arises in our mental world with the awareness that something is bothering us, making us unhappy. But that does not mean that a solution needs to focus primarily on changing our mental world.

Anxiety, depression, joy, enjoyment, and other feelings and thoughts take place in our mental world. In contrast, playing sports, watching video games, working, talking to people, and arguing with someone take place in our physical world.

The purpose of the Diagnosis skill is to determine whether the solution to our problem needs to take place primarily in our mental world or our physical world. This skill is often used by the Diligent Detective.

Here's an example of how we diagnose, or decide, whether a solution should focus on our mental, physical, or spiritual world. Let's say you're expecting a raise at work. Months go by, but the raise never materializes. Now you're really unhappy. You become negative at the workplace, and even at home, because of your anger about not being given the raise. While it's true that the failure to get the raise happened in the physical world, the feelings of unhappiness are actually occurring in your mental world. With the Skill of Diagnosis, you can decide whether to change your mental world, your physical world, your spiritual or religious world, or some combination of the three. You can take steps in your physical world by making the case with your boss for why you should get a raise. You can also take steps in your mental world to calm yourself through mindfulness and meditation. If appropriate, you could take the steps suggested by your spiritual or religious tradition.

For many of us, figuring out what needs to change and where—in our mental, physical, or spiritual worlds—can be very challenging. This is why millions of people have found comfort and guidance in the Serenity Prayer:

> **God grant me the serenity to accept the things I cannot change,**
> **Courage to change the things I can,**
> **And the wisdom to know the difference.**

It's not hard to see how the prayer could be rephrased for mindfulness.

> Use mindfulness to change my mental world,
> Kindness to change my physical world,
> And the wisdom to know which one to emphasize in the present moment.

## PUT INTO **Practice**

Describe a personal problem that is currently causing you to be unhappy or feel unfulfilled. Write about what part of that problem is occurring in the physical world, what part is in the mental world, and, if relevant to you, what part is in your spiritual or religious world. Describe possible solutions in your mental world, your physical world, and, if relevant, your spiritual world.

Describe the problem: _____

_____

How does it impact your mental world? _____

_____

Solution to the mental world problem: _____

_____

How does it impact your physical world? _____

_____

Solution to the physical world problem: _____

_____

How does it impact your spiritual world? _____

_____

Solution to the spiritual world problem: _____

_____

Once you are able to diagnose where your efforts for change need to start, you are better able to work on solutions.

### EXAMPLE

Eighteen-year-old Daniel wrote that he was able to change his mental world, which in turn changed his behavior and led to positive connections with others (changes in his physical world). It is unfortunate that so many of us have to be in deep unhappiness, for example, because of feeling inadequate, before we are motivated enough to change the way we live.

> *Once you are able to diagnose where your efforts for change need to start, you are better able to work on solutions.*

*I used to run from my self-induced feelings of inadequacy. I would run in any way that I could, no matter how irresponsible. My mind filled with thoughts of self-doubt, worried about disappointing those around me and not being worthy of compassion. After a poor academic running streak, I realized I had lost a sense of myself and finally reached out for help.*

*I realized that I had been keeping people at arm's length by not showing them my true self and would never admit to my inability to reach out to others for help. I would always show compassion, but never requested it from others because I felt like I didn't deserve it.*

*Building trust in others required me to step out of my comfort zone and take chances and risks, something I've never been fond of before. I stripped my mental image of myself as a slacker and good-for-nothing teenager and decided I would prove myself to others through meaningful action.*

*Now when I have an assignment to do, I have two reactions. It's as if I was split into two people. One person hears the assignment and instantly groans. They don't believe in me. My other person hears their groans, shakes them away, and tells me I have what it takes. I have to decide who I am going to listen to; which dog am I going to feed? If I commit myself and work hard to get things done well, I please the positive dog, and the dog that bit me starts to disappear. I'm learning more about myself and working harder every day to feed healthy habits, and as a result I have never felt more free, confident, and fearless. This mental change has also impacted my physical world. I am no longer afraid to ask for help. I now have a good support system of friends that I hang out with.*

### FROM THE OTHER SIDE

Here's how Tad answered the question above about changing his mental world:

*Knowing I'm in prison for a crime I didn't commit is tough! I must be brutal and stay away from dwelling on it. It's not a feeling of hatred. It just hurts. Only a person in my shoes could sympathize with me. That is why I got that little powerful saying written down where I can read it on a regular basis. I've shared it before, but it is worth repeating: "It's a smaller thing to suffer punishment than to have deserved it! The punishment can be removed, but the fault will remain forever!!"*

# Committing Yourself

Have you ever made a vow to yourself to change something in your life or improve in some way? Many people who make a New Year's Resolution are doing exactly that. In many cultures, when people make a serious commitment, they formalize that commitment with a vow. We say vows when we pledge our lives to a partner in marriage or when we swear to tell the truth when we testify in court. The Girl Scouts and members of many formal organizations recite promises or an oath, pledging to live up to the ideals of their group. Do you want to commit yourself to making kindfulness a central purpose of your life and to follow through on your kindful intentions? If so, we invite you to take what we call the Kindful Vow. The skills described in this chapter—Skills of Diagnosis, Action, and Character—can give you the strength needed to stick to your Kindful Vow.

# The Kindful Vow

> **I intend to be mindfully kind to myself.**
> **I intend to be mindfully kind in all my relationships.**
> **I intend to expand the reach of my kindfulness.**

The vow has three commitments. Let's take a closer look at each of them.

## *I intend to be mindfully kind to myself.*

It's easy to treat ourselves by splurging on a new app for our phone or indulging in a shopping spree. But is that the same thing as being mindfully kind to ourselves? Of course not. When we make this commitment, we are pledging to practice self-care that's grounded in pleasant, kind, and meaningful habits. At the same time, we are committing to get control of behaviors that are harmful to ourselves or others—such as excessive online gaming, overdrinking, overpartying, or overspending. **This commitment means we agree to look honestly at ourselves rather than indulging in self-centered worry, regrets, or distractions.** One young adult, in therapy for depression, said, "An added benefit in making these vows visible is that they require us to take a step back and learn to care more about ourselves. Instead of reacting to momentary strain with self-gratifying 'gifts,' we can take care of ourselves, which reduces depression and offers other benefits as well."

## *I intend to be mindfully kind in all my relationships.*

The Golden Rule tells us to treat others the way we would want to be treated. But the truth is that different people actually want different things. That is where the Platinum Rule comes in: **Treat others the way they want to be treated. The pledge to be mindfully kind in our relationships is about agreeing to focus with consideration on the other person. The key to this commitment is a special kind of deep listening: listening with the intention to understand.** When we stop interrupting or thinking about what we want to say, we will start to hear responses to important questions: Is the other person happy and experiencing comfort and joy? Do they need help with work, family, or other friends? Is there a way I can bring greater happiness or well-being to this person? Deep listening is especially important for a person we love.

*I intend to expand the reach of my kindfulness.*

As challenging as it can be to treat those closest to us with kindfulness, it's easy to forget about the people outside our inner circle. The kindful vow is about pledging to treat with kindness all living beings—people of different races, ages, political views, religions, genders, sexual orientations, education levels, economic status, and nationalities. And to consider how we can expand the reach of kindfulness to include those convicted of crimes, the unhoused, the disabled, and even our enemies. **Treating people with kindness does not mean we agree with what they say or do.**

## The Critical Role of a Mentor

Learning the Skills of Action, Character, and Diagnosis on our own is very challenging. In fact, learning any new complex skill all by ourselves is challenging. We can always use some help from a mentor, who might be a teacher, spiritual/religious guide, coach, family member, or friend. When we are fortunate, we benefit from multiple mentors in these different aspects of our lives:

- An inspiring teacher might help us learn to be a Diligent Detective or Wise Warrior, and to have a growth mindset

- A trustworthy and caring spiritual/religious guide can show us how to be a Kindful Practitioner who is humble and patient—in our mental world and in our physical world

- A conscientious boss can teach us to be responsible and cooperative

- A considerate friend can teach us about creating positive relationships

- An athletic coach might teach about nutrition, fitness, and how to be part of a team

### EXAMPLE

Belise, an East African refugee-immigrant, comments on the impact a mentor can have:

*Because my English was not fluent, I repeated kindergarten. Over the summer, Erin, an important person to me whom I consider my "bonus mom," worked tirelessly to teach me how to read. She taught me confusing words like which, rich, and witch. When we sat on the couch she would wait patiently as I sounded out each word, d-o-g. Because of her, I developed a love for reading, which greatly improved my English.*

**We should always be on the lookout for mentors to help us on our way to applying knowledge, skills, and values.** When a positive, constructive mentoring opportunity does arise, we should act decisively, showing our interest and respect for the prospective mentor.

**A NOTE OF CAUTION**

A critically important characteristic of a mentor is the mentor's values. Values are important because when we accept mentoring from a person, we open ourselves to the mentor. We become vulnerable and come to trust the mentor. If the mentor is exploitative rather than caring, we can be deeply harmed. On the other hand, a mentor with caring values is someone we can turn to in difficult times for advice and comfort. A good mentor also benefits by learning from those they mentor, as illustrated by what Doug has learned from the imprisoned men he mentors.

PUT INTO **Practice**

Think about the mentors you have had, past and present. Think about one who made a difference in your life and describe them.

_____

_____

Do you have a need for a mentor at this time of your life? If so, describe an area of your life in which you would like to have one.

_____

Do you know someone you would like to be a mentor to you? Describe that person.

_____

# Wrapping Up

In the first chapter, you learned about the benefits of both kindness and mindfulness. In this chapter, you've learned about the types of skills (Action, Character, and Diagnosis) that will support you as you form the foundation for your new, more kindful self. You will especially need to focus on the Skills of Character because developing these skills can take lots of time and much effort. Spending the time and making the effort will be worth it. A strong foundation can ultimately lead to close, caring relationships and authentic happiness; it's the beginning of forming kindful habits that then can support you within a more expansive and inclusive community.

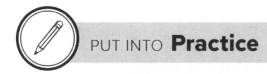

## PUT INTO **Practice**

Are you ready to take the Kindful Vow? Maybe you are ready to take only one part of the vow—to be more kindful to yourself. Or maybe you want to take the vow for only a week or month. You can take the vow alone, with an important person in your life, or as part of a group. Before you begin, strengthen your commitments by making the three parts of the vow more personal and specific.

Write down the commitments you are willing to make on a piece of paper or on your phone. Then add a few words about what you will do to carry out those intentions:

I _____ , commit to the following:

I will be more kindful to myself by . . .

I will be more kindful in all my relationships by . . .

I will extend the reach of my kindfulness by . . .

When you're satisfied with your new commitments, sign your name and the date on the piece of paper or on your phone. Now you're ready to make the Kindful Vow by repeating out loud what you have written. Display your vows so that you will see them several times a day.

## Time for Reflection

Think about each statement and then circle Yes or No.

| | | |
|---|---|---|
| I feel grateful for people and pets I care about. | Yes | No |
| I feel grateful for something that went well today. | Yes | No |
| I feel grateful for what I can do with my body and mind. | Yes | No |
| I feel grateful for people who help me and others. | Yes | No |
| I feel grateful for my beliefs that give me purpose and meaning. | Yes | No |
| I feel grateful for having fun and laughter. | Yes | No |
| I feel thankful for the earth and universe. | Yes | No |

# Build Kind Habits

*Construct walls to support a house of kindness.*

---

Chapter 3: Expand Your Idea of Kindness

Chapter 4: Increase Your Kindness

---

Scientific findings: 17
Real-world examples: 23
Opportunities to apply what you are learning: 20

### Teachings from the World Religions

Christianity: "Give away your life; you'll find life given back, but not merely given back—given back with bonus and blessing. Giving, not getting, is the way. Generosity begets generosity." (MSG: Jesus, Luke 6:38)

Buddhism: "If you knew what I know about the power of giving, you would not let a single meal pass without sharing it in some way."

Judaism: Rabbi Akiva taught: "Love your neighbor as yourself" (Leviticus 19:18). This is the most important rule in the Torah. (Jerusalem Talmud Nedarim 30b commentary)

Taoism: "Kindness in words creates confidence. Kindness in thinking creates profoundness. Kindness in giving creates love." —Lao Tzu

Hinduism: "The great secret of true success, of true happiness, is this: The man or woman who asks for no return, the perfectly unselfish person, is the most successful." —Swami Vivekananda

Native American: "Teach us love, compassion, and honor that we may heal the earth and heal each other." (Ojibwa prayer)

Chapter 3

# Expand Your Idea of Kindness

*Constant kindness can accomplish much. As the sun makes ice melt, kindness causes misunderstanding, mistrust, and hostility to evaporate.*

Albert Schweitzer

If you watch preschoolers at a playground, it doesn't take long before you see both kind and unkind actions, such as one child allowing another to go first on a slide or a child pushing another out of the way to get to the swing first. But is our behavior much different? What makes one child or person kind enough to allow someone else to take their place in a line or to give up a seat on the train to an elder? Is being kind part of our DNA—are we born wanting to be kind? Is it learned? Can we change the habit of always wanting to be first?

**instinct**

An inborn response to a specific type of situation.

Only recently have scientists recognized that kindness is an instinct.* In his book *Born to Be Good: The Science of a Meaningful Life*, professor Dacher Keltner explains that in order to survive, early humans had to cooperate and be kind to each other, and these traits of cooperation and kindness continue as part of our hereditary makeup today.[1] In our modern world, the feel-good chemicals released in our bodies when we practice kindness, along with the social rewards we enjoy for being kind, contribute to our happiness and encourage us to continue to act with kindness.

## The Many Ways to Practice Kindness

In this chapter, we will focus on ways to expand our capacity for kindness. As we progress through the book, we will see more and more the relationship between mindfulness and kindness.

### EXAMPLE FROM AN AUTHOR

How Doug learned about an unusual form of kindness:

*When I was 10 years old, my family was driving through the Smoky Mountains. The fog became so dense we could not see the road. We parked the car at a truck stop, along with many other cars that had pulled off and were waiting for the fog to lift. Then, in what I later realized was an act of kindness and courage, a boy in a car in front of us leaned out his window and shined a powerful flashlight down on the center line of the highway so the car's driver could steer to stay on the road. After the boy's car pulled out and away, a wagon train of cars followed, each barely able to see the red taillights of the car in front of them.*

*I learned that kindness can have a ripple effect. The boy shining the light ended up helping not just his family but also the many cars behind him. With the help of the flashlight, many people were able to safely navigate through the fog.*

✦ ✦ ✦

Doug's experience is a great analogy for mindfulness. The thick fog of the mountain is rather like confusion in our mind that at times keeps us from seeing an opportunity for kindness along the centerline

---

* Most religions have recognized the good of humans for centuries, for example, Genesis 1:27: "So God created man in his own image, in the image of God he created him; male and female he created them."

of our lives. Mindfulness is like the flashlight that allows us to move safely through the fog and bring the cars down the mountain. Later we will work on developing our mindfulness, but right now, we'll discuss more about kindness.

## —Key Idea —

There are many elements or different ways to think about kindness. In this chapter, we will look at three important elements for practicing kindness: feelings of compassion, feelings of gratitude, and acts of altruism. As we progress through later chapters, we will bring in additional elements of kindness.[†]

# Compassion

**compassion**

Sympathy (understanding) and empathy (sharing the feeling) for the pain and unhappiness of others, often combined with a desire to help.

Compassion is of great value because it means we understand and have empathy for the situation another person is facing and the feelings of the other person. Compassion is a beginning step to genuine kindness because it allows us to connect with and understand those in need. The ability to sympathize, and also to understand the feelings of others, helps us take the next step in kindness by providing people with help they may need. How do you feel when you are hurting inside and someone offers you compassion? How does it feel when you are kind toward someone who is hurting?

### EXAMPLE

How a boyfriend's compassionate act of kindness affected Sally after she hurt herself:

*I had everything a girl could ever want, the perfect life. I had just moved out of home and in with my boyfriend, who was the perfect man. I was studying at university, had a wonderful family, and went out with my friends every other night. But I was broken inside. I felt like it all meant nothing, that the pain was going to eat me up.*

*It wasn't that I wanted to be dead, but more that I didn't want to continue living. It was such a complicated feeling that followed me everywhere I went, hanging over every move I made. Eventually, I stopped leaving the house at all. One night my boyfriend went out to work, and I couldn't deal with the loneliness anymore, so I pulled out a bottle of wine and drank the whole lot. Then I hurt myself. He found me on the floor. It was such a simple action on his behalf, and I don't think he will ever know how much it meant. He pulled me from the floor into his arms and cried. He cried because he felt my pain just as much as I did, I*

---

† There are seven elements, or seven different ways, to think about kindness. Four of the ways are internal—or mental—ways of thinking and feeling: forgiveness, gratitude, empathy, and compassion. The remaining three are external—or physical—acts: acts of altruism, acts of generosity, and acts of cooperation. Throughout the book, we will give examples of all the elements of kindness. In this chapter, we will discuss only three of the elements: feelings of compassion, feelings of gratitude, and acts of altruism.

*just hadn't realized that he could see it. I thought I was doing such a great job of holding it all together, of hiding my pain, but really he was sharing it with me."\**

❖ ❖ ❖

For the boyfriend to be genuinely kind, he would support Sally in seeking professional help so she would not hurt herself in the future.

It is important to note that whether an act is genuinely kind or not depends on the other person—and what they actually need. Being mindful means we pay attention to and are aware of what a person needs and wants. Sally's need was not obvious to her boyfriend until she hurt herself. Possibly Sally's boyfriend could have noticed her need before she hurt herself, but oftentimes there are no indications that a person is contemplating self-harm. When we're being mindful, we use our Diligent Detective and Wise Warrior to help us seek appropriate ways to be a Kindful Practitioner.

### EXAMPLE

A young woman describes how to take into account another person's needs when being kind:

*I grew up in a family that generally had two ways of responding to stressful situations that happened in our family. Several of my aunties and my grandma always thought that good home cooking was the place to start, so they were always trying to feed you to make you feel better. They believed there was nothing like comfort food to show compassion for someone else's troubles. Others in our family didn't want to eat when they were upset, but instead just needed to vent and get it all out. This had to happen before they could calm down and think clearly about a solution to their problem. So now whenever someone is upset, I always ask, "How can I help you? Do you just need to vent or do you need me to bring you something to eat?" I've learned that it is more important to take into account the other person's needs than to just jump in and do what would make me feel good. I've found this is certainly more helpful than trying to force feed someone who just wants to talk. It also makes me feel better about myself for "helping" in a truly helpful way.*

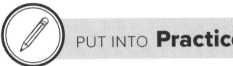

## PUT INTO **Practice**

Describe a situation in which you wanted to be kind but were not sure how to be kind.

_____

_____

Did you try to be kind anyway? What happened?

_____

_____

---

\* Personal story from Beyond Blue website: https://www.beyondblue.org.au/who-does-it-affect/personal-stories/story/sally

# Self-Compassion

**self-compassion**

Being warm and understanding toward ourselves when we fail or feel inadequate, rather than ignoring our pain or attacking ourselves.

Later chapters go into great detail about teaching self-compassion—which we also call self-care and being kind to ourselves—by managing our stress, obtaining the education and skills needed for a job, and getting the right amount of sleep, exercise, and healthy food. Our ability to achieve lasting happiness and peace of mind is closely tied to our self-care and our ability to have warm, close relationships. As a young adult wisely told us, "Taking care of ourselves . . . allows us to see beyond ourselves and develop close, caring relationships with others."

 PUT INTO **Practice**

Have you been compassionate to yourself ? If not, name a way in which you have not been compassionate to yourself.

_____

_____

 PUT INTO PRACTICE **Journal**

### *Mindful Breathing*

Are you ready to change your breathing exercise? From now on, instead of counting your breaths, pay attention to the physical sensations—the movement of your chest and abdomen as you inhale and exhale. We'll call this mindful breathing. Without counting, you may notice more negative thoughts. Don't give in to distractions; just return your attention to the physical sensations of your breathing. If it helps, put a hand on your chest and abdomen so you literally feel the inhaling and exhaling.

Do this new mindful breathing exercise 2 times a day for 2 to 3 minutes for 5 days, then, on page 279, write about the effect of this breathing exercise on how you feel.

# Gratitude

**gratitude**

One of the most powerful kind feelings, gratitude involves being aware and thankful for all the positive things we have in life.

There are many things we can be grateful for. We can be grateful for the earth, people and pets we care about, things that go well in our day, what we can do with our body and mind, people who help us, our beliefs that give us purpose and meaning, our ancestors, and for being able to have fun and laugh.

Many cultures have rituals and celebrations to express gratitude to their ancestors and for the land and earth. Indigenous cultures often express feelings and perform rituals of gratitude for negative as well as positive experiences. The cultures recognize that even negative experiences can provide positive opportunities when a person has a growth mindset and is open to new possibilities. In Native American and other Indigenous cultures, even death is viewed with a sense of gratitude because it is accepted as a passage to the next world or the next step in life. This is illustrated by a quote from a traditional teacher and healer of the Mohawk Nation:

> We understand who we are
> We know where we came from
> We accept and understand our destiny here on Mother Earth
> We are spirit having a human experience[2]

The stronger and more often we recognize our feelings of gratitude, the more frequently we are likely to act with kindness. Multiple studies have shown that feelings of gratitude foster the intention to be kind and increase the help we give to others, even strangers.[3] Interestingly, researchers indicate that writing in a gratitude journal activates the "generosity" portion of the brain.[4]

## EXAMPLE

A young adult Indigenous leader comments on gratitude:

*We show gratitude for all that the earth has provided us. When we start with gratitude toward the basics, the extraordinary earth, everything else seems to fall away. Money, people's opinions of us, grades, or politics, all of this suddenly doesn't seem so important when we show gratitude for the natural world.*

◆ ◆ ◆

Researchers report that grateful people experience higher levels of positive emotions such as joy, enthusiasm, love, happiness, and optimism. Gratitude helps protect us from the destructive impulses of envy, resentment, greed, and bitterness. People who experience gratitude can cope more effectively with everyday stress, show increased resilience in the face of trauma-induced stress, recover more quickly from illness, and enjoy more robust physical health.[5]

*EXAMPLE*

Athletes are discovering that the practice of gratitude has benefits that enhance not only their mental health, but their athletic performance as well. An Instagram post from *Runner's World* asked how runners get through the rest of their long runs after they hit a wall (usually about mile 20 in a 26-mile marathon) and feel exhausted. One runner, Melissa Emery, talked about the importance of gratitude:

*Once I hit a wall, I spend the next mile focusing on the things I am grateful for. "I am grateful for this beautiful view, I am grateful for the sidewalk, I am grateful for the sun, I am grateful for my legs, and even though they hurt, I know I can do this, etc." By the time the mile ends, the wall has been lifted and I continue on.*[6]

## PUT INTO **Practice**

If you seldom actually feel grateful, try this activity: Visualize something or someone very important or meaningful to you—like your partner, sibling, parent, friend, pet, or even the car that takes you places, the home that shelters you, natural settings such as mountains and rivers, or the computer that makes it possible for you to work and play. Imagine something happens beyond your control that removes this important something. How does that make you feel?

_____

_____

Now, remind yourself that it has not been taken away. Do you feel gratitude?

_____

A teenager who tried this challenge said: "I found the practice of imagining your life without something as a way to find gratitude was really useful. It's something that I think would resonate with everyone! We get used to the things and people we enjoy and forget how much they've improved our life and how we should show that gratitude."

## PUT INTO **Practice**

Write about two things you are grateful for today.

_____

_____

# Altruism

---

**altruism**

   Acting out of selfless concern for the well-being of others.

---

We can group acts of kindness into four categories. In this workbook, we will refer to these four ways of acting with altruistic kindness as the four kindness skills:

- Showing appreciation
- Giving help
- Being friendly
- Reaching out to those in serious need

## *Examples of the Four Kindness Skills*

Table 2.1 on pages 52–53, prepared for middle school, provides examples of the four ways we can act with kindness. Examples are shown for different places in school (or in the workplace).

Some kind acts have a greater impact than others on the giver and receiver of the kindness. Think about how delivering a hot meal and a hug to a family whose house was destroyed in a fire would be more meaningful than just dropping off a can of beans for a food drive. How does it feel when you are the giver, putting others first?

All acts of altruism have value and meaning. Even small acts contribute to building meaningful kind habits and impacting the world around us.

### EXAMPLE

Honduran Yanelle Cruz received small acts of heartfelt kindness (friendliness and help) when she traveled from her home in Honduras to Beijing, China, on a cultural exchange program:

*I was born and raised in Tegucigalpa, Honduras, and I am obsessed with my homeland. When I was in high school, I had an opportunity to travel to Beijing, China, over the summer to attend a cultural exchange conference. It did not take long for me to realize I didn't need to speak Mandarin to communicate kindness to my tour guides or to the lady who cleaned my hotel room every day. The things I remember most about my trip were the small moments, like when a woman offered me her water bottle after I ran out of water climbing the Great Wall. Or strangers who saw me awkwardly try to take selfies and offered to take my picture instead. Little acts of kindness like those would seem insignificant when you're home and living your daily routine, but when you're in a place that's completely unknown, they can provide a strong sense of comfort.*[7]

✦ ✦ ✦

Heartfelt kindness has a deeper and more lasting impact, not only for the recipient, but also for the giver. So, what makes an act of kindness heartfelt? Three things: the recipient's need is significant, the giver fulfills that need, and the kindness "transaction" happens on a personal level, ideally face to face.

## EXAMPLE

When the Romero Vasquez sisters gave some food to hungry immigrants traveling across Mexico on the roof of a train, they didn't think much of it. They were just afraid their mother would be mad at them for giving away their breakfast. Little did they know that 19 years later, with their mother's help, their small act of kindness would become Las Patronas, a charitable organization in Veracruz that's helped thousands of migrants. And in 2013, they received Mexico's most prestigious human rights prize, the Premio Nacional de Derechos Humanos.[8]

## EXAMPLE

There were two juniors in high school, Latisha and Stefan. Latisha was active in her school's Black Student Union and NAACP youth chapter. She noticed that Stefan was becoming increasingly isolated, so she invited him to attend some Black Student Union and NAACP youth chapter activities. She learned that Stefan was in a terrible foster home setting and was becoming increasingly depressed, which led to a drop in his grades. His birthday was coming up, and he was desperate to play sports but lacked the $300 fee. When Latisha told her mother about Stefan, her mother said she would pay the $300 and see if she could be his foster parent.

## FROM THE OTHER SIDE

Doug learned about heartfelt kindness through his correspondence with prisoners, since every time one of his prison friends described an act of kindness, it almost always involved a personal connection as well as meeting a significant need. Sometimes a heartfelt act of kindness follows an act of forgiveness, and even the smallest acts (friendliness) can have big impacts. Imagine, for example, a newly hired restaurant server who spills syrup all over you, but instead of becoming angry, you forgive the person and do not create a fuss. Below is how Roy forgave a guard who made a mess in his cell:

*A new guard just started working for ADC and it was her first night at work. She dropped my breakfast into my cell before I could get to it. Oatmeal and syrup went everywhere and that included on me, from the waist down. She was almost in tears and I said, "Ma'am, please relax because the world ain't gonna end over small shit like you dropping a tray and painting me with oatmeal and syrup." I said it with a smile on my face. The sergeant over the shift came over and thanked me for being kool about the accident and not clicking or snapping on the new officer.*

**TABLE 2.1**    *Four Ways We Can Act with Kindness in Different Settings*

|  | Classroom | Cafeteria |
|---|---|---|
| **Be friendly** | • Smile<br>• Greet—Say Hi<br>• Learn everyone's name<br>• Make positive comments<br>• Compliment<br>• Listen carefully<br>• Look at the person speaking | • Smile<br>• Greet—Be welcoming<br>• Speak about positive things—don't gossip<br>• Listen and let others talk<br>• Let someone go ahead of you |
| **Offer help** | • Say, "Can I help …"<br>• Offer to share, "I have an extra pencil you can use."<br>• Volunteer to help other students<br>• Offer to help a teacher | • Help new students learn cafeteria routines<br>• Do your part to help at clean-up times<br>• Put lunch boxes, trays, and trash in the right place<br>• Invite someone new to sit with you |
| **Show appreciation** | • Say thank you to teachers and students for their efforts<br>• Comment on others' thoughtfulness<br>• Comment on things you are grateful for: "I'm happy when …" "I feel good about …"<br>• Say thank you to others who help you. Accept help graciously. | • Comment positively on food, "I love the salsa you made today"<br>• Say please and thank you to cooks, food servers, and preparers<br>• Make comments about things you are grateful for<br>• Notice and kindly comment on other people's thoughtfulness and friendliness |
| **Reach out** | • Offer to help students who are struggling<br>• Encourage students who seem frustrated, "We can do it!" Then help them with their work.<br>• Partner with students having difficulty | • Ask if you can sit with students who seem upset. Reach out to students having difficulty.<br>• Give a compliment, "I like …" |

| Hallways | Buses | School Grounds |
|---|---|---|
| • Smile<br>• Greet—"Nice to meet you."<br>• Say Hi, wave, high-five as you pass in the hall<br>• Make positive comments<br>• Compliment<br>• Listen carefully | • Smile<br>• Greet<br>• Make positive comments<br>• Compliment<br>• Listen carefully<br>• Invite someone to sit with you | • Smile<br>• Greet others when you arrive<br>• Wave, say "good-bye" or "have a good day" as you leave school<br>• Make positive comments<br>• Compliment |
| • Accompany students who are new in the school<br>• Help students with heavier burdens<br>• Help students who are lost<br>• Help students pick up any things that have fallen<br>• Hold doors open | • Offer a more convenient place to sit for people who need it<br>• Assist people who are having difficulty carrying things | • Offer to help new students who are unfamiliar with school grounds<br>• Pick up garbage<br>• Put equipment away<br>• Explain the rules of a game if someone is new |
| • Thank others for being cooperative<br>• Thank others for being friendly<br>• Compliment artwork or displays | • Thank others for being cooperative<br>• Thank others for being friendly<br>• Smile and thank drivers and assistants | • Thank teachers and aides for their efforts<br>• Acknowledge students when they are being positive<br>• Congratulate students for a good game, "Nice game ..." "Way to go."<br>• Thank other students, "Thanks for letting me join in." |
| • Accompany students who are often picked on or are unpopular<br>• Support students who are being bullied | • Share a seat with students who are excluded. Introduce yourself and ask their name, "Hi, I'm Jane, what's your name?"<br>• Sit and talk respectfully with everyone, including students who are excluded or discriminated against | • Invite kids who are often excluded to play with you. Let others join your team no matter what.<br>• Encourage students who struggle, "Way to go!" "Good job!" "Great hit!" "You'll get it next time." |

## PUT INTO **Practice** 🖉

Think about an act of heartfelt kindness you've experienced, either as the giver or the receiver, or as a witness. Write a description of what happened, including the significance of the receiver's need, the impact on the people involved, and how it made you feel.

_____

_____

_____

Indicate which of the four kindness skills were involved: showing appreciation, giving help, being friendly, or reaching out to those in serious need.

_____


## *Volunteering*

Probably the best example of applying all four kindness skills is through volunteering. In most types of volunteering we reach out to those in need, are friendly, give help, and show appreciation for the opportunity to be kind.

Numerous studies have shown that volunteering, when done with altruism, offers powerful benefits to the person doing the volunteering as well as to the recipient. For example, in one study, tenth-grade students who volunteered with elementary students every week for two months had improvements in heart health. On the other hand, tenth-graders who did not volunteer did not have those benefits.[9]

One of the unexpected important benefits of volunteering is that the person who does the volunteering often learns gratitude. A young volunteer, tutoring a child from an immigrant family, spoke of how he learned about the violence the family had been subjected to in their home country and felt gratitude for being able to live without daily fears of being subjected to violence.

### FROM THE OTHER SIDE

Tad, who is an exceptional artist and one of the coauthors of *Saint Badass*, describes how he volunteered to show kindness by helping a friend in prison and encouraged this friend to share kindness with others in turn. Tad did not ask anything for himself:

*A friend of mine was going home from prison and wanted me to draw his two girls and two sons some pictures. It took me two and a half weeks of drawing. The last one was a Roman aqueduct in France and the Sydney Opera House in Australia; that took me 18 hours to draw and four hours to shade. Then I added the North and South Constellations at the top and bottom. On the front I drew the seven continents and five oceans. Basically, not only were they nice drawings, but they were educational. When I was asked by my friend how much he owed me, I said, "Nothing. It's for your children. When you get out, stay out, and if you can help someone one day, do so." He was amazed. Even his own Homeboy had charged him.*

*EXAMPLE*

College advisor Jody Bothe describes how she encourages teens to be kind by volunteering:

*I am constantly supporting them to find a volunteer activity to personally connect with and to then do it deeply. It's more about depth, not breadth, of volunteer activities. Don't show me a list of 10 different short-lived volunteer activities where you spent a minimal amount of time being directed by someone to do something specific. Show me where you put in your time and then lifted the activity to a higher level; display some leadership and ownership. For example, maybe you love to play soccer. OK, now turn that into something more. Since you are already connected to the activity, that is a start. Now find a way to play soccer with a community of people who will benefit from your enthusiasm and expertise. For example, start a free summer soccer camp for poor children, fundraise for soccer balls for those who can't buy one, etc.*

*EXAMPLE FROM AN AUTHOR*

Doug describes how volunteers and unhoused people were affected by heartfelt kindness of food and shelter.

*Each winter in Eugene, Oregon, where I live, a community organization works with a number of churches to provide shelter for unhoused people when the temperature drops below 32 degrees. The program houses more than 500 people some nights. The organization depends on volunteers to be able to provide this service. I served dinners during evening shifts. The supervisor told the volunteers how much it means to the clients to receive a smile and a sincere greeting. I noticed that some volunteers were touched by their experience providing food and shelter to unhoused individuals. They would no longer see the homeless as a type of undesirable person but rather as a collection of individuals, each with their own story of hardship.*

Volunteering sincerely to help people with serious needs can awaken our compassion for those individuals and can intensify our gratitude for the good things in our lives.

PUT INTO **Practice**

Describe how you might use one of your skills by volunteering to help others learn that skill, such as in Jody Bothe's soccer example.

| Skill | Volunteering Opportunity |
|-------|--------------------------|
| _____ | _____ |
| _____ | _____ |
| _____ | _____ |

# Altruism Mistakes

Altruism seems simple and straightforward—we simply apply the four kindness skills. But to be truly altruistic, we need to avoid common mistakes people make when trying to be altruistic. We will discuss four altruism mistakes: 1) refusing to receive kindness, 2) failing to recognize when an act is genuinely altruistic, 3) believing kindness must be nice, and 4) faking altruism.

## Refusing to Receive Altruistic Acts of Kindness

Most people are not aware that one of the most important acts of kindness we can do is to accept kindness from others. Feeling compassion, we recognize that when we receive the kindness of another person, that person can experience the warm feelings that come from a generous act. Whenever we get the opportunity, we can be kind by giving others the opportunity to be kind to us. Receiving as well as giving kindness is important to our lives in many ways, most importantly in contributing to closer relationships, better health, and greater happiness.

Some people who are especially kind have difficulty receiving kindness. This reluctance might come from their need to be independent and therefore not need kindness from others. Or maybe reluctance comes from not wanting to feel obligated to the person giving the kindness; they believe that if they receive a kindness, then they owe that person a kindness. Do you find it hard to receive kindness from others? If you recognize your reluctance to accept kindness, take on the role of the Wise Warrior to overcome the reluctance. Remember, when we accept the kindness and express our gratitude, we are being kind to the giver of the kindness.

### EXAMPLE

Doug's wife, Linda, was waiting in line at a coffee shop. When she completed her order and reached for her wallet, the man behind her reached for his wallet to pay for her coffee. When she protested, he explained that he liked to buy coffee for other people because it helped him take his mind off his own worries. Linda realized that accepting the coffee would actually be an act of kindness toward this stranger.

 PUT INTO **Practice**

Have you ever refused to accept an act of kindness, even something simple such as someone offering you a part of their lunch? Describe the offer of kindness.

_____

How did you feel after you refused?

_____

How do you think the other person felt?

_____

# Failing to Recognize When an Act Is Genuinely Altruistic

While the first altruism mistake is refusing to accept an act of kindness, the second mistake is failing to recognize an action as being genuinely kind. Many of us have spent part of our lives in unkind environments. Previous experiences can leave us suspicious of acts of kindness. We often assume that seeming acts of kindness by someone we are not very close to are in fact unkind.

*EXAMPLE*

A teenager who has experienced racial profiling throughout his life explains why he has a hard time recognizing kindness.

*One night my mom was short a can of chicken stock. I was allowed as a child to walk to the nearby 7-Eleven to get a can. After staring at the same shelf for 5 minutes, I found the right can. But at the register, my mom's credit card was rejected. Confused, I tried again. All I knew was that I needed to get this can of soup and make it back home before it got too dark. The card didn't work at all, so I realized I would have to return home empty handed. Defeated, I plopped the can back on the shelf. As I walked out of the store I heard the deepest "WAIT" escape a man's voice. That was enough to send fear through my body and I ran. Frantic and out of breath, I returned without the can of soup to a very confused mother. Together we walked back to the store and there was the man who had yelled. He told us he was just trying to help and had paid for the soup. From that young of an age I had assumed someone was out to hurt me, instead of help. I laugh looking back at it now, but I remember the fear. It can be hard to separate those who are out to get you from those who want to help you. Growing up as a person of color, you are taught to have your guard up constantly. I wish I could go back now to thank that man. Unfortunately, I still find that as a person of color I need to have my guard up, but I try to be mindfully aware of all that is happening before interpreting a person's intended act of kindness as not being sincere.*

✦ ✦ ✦

As we continue through the workbook, we will learn to use our Diligent Detective to better judge when we are being genuinely kind and when others are being genuinely kind. In the final chapters of this workbook, we will learn about challenges faced by those who often are discriminated against. This knowledge will be very valuable, particularly to those of us who are not targets of discrimination, to make sure that acts of kindness are really altruistic acts of kindness. These chapters will also be valuable for those of us who are victims of discrimination in learning to understand.

PUT INTO **Practice**

Have there been times when you meant to do something kind, and your kind gesture was rejected by the intended recipient of your kindness? If so, describe what happened and tell why you think your kindness was rejected.

_____

_____

**Have there been times when you rejected an intended act of kindness from someone else? If so, why did you reject the act of kindness?**

_____

_____

## Believing Kindness Must Be Nice

The third mistake is misunderstanding the ways kindness can be expressed, in particular believing that kindness must always be nice. Being nice is when you are polite to people and treat people pleasantly. Of course, we want to be nice by being pleasant and agreeable. But in some situations, it is not necessary to be polite to be kind. We are being kind when we care about people and show we care by acting with altruism. Sometimes we can be kind to someone even though we aren't being nice to them. For example, frequently reminding a close friend to do their physical therapy exercises prescribed after an accident might seem like nagging. Nagging is not nice, but in this case the reminders can be kind, especially if the person needs the physical therapy to recover and walk again. Upsetting someone, for example, by what appears to be nagging, creates an uncomfortable situation, but it can be the kind thing to do if it helps the person build a kind habit—such as doing critical physical therapy exercises—and break a harmful unkind habit—putting off important responsibilities such as doing their physical therapy exercises. This is not to advocate for confrontations with people in the name of kindness. The point is that sometimes when we need to be kind, the help we give may not appear to be nice.

### EXAMPLE

In his early twenties, Derek got a job as an assistant to a skilled metal worker, who allowed him to sleep in an unused space in his workshop, rent free. When Derek received his first paycheck, he said he could not accept it because the free rent was worth more than the pay. His boss said, "You can't only give. You must learn to receive or else other people will not be able to give." The boss then told Derek he had to move out and find a new place to live. It was his boss's way of showing him, in a very forceful manner, that he should not refuse kindness. In looking back at the incident, Derek wrote this surprising explanation: "They were good people. I doubt I would remember the lesson if they just said you have to give and you have to receive. I remembered it because of the intense way they did it." Derek's point was that his boss's seeming cruelty was actually kind because it was necessary for Derek to learn the importance of accepting kindness, a lesson Derek has never forgotten. Derek felt the 'not-nice' eviction helped him become a better person. If you act with kindness that is not nice, be sure to explain why the act was actually kind. Derek's boss could have told Derek that evicting him was intended to be an important kindness lesson about receiving kindness. Fortunately, Derek figured it out on his own.

✦ ✦ ✦

In the example below, a recent high school graduate is given advice that makes her feel bad, but later she realizes the advice was kind.

### Example

Belise, an East African refugee-immigrant explains how *nice* differs from *kind*:

*Unlike my parents, I have the ability to attend college, and one of my own choosing. This has been a dream of mine since I was a young girl. So, when senior year rolled around and college application season arrived, I began applying to all my dream schools. A friend of mine who was helping me said, "You need to start applying to more safety schools. You are not going to get into all or any of these high-end schools." I was taken aback by her comment. It was not nice, but it was kind. She was thinking of my future and the negative effects that would occur if I only applied to difficult schools and ended up without any colleges that would accept me.*

✦ ✦ ✦

We can avoid the mistake of believing kindness must be nice in two ways, first, by how we receive a seeming unkindness and second, by how we deliver a kindness that could be seen as unkind. When we receive a seeming unkindness, we can be mindful of the intent of the person who thinks they are being kind. Reflect on the content of the action to see if it might be kind. If necessary, take on the role of the Wise Warrior to stop reacting in anger to the not-nice act of supposed kindness.

The second way to avoid the kindness-must-be-kind mistake is to learn how to deliver our kindness in the nicest possible manner, even though the content appears to be not-nice, as illustrated by Belise's friend. We may need to take on the role of the Diligent Detective to figure out how to give advice that is caring and gentle, even though it may be delivering a message the recipient may not be happy to hear.

## Faking Altruism

The fourth mistake might be thought of as the result of not feeling compassion. When we give help to others and expect something in return, we are not practicing altruism. We are engaging in a trade: We will do something for someone. Then that person will do something for us. Trading is fine and even necessary, and can be kind. But trading is not an act of altruism. With altruism, we expect nothing in return. Altruism comes from compassion. Making a trade and thinking it is altruism is fake altruism. In one study, researchers investigated 50 years of data on more than 10,000 Wisconsin high school students as they aged and found that the people who volunteered lived longer.[10] Then the researcher looked more closely and found that people benefited more from volunteering when their kind acts were based on altruism and compassion—as opposed to faking altruism. The selfish volunteers, lacking compassion, lived no longer than the individuals who did not volunteer at all.

Faking altruism means we act nicely for selfish reasons, like wanting to be a member of the National Honor Society, building up a resume, impressing friends, or converting others' beliefs about religion or politics. A high school member of the National Honor Society had this to say about the problem of being compelled to volunteer: "There's a 10-hour minimum volunteer requirement each semester, and I find a lot of my friends don't have any heart in their volunteering."

As we learn more about mindfulness and compassion, we can avoid the mistake of faking altruism. Mindfulness will help our Diligent Detective determine if our act of intended kindness stems from compassion and is altruistic. Doing the exercises in this workbook will help develop our compassion as we hear more stories that make us care about people and that will increase our concern and empathy for the troubles others are having. And we will become more aware of how our kindfulness can help them.

## PUT INTO **Practice**

Write about how you have acted with kindness. Give one example where you expected to receive something in return for being kind.

_____

_____

Write about a time when you offered someone kindness with altruism, without any selfish expectations.

_____

_____

How did each of these situations make you feel?

_____

_____

# Cycles of Mindfulness and Kindness

As we go through life, we alternate between being more mindful and kind (with compassion, gratitude, and altruism) and being less mindful and kind. Not surprisingly, a purpose of this workbook is to help you spend more of your day (and life) in a cycle of mindful kindness.

## The Mindful-Kind Cycle—Key Idea

Kindness in the forms of compassion, gratitude, and altruism sets the stage for us to enter the mindful-kind cycle. When we are mindful, we are more aware of the opportunities to be kind and more able to carry out acts of kindness. Carrying out acts of kindness makes us feel good. When we feel good, we are more likely to carry on our mindfulness, which in turn makes us more ready to see and carry out opportunities to be kind.

### FROM THE OTHER SIDE

Roy, the first person at Tucker Max with whom Doug corresponded, taught mindful kindness to Tad, who is teaching mindful kindness to two other prisoners, Chris and Tex. Here, Tad describes how he taught the mindful-kind cycle:

*Chris, me, and another guy in this barracks named Tex are pretty close. I will deliberately take myself out of certain situations so I won't be recognized for doing a kind act, e.g., I know Tex is out of coffee. I'll send him some and tell him, "It's from Chris." Tex will send me something (when he can). And I'll send it to Chris and tell him, "It's from Tex." Some would say, "I'm purposely lying." But I don't see it like that. These two guys have life in prison. They're never getting out. Me, I'll soon be gone. I just want to help build a solid bond between two people. That's my intention! So after I'm gone, they will continue to be there for each other.*

## The Unmindful-Unkind Cycle—Key Idea

When we are unmindful, we are less aware of the consequences of our unkind habits. We are not being sensitive to the harm we are causing ourselves and others. If we were aware of the harm we are causing, we would probably be motivated to stop causing the harm. But being unaware means we are more likely to continue being unkind. If we are unaware of how we are harming others, we are also unlikely to be aware of opportunities to be kind. In the unmindful-unkind cycle, our unkindness triggers feel-bad chemicals and our lack of kindness deprives us of the feel-good chemicals. Acting unkindly leads to damaged personal connections and personal isolation. When we are caught in the unmindful-unkind cycle, we are often consumed by negative self-talk. We often feel depressed and closed in by our own miserable, negative self-talk. We may use aggression, drugs, alcohol, and other unkind habits to stop the negative self-talk.

The chapters in Part 4 of the workbook explain how the Diligent Detective and the Wise Warrior work together to identify and get rid of our unkind habits and help us stay out of the unmindful-unkind cycle.

**negative self-talk**

> Mental chatter about our problems that often reads like a list of complaints about what we want but can't get and about what we get but don't want.

*EXAMPLE*

Victor, a teenager, reflected on his experience of the unmindful-unkind cycle:

*Sometimes I'm just happy, and being kind to other people and myself just comes as second nature. Other times, I'm just really angry with myself, which causes me to be blind to other people's problems. For me personally, I usually don't realize it until after the fact, and by that point I realize I've wasted a lot of time, which makes me even more angry with myself. If people are more aware when they're about to fall into one of those cycles, it can help them be more kind to themselves or nudge them to do an activity that relaxes them.*

✦ ✦ ✦

As you read this book and do the exercises, you will learn to answer this question: What can we do in our daily lives to spend more of our time in the mindful-kind cycle? The answer is simple: Build more kind habits and decrease or eliminate unkind habits. With the right effort in working on the mindfulness and kindness exercises, you will in fact spend more of your time in the mindful-kind cycle.

PUT INTO **Practice**

Describe a time when you found yourself in a mindful-kind cycle and how it made you feel.

_____

_____

Then describe a time when you found yourself in an unmindful-unkind cycle and how it made you feel.

_____

_____

# Wrapping Up

Chapter 1 introduced mindfulness and kindness. Chapter 2 explained the Skills of Action—the ability to assume the different roles one needs on the path to lead a loving, healthy, and happy life (Kindful Practitioner, Diligent Detective, and Wise Warrior); Skills of Character—the ability to develop an attitude that supports us in making change (Growth Mindset, being Responsible, Patient, and Humble); and the Skill of Diagnosis—the ability to determine whether the challenge we face requires us to act primarily in our mental world, physical world, or possibly, our spiritual or religious world. Chapter 3 expands our ideas of kindness in several ways:

- Explaining our basic instincts that include kindness

- Describing the different forms kindness can take: compassion, gratitude, and altruism

- Giving examples of four ways to act with altruism: give help, be friendly, show appreciation, and reach out to those with serious needs

Four altruism mistakes were spelled out: 1) refusing to receive kindness, 2) failing to recognize when an act is genuinely altruistic, 3) believing kindness must be nice, and 4) faking altruism.

Finally, compassion, gratitude, and altruism in the form of kind habits lead to a mindful-kind cycle. In contrast, unkind habits which greatly limit our compassion, gratitude, and altruism lead to the unmindful-unkind cycle.

## ☑ *Checking In*

Are you remembering to practice your mindful breathing? As you progress through the workbook, you will find that mindful breathing is a building block for more advanced mindfulness practices and also is an invaluable tool to help you deal with difficult situations. So do the best you can to practice mindful breathing each day. As you practice, tune in to how this breathing practice makes you feel.

# Time for Reflection

On a scale of 1 through 4, how interested are you in spending time on the following practices?

|  | Not Interested 1 | Some Interest 2 | Interested 3 | Very Interested 4 |
|---|---|---|---|---|
| Becoming more compassionate | ☐ | ☐ | ☐ | ☐ |
| Naming what I am grateful for and experiencing more gratitude | ☐ | ☐ | ☐ | ☐ |
| Volunteering | ☐ | ☐ | ☐ | ☐ |
| Being better able to receive kindness | ☐ | ☐ | ☐ | ☐ |
| Becoming a better Wise Warrior: Have the courage to go outside a comfort zone to take action | ☐ | ☐ | ☐ | ☐ |
| Becoming a better Diligent Detective: Get the information needed to make a constructive decision | ☐ | ☐ | ☐ | ☐ |
| Becoming a better Kindful Practitioner: Act with kindness and mindfulness many times every day | ☐ | ☐ | ☐ | ☐ |

Write about how you have been kind at least one time in one of these ways:

- Be friendly
- Give help
- Show appreciation
- Reach out to those with serious needs

_____

_____

Chapter 4

# Increase Your Kindness

*If you want to lift yourself up, lift someone else up.*

Booker T. Washington

To have a meaningful, healthy, happy life, we need to receive kindness and show kindness. Four ways to do this are: giving help, showing appreciation, being friendly, and reaching out to those with serious needs. We also want to show kindness often. For example, in stable and happy close relationships, there are many positive comments and activities every day. Most of them involve three of our four kindness skills: helping, showing appreciation, and being friendly. In fact, in stable and happy marriages there are five times as many positive comments/activities as negative comments/activities.[1] These kind comments and activities build personal relationships, not only in a marriage, but with partners, family, friends, groups with mutual interests, and others in our surroundings. Most of this workbook is about relationships with those closest to us; however, later chapters describe how to expand our kindness throughout our community and how to expand the reach of our kindness to those with serious needs.

> " *Three things in human life are important. The first is to be kind. The second is to be kind. And the third is to be kind.* "
>
> — Henry James

### EXAMPLE

Victor, a high school student, explains how to act with kindness more often:

*I think people think of themselves as kind, but they don't really go out of their way to be kind. They don't think to show it to people they don't know or classmates who were mean to them first. We should be aware of the things around us because we are often too caught up in our own fears and doubts to notice others whose day would be so much better with kindness. I think it's also important to emphasize that kindness is also the small things in life, like giving a smile in the hallway or remembering someone's birthday. I think a lot of people have stereotypical thoughts of kindness being, for example, helping someone pick up their stuff when they've dropped it. I don't think you should wait for something bad to happen to offer kindness.*

In the last chapter we expanded our ideas about why and how to be kind. This chapter describes how to put those ideas into action. While there are many ways to build kind habits, this chapter will discuss just three ways: practicing quick acts of kindness, using pleasant kind habits, and using kind communication habits. The chapter will conclude with a section about how to make plans to help us be successful in developing our kindness skills.

## Kindness Begins with You

Small acts of kindness are an excellent way to start increasing your kindness. And small acts of kindness make a difference. A wealth of ideas for small, random acts of kindness can be found on the website Randomactsofkindness.org. Below are some specific ideas for how to be friendly, help, show appreciation, and reach out to those with serious needs. The first group includes things you can do quickly at any moment. The second group (not-so-small acts of kindness) includes acts that may need some planning and that you might do over an extended amount of time:

## A. Quick Acts of Kindness

1. Take a walk with a lonely classmate or co-worker. (reach out)
2. Buy someone a lunch or a snack at school or work. (be friendly)
3. Surprise someone with something they like to drink, like coffee or tea. (be friendly)
4. Listen deeply to a friend or coworker as they work through a personal problem. (reach out)
5. Hold a door open. (help)
6. Give what you can to an unhoused person. (reach out)
7. Text someone who would like to hear from you. (be friendly)
8. Ask someone how their day is going. (be friendly)
9. Smile at people. (be friendly)
10. Make someone laugh. (be friendly)
11. Give high-fives. (be friendly)
12. Clean up trash when you walk on the beach or in your neighborhood. (help)
13. Respond with an open ear and nonjudgmental comments. (be friendly)
14. Lightly joke around to help create a good mood. (be friendly)
15. Like someone's Instagram pictures. (show appreciation)
16. Smile, make eye contact, or show attention, and say hello to someone you don't know. (be friendly)
17. Say someone's outfit is cool. (be friendly)
18. Return shopping carts for people at the grocery store. (help)
19. Put positive sticky notes on someone's car, locker, or desk. (be friendly)
20. Take out the trash. (help)
21. Put a note on somebody's desk telling how they support you. (show appreciation)
22. Give genuine compliments to those you hardly know, like a waiter or bus driver. (show appreciation)
23. Buy a gift card for a homeless person. (reach out)

## B. Not-So-Small Acts of Kindness

1. Support a sick friend, relative, or coworker. (reach out)
2. Volunteer at a homeless shelter. (reach out)
3. Visit several times with an elder. (reach out)
4. Make dinners for a family or friend who is having medical problems. (reach out)
5. Remember to send a text or card on the birthdays of your family and friends (requires making a list on your phone's calendar app). (be friendly)
6. Write friends about things you like about them. (show appreciation)
7. Email or write to a former teacher who made a difference in your life. (show appreciation)
8. Send a thank-you note to let someone know you appreciate something kind they have done. (show appreciation)
9. Give someone a list of all they've done that you're grateful for. (show appreciation)
10. Acknowledge someone publicly in front of friends or coworkers for the kind things the person has done. (show appreciation)

## PUT INTO **Practice**

Select and write 5 items from the list above that you want to do more often. Explain why you want to do them more often.

_____

_____

_____

_____

_____

# Pleasant Kind Habits

In an ideal world, we would find all our kind habits enjoyable to do. However, in our real world, we are likely to find that some kind habits are not fun for us; for example, while some people enjoy jogging, we might jog to take care of our health but find it unpleasant. Or we might limit the calories we eat to reduce our weight but feel bad as we see others eating ice cream. Or we may spend considerable time shoveling snow from an older neighbor's house but find doing so unpleasant.

Fortunately, most of us have kind habits that we find pleasurable or gratifying. We call these Pleasant Kind Habits.

**pleasant kind habits**

> Kind habits that bring joy, appreciation, and enrichment to our life, help sustain us during dark times, and buffer us against addictive behavior.

The pleasant events we experience each day improve our mood and our well-being, and can decrease our anxiety and depression.[2] Pleasant Kind Habits do more than make us feel better. They also can serve to energize us and fortify our intention to be a Kindful Practitioner who acts every day with mindful kindness—toward ourself and others. On the other hand, kind habits we find unpleasant may often be very important but may not elevate our mood.

The point is that **all kind habits are helpful. If they are pleasant, they can boost our mood. If they are unpleasant, they are unlikely to boost our mood at the moment but are helpful over the long run.** Being able to engage in our pleasant, kind habits can often make us feel better when we are anxious or feeling slightly depressed. Have you ever felt a release from anxiety when you engage in a pleasant habit? Describe that sense of release. When we feel better we are less likely to engage in negative behavior.

*EXAMPLE*

Here's how a high school student found pleasure and stress reduction through his pleasant kind habit of dancing:

*In the beginning of my junior year of high school, I had a lot going on. I had music practice, dance classes, learning to drive, challenging courses, and social drama at school. All of those things felt like they were constantly on my mind. I have a very chatty brain; I'm constantly thinking something, and typically it's about what is stressing me out. Luckily, dance has always been a great outlet for me; I've been consistently dancing for almost 10 years now. Tuesday and Wednesday nights, I could leave all of my worries at home and focus solely on my body, the music, and exercise. I literally felt physical relief from my stress during warmups. Going home, I felt like a new person—ready to take on my responsibilities and start fresh. After that tough period, I'll never forget how much dance can do to ground me!*

✦ ✦ ✦

An often underappreciated type of pleasant kind habit is spending time in nature, which seems to help relieve stress and anxiety, improve our mood, and boost feelings of happiness and well-being.[3] Just living in greener areas seems to produce a range of health benefits.[4] For a comprehensive summary from science about the value of spending time in nature, read *The Nature Fix: Why Nature Makes us Happier, Healthier, and More Creative.*[5] Most cities have parks where we can enjoy nature. We can bring nature into our homes with house plants, and, if we have the space, we can plant small gardens in our yard, on our deck, or on our apartment patio.

## Kind Habits Inventory

Find the Kind Habits Inventory. It lists examples of kind habits that can contribute to us living a happy, healthy life. Two aspects of kind habits are 1) whether they are pleasant or unpleasant, and 2) their importance. Some kind habits are pleasant, while some are not. On the other hand, every kind habit is important, but some habits are more important than others. As you read the Kind Habit Inventory, think how important each habit is to you and if you consider it a pleasant habit.

PUT INTO **Practice**

On the Kind Habits Inventory on the next pages, write **P** next to ten kind habits that you feel are pleasant. You can also add a pleasant kind habit to the inventory and mark it with a **P**.

Write **I** next to the five habits that are most important to you. You can add a kind habit that is important to the inventory and mark it with an **I**.

Write the habits that have both a **P** and an **I** in front of them on your phone or on a piece of paper and post it where you will see the list every day.

## Kind Habits Inventory

1.  **Kindness to Yourself**

a. Physical Health

\_\_\_\_\_  I exercise and am physically active.

\_\_\_\_\_  I get enough sleep.

\_\_\_\_\_  I eat healthy food and drink an adequate amount of water.

b. Mental Health

\_\_\_\_\_  I act with mindfulness.

\_\_\_\_\_  I meditate.

\_\_\_\_\_  I pursue education and develop skills so I can find suitable employment.

\_\_\_\_\_  I spend time in nature.

\_\_\_\_\_  I sing, listen to music, play a musical instrument, or make arts and crafts.

\_\_\_\_\_  I set aside more time and energy to get my work done.

\_\_\_\_\_  I am courteous when I am driving, shopping, and talking on the phone.

\_\_\_\_\_  I manage my stress effectively.

\_\_\_\_\_  I forgive myself when I make errors.

\_\_\_\_\_  I have a mentor with expertise to help me build important habits in my areas of interest (not limited to kindness).

\_\_\_\_\_  I have hobbies and interest areas that bring me enjoyment.

\_\_\_\_\_  I practice cultural traditions.

c. Spiritual/Religious Health

\_\_\_\_\_  I find purpose in my religion/spiritual practice.

\_\_\_\_\_  I find moral guidance in my religion/spiritual practice.

\_\_\_\_\_  I find comfort in my religion/spiritual practice.

\_\_\_\_\_  I find friendships through my religion/spiritual practice.

**2. Kindness with Friends and Family**

\_\_\_\_\_  I am friendly, respectful, and kind with all members of my family and friends.

\_\_\_\_\_  I help family and friends without being asked.

\_\_\_\_\_  I help family and friends weaken unkind habits.

_____ I show appreciation to those who help me or who I see helping others.

_____ I encourage others as they work toward a goal.

_____ I respond with positivity when others say something to me.

_____ I make the effort to engage in activities that my good friends highly value, which might involve learning new skills.

_____ I am forgiving of others.

_____ I attend community gatherings with my family and friends.

3. **Kindness at School and/or Work**

_____ I am friendly, respectful, and kind when I speak with others.

_____ I help others who are stuck on a school or work assignment.

_____ I assist with physical tasks when help is needed.

_____ I show appreciation by complimenting the good work of others and by focusing on my group's success rather than my own (when the group succeeds, so do I).

_____ I attempt to consistently be a good example of mindful kindness to classmates or coworkers.

_____ I make people smile and feel accepted.

_____ I am open to new ideas.

_____ I try to include people usually not included in activities. I try to never leave anyone out.

_____ I try to create a good relationship with my teachers or supervisors.

_____ I intervene if someone is being bullied or not respected, even if it's out of my comfort zone.

_____ I show appreciation to those who help me or who I see helping others.

4. **Kindness to Those in Serious Need**

_____ I act respectfully and kindly when interacting with those with serious needs.

_____ I give direct support to those in need—for example, money, food, gloves, or other warm clothing to an unhoused person in cold weather.

_____ I volunteer to help children and families in need in any way I can.

_____ I volunteer to help children who are abused or lacking a caring adult.

_____ I am respectful and helpful to people who migrate to the United States.

_____ I join or support organizations that provide help to those with serious needs.

## PERSONAL CHALLENGE **Journal**

For 5 days, make a tally mark next to each pleasant and important kind habit every time you engage in that kind habit. Then, on page 279, write about how you feel after engaging in your pleasant and important kind habits for 5 days. Continue to review your list even after you stop making tally marks.

# Kind Communication Habits

Learning to act with small kindnesses is relatively simple compared with learning habits of kind communication. The way we communicate with another person greatly influences the quality of our relationship with that person. Communicating with kindness depends on developing habits of caring communication (verbal and nonverbal) based on vulnerability and respect. Kind communication habits enable us to act with friendliness, show appreciation, give help, and reach out to those with serious needs. **Learning kind communication habits is important in all parts of our lives: at home, at work, with our friends, at school, and anywhere we are meeting with people.** The first two important kind communication habits we will discuss are communicating with vulnerability and communicating with respect.

## Vulnerability

### communicating with vulnerability

We share our personal feelings and thoughts so we can build a closer relationship with another person. Communicating with vulnerability is risky because our feelings might be hurt and our thoughts might be judged negatively.

When we communicate with vulnerability, we are honest and open—even though we could be hurt emotionally by the criticism we hear. At the same time we are careful not to hurt other people's feelings. When communicate openly and honestly, we are brave, telling how we feel and/or what we want, for example, using sentences that start with: *I want, I hope, I need*. In difficult situations, we might begin our communication with a statement of vulnerability—for example, by saying how it makes us feel to share what we are going to say. In requesting a favor, we might begin our communication with a statement of vulnerability—for example, "It's hard for me to ask this favor, and I will understand if you say no." By being open about our feelings and speaking in a kind manner, we hope that the other person will respond with vulnerability and kindness as well. When we communicate with vulnerability, we are taking a risk because the other person could respond in a hurtful way.

Here are some examples of communicating with vulnerability.

| | |
|---|---|
| Telling others how they have upset you | I feel badly for not letting you know that I was upset when you laughed at the idea I shared with our instructor. |
| Telling others that you are afraid that what you are going to say may upset them or make them angry | I hope what I am going to say does not upset you. I feel I must say it if I am going to be a good friend. |
| Sharing with someone something from your childhood that you would normally hold back | My father drank too much, so I don't want to be around people who drink too much.<br><br>My brother would say mean things to our mother, so I don't like being around people who are mean. |
| Reaching out to someone you haven't talked to in a while and would like to reconnect with. | I hope you are still willing to be friends even though I have not contacted you for a long time. |
| Sharing your positive feelings that you have not yet communicated | Even though we have not known each other for very long, I want you to know I enjoy spending time with you. |
| Admitting a fear | When I would hang out with friends in high school, I was punished for admitting that I was scared, so now I have difficulty expressing fear. |
| Admitting a regret | I put off visiting my grandmother when she was in the hospital and never got to tell her how much I loved her before she died. |
| Admitting something that is worrying you | I'm afraid that if I make them angry, they will hurt me. |

*Note:* When you communicate with vulnerability, your intention is to improve a relationship. To be honest with a person in a mean, cruel manner is not communicating with vulnerability. For example, saying "You are an awful, selfish person who cares about no one but you" is not vulnerable communication.

 PUT INTO **Practice**

Describe a time when you were not open and honest in your communication. You did not communicate with vulnerability

_____

_____

How did you feel when you were not open and did not communicate with vulnerability?

_____

Describe a time when your communication did include how you really felt. You did communicate with vulnerability.

_____

_____

How did you feel?

_____

Why do you think that being vulnerable might improve your relationship?

_____

_____

 PERSONAL CHALLENGE **Journal**

Have a conversation in which you communicate with vulnerability, sharing one of your regrets, worries, or fears. On page 280, describe what happened during this conversation.

Showing vulnerability is difficult in some cultures. A Latinx community leader commented, "Sometimes in order to survive school, racist people, or other dangers, we build these walls and learn not to show vulnerability."*

### EXAMPLE

A young adult describes how honest communication strengthened a friendship:

*I have been friends with my best friend since kindergarten. Our relationship when we were younger was a bit rocky; we would fight over little things, as kids do, but we never really talked about those problems with each other. In middle school, we both sort of "discovered" the internet, social media, and things like that. Middle school is a huge time of change for kids, and a habit I noticed her taking on was using curse words super frequently.*

*I had no problem with her cursing in general, but she sometimes directed it at me, like calling me "bitch." She used them as terms of endearment (like some people do), and I knew that! But for some reason, I felt really hurt whenever she said that, and I worried that maybe she was secretly actually angry at me.*

---

\* For a more in-depth explanation of vulnerability, watch "The Power of Vulnerability," a TED Talk by Brené Brown, Ph.D., in which she discusses what she has found and learned from her long research into human connection, specifically about the concept of vulnerability and its essential role in our everyday life.

*One day, she exasperatedly called me bitch, and I finally told her, "Hey, I know you say that with love, but I feel bad when you call me bitch. Could you please not call me that?" She hadn't realized how I felt, and stopped calling me words like that. It sparked a new era in our friendship, where we came to each other about our issues and solved them together instead of ignoring them. Many years later, we're still the closest friends!*

 PUT INTO **Practice**

**Describe a time when a conversation you had could have gone better if you had communicated with vulnerability.**

_____

_____

## Respect

We cannot have a close, caring relationship unless we show that we actually, truly care about the other person. We show respect by demonstrating our genuine interest in what the other person has to say, which is at the heart of what it means to be friendly in a deep way. For example, when we are conversing we can make it clear that we are fully involved in the communication, not daydreaming about other things or letting our attention wander.

Showing someone we find them worthy of our attention is being respectful; it's how we demonstrate we genuinely want to learn about the person. We also show respect by being curious about the person because we want to be able to talk about something the person cares about. We use appropriate eye contact, tone of voice, and body language to show our sincerity. Being curious signals our interest not only in another person but also in the world around us. We show our curiosity by giving feedback in the form of asking to hear more, nodding in agreement, making an encouraging comment, and offering relevant information. Being aware and sensitive helps us notice the positive and appreciative affect our attention has on others and ourselves.

Communicating respect to someone else takes a variety of forms depending on our culture. For example, in some cultures, men of the same sex come very close to each other when talking, often laying their hands on each other's shoulders and embracing when meeting with kisses on either cheek. In China, Vietnam, and Cambodia, direct eye contact with a stranger can be seen as disrespectful. And in Japanese culture, hand shaking or other close touching as a greeting is replaced by a distanced bow.

## Body Language

Body language is another important aspect of a caring conversation. In Western cultures, we show respect by facing someone, or possibly leaning forward slightly to indicate interest. In contrast, if we are looking at something or someone else other than the person we are talking to, our body language shows a lack of interest in the person, and the person is likely to not respond in a positive way during the conversation.

Another example of negative body language is talking with our arms tightly crossed across our chest, which often indicates impatience or irritation.

Physical contact is also an important aspect of body language, but it's prudent to be sensitive to whether or not the other person will be receptive to physical contact, such as a hug or touching their arm. Some people may be very receptive to physical contact while others are made extremely uncomfortable by physical contact. In a close relationship with a partner, physical contact such as holding hands can be very comforting. One study found that when one partner was in pain, the pain decreased when the other partner held their hand.[6] Moreover, hand-holding partners tended to have their breathing rates and heart rates become similar to each other. Similar rates are also produced when a group of individuals watch an emotional movie or sing together.

## Conversing with a New Person

In classrooms or workplaces, individuals can get to know each other because they spend day in and day out seeing each other. When we meet a person for the first time, however, we don't know enough about the person to open up or be vulnerable or to ask a caring question to start a conversation. And if we're shy, it's even harder to make the first move.

It's not easy to talk with a new person. If we ask too many questions, they may feel we are grilling them. If we ask too few questions, they may feel we are not interested in them. Sometimes, we can prepare ourselves in advance by finding a topic of mutual interest, which might be about family, work, hobbies, physical activities, or their community. The goal is to share information back and forth. If it is obvious the person is not interested in a topic, we need to switch to another topic.

Always remember, whether we are talking to a friend of 20 years or 20 days, we cannot fake a caring question; it's important that we really care and act with genuine interest. It might seem surprising, but being curious is exceedingly important to show you really care about getting to know the person. When we are curious, we are interested in what the person is talking about.

### EXAMPLE FROM AN AUTHOR

Doug recalls a conversation he had with a stranger at a party.

*At a party, I began a conversation with a fellow guest who I had never met before. She mentioned she was an elementary science teacher. I told her I am particularly interested in life sciences. She responded that she recently taught her class a unit on the Pacific lamprey. I asked her questions about the Pacific lamprey and found that she was passionate about the lamprey. (The lamprey is a species that is 450 million years old, living long before the dinosaurs. They are blind and toothless for the first seven years of their lives. The species is of central importance, in a spiritual and practical sense [food], to numerous indigenous groups in the Pacific Northwest.) My interest increased her passion and made clear my respect for her and her thinking.*

## PUT INTO **Practice**

Imagine you are meeting someone for the first time. List four simple questions you might ask.

_____

_____

_____

# Six Communication Habits for Responding during a Conversation

Kind communication habits allow us to keep a caring conversation going. In the extended example below, a worker makes a comment about sleeping poorly because of worrying about a problem at work. In the table **Examples of Six Kind Communication Habits**, the responses of his office friend illustrate each of these six kind communication habits. These six habits enable us to showing respect and vulnerability and also to use body language. These six habits are also ways of being friendly, offering help, showing appreciation, and reaching out to those with serious needs.

## — *Role-Play* —

For this role-play exercise, find a partner for practicing kind communication habits. To get a feeling for what it means to role-play, you and your partner can take the roles of the worker and the friend shown in the table **Examples of Six Kind Communication Habits.** Read the words in the example, with one of you reading the lines of the worker and the other reading the lines of the kind friend.

*Examples of Six Kind Communication Habits*

| **Kind Communication Habits** | Example: A worker is telling his friend about his trouble sleeping because of a problem at work. |
|---|---|
| 1. Give feedback in the form of asking to hear more. | Worker: I seem to worry a lot of the time. Lots of nights I can't sleep.<br><br>Friend: My worries sometimes keep me awake at night. Do you know what is bothering you? (friendliness) |
| 2. Indicate understanding of what you are hearing. | Worker: My supervisor seems to always be criticizing me about the quality of my reports and not getting them in on time. I'm worried I might lose my job.<br><br>Friend: I can see why you are worried. (friendliness) |

| 3. Make an encouraging comment, offering interesting and relevant information. | Friend: A couple of years ago my boss was giving me a hard time. It worried me a lot. I found a job counselor who helped and also a book on getting along with your boss. I'll get you that information if you are interested. (offering help) |
|---|---|
| 4. Respond in a kind, supportive manner to requests. | Worker: I can't afford a counselor but I would really like to see the book. After I look at it, can you tell me what advice your counselor gave you?<br><br>Friend: I'd be happy to go over what my counselor told me. I even kept some notes I can give you. (offering help) |
| 5. Demonstrate your caring by being more considerate than usual when the other person is having a hard time. | Friend: I know you are stressed out about finishing your reports. Would you want me to organize the information so you can finish them quicker? (offering help) |
| 6. Be gentle in conflict. Avoid criticism or blame, and instead focus on your own feelings or needs. | Worker: Don't bother. I don't think there is any way to fix my mess in time. Besides, it's my responsibility, not yours!<br><br>Friend: I value your friendship. I really want to help if I can. (showing appreciation) |

## — Role-Play —

With the same partner, decide on two kind communication habits that will be the most helpful to you. Mark those habits with an **x**. Then create a situation in which you can practice those habits. Do the role-play and describe how you used each of the habits you marked with an **x**.

| Kind Communication Habits | How We Used the Habit |
|---|---|
| ☐ Give feedback in the form of asking to hear more. | |
| ☐ Indicate understanding of what you are hearing. | |
| ☐ Make an encouraging comment, offering interesting and relevant information. | |
| ☐ Respond in a kind, supportive manner to requests. | |
| ☐ Demonstrate your caring by being more considerate than usual when the other person is having a hard time. | |
| ☐ Be gentle in conflict. Avoid criticism or blame, and instead focus on your own feelings or needs. | |

# Unkind Communication Habits

To keep from falling into unkind communication habits during a conversation, we should be aware of the common unkind communication habits so we can try to avoid them. Which of the following unkind communication habits have you been subjected to or used with others: judgmental comments (especially contempt and ridicule), ignoring what the person says, giving unasked-for advice, and rushing the conversation? How did it make you feel to carry out that unkind habit(s)? Such unkind communication habits are usually conversation stoppers. The Unkind Communication Habits table illustrates examples of these unkind communication habits.

| Unkind Communication Habits | Examples of unkind responses by a coworker to this statement by a nurse: "I seem to worry a lot of the time. Lots of nights I can't sleep." |
|---|---|
| Ridicule | Unkind coworker: Do you think you are the only person who worries? Get over it and then you can sleep. |
| Ignore | Unkind coworker: I started a great new Netflix series last night. |
| Give unasked-for advice | Unkind coworker: You stay up too late. Get real. Go to bed earlier. |
| Rush the conversation | Unkind coworker: Yeah, lots of people have things to worry about. I'm hungry. Let's get some food. |
| Blame | Unkind coworker: It's your own fault. You need to quit messing up your life. If it's not one thing, it's another. |

## — Role-Play —

For this role-play exercise, find a partner for practicing unkind communication habits. Use the table above. One of you takes the role of the nurse and says this statement: *I seem to worry a lot of the time. Lots of nights I can't sleep.* The other person reads the unkind responses. Even though it is just a role-play, think about how these comments would make you feel if you were the nurse. Then trade roles. The unkind person becomes the nurse. And the person making the nurse's statement says the unkind responses. The person who hears the unkind statement says how it makes them feel.

# Guidelines for a Difficult Conversation

When you are likely to disagree with someone, being aware of how and when to use kind conversation habits, as well as how to avoid unkind conversation habits, is important. During difficult conversations, we need to consciously think about what we will say. Using these six questions can help guide us in difficult conversations:

1. Am I calm and mindful before I say anything? Comments made during great anger or resentment can cause lasting harm to a relationship.
2. Is what I am going to say true?
3. Is what I am going to say (or do) helpful? Will it be beneficial?

4. Is this a good time to say it (or do it)?

5. Will what I say (or do) bring people together or divide them?

6. Will I cause harm by not speaking up (or acting)?

The disagreement may be personal in nature or relate to content from work, school, current events, politics, or religion. We show that we respect the person we are disagreeing with by being thoughtful about what we say.

## PUT INTO **Practice**

Describe a conversation you have had that went well because you used kind conversation habits and avoided unkind conversation habits.

_____

_____

Identify which types of communication habits you used effectively.

_____

Also, describe a conversation you have had that went poorly because you did not use kind conversation habits but instead used unkind conversation habits. Identify which unkind communication habits caused the conversation to go badly.

_____

_____

How did you feel when things went poorly? How about when they went well?

_____

_____

## Creating Situations That Encourage the Use of Kind Communication Habits

Any time people come together, whether in a classroom or office staff meeting, it is desirable to create an environment that encourages people to apply their kind communication habits. In some work settings, ground rules are established ahead of time calling for the use of kind communication habits.

Before going to a meeting that will involve strongly differing opinions, we can employ our Diligent Detective skills to do research on the topic to be discussed and if possible, to learn about the reasons why people might have a different opinion than ours. This knowledge prepares us for the meeting so that we will not be caught off guard and increases our ability to use our kind communication habits and not become defensive and use unkind communication habits.

***EXAMPLE***

A school provides students the opportunity to practice kind communication habits through morning meetings that use mindfulness techniques to generate a constructive, harmonious classroom climate.

An atmosphere that nurtures mindful communication is part of daily meetings in this classroom. The room's mood is altered when classroom overhead lights are dimmed and soft lamps, strings of tiny lights, and gentle instrumental music are used to create a calming atmosphere. Students sit in a circle and the facilitator asks them to take deep breaths in and out and in and out again. She suggests they close their eyes. Then, after a minute of silence, she asks these caring questions: "How is it going today in class? What have you done to help yourself and others? How have you been mindful?"

Students share things such as "I am getting better at keeping my hands to myself, and that has helped others feel better about being my friend" and "I came to class feeling sad today because my parents had a bad fight. It made me feel like I didn't want to do any work, but my friend asked me about my mood, and when I shared my feelings, I felt better and started to focus on classwork." After a student speaks, the others acknowledge the speaker by saying, "I see your face." Although the "I see your face" response might seem artificial, it works to create a sense of being heard and being accepted.

✦ ✦ ✦

*Note:* In this workbook, we introduced you to a variety of mindful conversational skills. You may have found some of these skills of particular interest and want to learn more about them. A book that may be helpful in learning more about mindful conversation skills is *The Five Keys to Mindful Communication: Using Deep Listening and Mindful Speech to Strengthen Relationships, Heal Conflicts, and Accomplish Your Goals* by Susan Gillis Chapman (2012, Penguin Random House).

# Making a Kindness Plan

Often, implementing our desire to be more kind about something we consider important is not easy. We may begin a new activity, but only continue doing it for a couple of days. The purpose of a kindness plan is to help us build a kind habit that will become an important part of our life.

Here is a sample kindness plan made by a teenager named Sarah. Following this example is a blank plan for you to use. The questions in this sample are the same questions you will see when you write your kindness plan.

1. What is the kind habit you have chosen to develop?

   *Actively paying attention to others who I interact with, showing them that I am giving them my full attention when they are talking to me. This will show them that I care about what they have to say instead of being distracted by other people or things (like my phone).*

2. How are you hoping to help others by strengthening this habit (or engaging in this activity)?

*By giving my friends and classmates my full attention when they are talking to me, I am showing them that what they have to say is important.*

3.  Who will you ask for support, if anyone? What kind of support will you ask for?

    *I will ask my friends to remind me to put away my phone while I am talking to them or others, and to notice if I am giving the other person good eye contact.*

4.  What Diligent Detective work will you need to do, if any?

    *I need to learn how to put my Apple Watch in a Do Not Disturb setting quickly and easily so that my watch won't distract me with texts and calls from my phone. I'll also ask my friends whether they have experienced good eye contact and communication from me.*

5.  How, if at all, will you use the mind of the Wise Warrior?

    *I will make an honest effort to put my phone away and look people in the eye while they are talking to me.*

6.  What Skills of Character (growth mindset, responsible, patient, and humble) will you need most?

    *I need to realize that I can accomplish this goal. Having people look me in the eye when I'm talking to them makes me nervous sometimes, and I forget what I'm going to say, so I need to be responsible for what I'm saying and thinking when this happens. I need to be humble if and when friends remind me to put my phone away or notice I'm distracted. I also need to stay humble if they tell me I didn't use good attention skills. I need to be patient and realize that improvement takes time.*

7.  What action will you take to build the kind habit in your mental world?

    *I will notice how others respond and interact with me when I give them my undivided attention.*

8.  What action will you take in your physical world?

    *I will find a special pocket in my backpack for my phone and will use a quick Do Not Disturb setting on my watch (Airplane Mode).*

After the plan was made, Sarah started doing what the plan says. After acting on the plan for several days, Sarah looked back at it and responded to follow-up questions.

1.  What happened as you tried to implement your kindness plan?

    *Several times, I tried putting my watch on Do Not Disturb but couldn't figure it out. As a result, I looked like I was more worried about what was happening on my watch than paying attention to the person talking to me.*

2.  How did you feel as you implemented your kindness plan?

    *It was embarrassing. I looked like a jerk.*

3.  What adjustment, if any, did you make?

    *I practiced changing the setting on my watch over and over and over again until I thought I could do it quickly. Then, I asked my brother to stand in front of me and to start asking me questions while I did it, so I could try doing it under the pressure of someone wanting my attention. I eventually got it, but it was so stressful!*

4.  What adjustment will you need to make next?

    *I will see how well I do in my next conversations. If I still have difficulty, I will ask one of my friends to practice with me.*

## Write Your Kindness Plan

The first thing to think about in creating a kindness plan is deciding which kind habit you want to work on. Look back at the Kind Habits Inventory starting on page 69 and find all of the habits you marked with an **I**. Write them below, then circle the kind habit you are most interested in building.
Your Important Kind Habits:

1.  _____

2.  _____

3.  _____

4.  _____

5.  _____

When developing a plan, be realistic about your expectations. You might learn a new simple kind habit over a few weeks; for example, expressing your appreciation for the kindness you receive from someone close to you. A kind habit that requires significant changes in how you live your life can easily take much longer; for example, establishing and refining your kind and mindful communication habits. Remember to use the Skills of Action you learned about in Chapter 2. For example, there are many times we need to be a Wise Warrior—we know how to act with kindness, but we do not feel like doing it. Be the Warrior and do the kind act.

After working on your plan for several days, you will look back at your plan and answer follow-up questions regarding how well your plan is going and what changes may be necessary. As you continue to work on your plan, return to these follow-up questions every week or so to determine if changes are needed. Give yourself some time—whether it's a few days or a few weeks—to let your plan unfold. This is important because some kindness plans will only happen in certain situations—for example, being kinder to other motorists when you are driving or learning to be kinder to a coworker or a fellow student who bugs you.

If you find yourself frustrated or losing motivation in building the new habit, consider working with a friend or group. This may add fun, support, and accountability to your efforts to change. You can discuss your progress and ideas, get a fresh perspective, and make a commitment to check in with each other about following through on your plans. You can also use these meetings to practice kindness to yourself and others by celebrating successes and being gentle with perceived failures. If you try those steps with the mindset of the Wise Warrior and still feel frustrated after trying for a couple of weeks, you might want to create a new plan.

## PUT INTO PRACTICE **Journal**

Go to page 280 and write your kindness plan by answering the questions.

## PUT INTO **Practice**

### *Mindfulness Using Our Senses*

Chapters 1 and 2 introduced you to the practice of mindfulness by counting your breaths. In Chapter 3, you stopped counting your breaths and instead focused on the physical sensations of your breathing—the movement of your chest and abdomen as you inhale and exhale. The following mindfulness exercise does not involve attending to your breathing. Instead, you focus on your senses of hearing, taste, and body awareness. Focusing our attention on our senses can be a valuable tool in helping us be calm. The next part of the workbook explains how and why using our senses in this particular way is a key to developing mindfulness and calm.

- For 10 seconds, focus entirely on what you hear wherever you are. When you focus entirely on what you hear, is there any attention left over for thoughts?

- Look at the palm of your hand and notice how the lines go in different directions.

- For 10 seconds, shift your attention to the sensations in your own body, for example, a pain or where your feet contact the floor. Focus on those bodily sensations and your presence within those surroundings.

After completing these experiences, write about how these three experiences made you feel and think.

_____

_____

_____

## PERSONAL **Challenge**

You have already written a plan to work on a new kind habit. But maybe you are interested in doing something in addition, something bigger than working on one kind habit. Here are some ideas:

- Learn new ways to be kind from books, articles, social media, TV, movies, and the actions of kind people.*

- Join or create a kindful club. Chapter 13 provides a list of clubs for teens and young adults that focus on kindness. A supportive group of friends can create a kindness club by meeting to check in about their lives, discuss what they have learned recently about mindful kindness, and share how members are doing with their kindness and mindfulness (which can include gentle accountability). The kindness club Doug participates in includes a few close friends who meet once a month at one of their houses, meditate for 20 minutes, and have a snack while they discuss what they have been working on in the areas of kindness and mindfulness.

- Join a spiritual, religious, or support group, virtually or in person, for fellowship that encourages you to carry out your kindful intentions.

Do any of these kindness activities interest you? If so, write about how you might engage in that activity.

_____

_____

## ━━━━ Wrapping Up ━━━━

In Chapter 3, we learned about the many different forms kindness can take. In this chapter, we began with how to use the four kindness skills in small ways, what pleasant kind habits are and why they are important, and different aspects of kind communication habits: Guidelines for a Caring Conversation, Six Communication Habits for Responding During a Conversation, and Unkind Communication Habits to Avoid. Finally, we learned how to make a plan to build new kind habits.

---

* For suggested books, moves, and songs about kindness, visit this website: https://www.spreadingkindnesscampaign.org/books-more/

☑ *Checking In*

Are you taking the time you need to digest the material and complete the exercises? If not, you might consider spending several days or even a week on a chapter, setting aside time each evening for reviewing what you read, and doing exercises. Another approach is to read through the chapter without doing the exercises, then go back through the chapter a second time and do the exercises. Or you can go through the exercises with a friend or as part of a group. As you work on an exercise or a new habit you might find out it's much harder than you guessed. It's not important to feel you have to get something right the first time. Kindness isn't a competition with others, or with yourself. In fact, kindness leads to cooperation, which allows us to develop close, caring relationships. In addition, kindness is central to seeing the needs of another person and being able to connect with that person.

# Time for Reflection

Reflect on whether you are enthusiastic about acting with kindness more often and then circle your level of enthusiasm.

Not very enthusiastic    Somewhat enthusiastic    Mostly enthusiastic    Very enthusiastic

• • •

Think about each of these statements and then circle Yes or No.

| | | |
|---|---|---|
| I feel grateful for the people and pets I care about. | Yes | No |
| I feel grateful for something that went well today. | Yes | No |
| I feel grateful for what I can do with my body and mind. | Yes | No |
| I feel grateful for the people who help me and others. | Yes | No |
| I feel grateful for my beliefs that give me purpose and meaning. | Yes | No |
| I feel grateful for having fun and laughter. | Yes | No |

• • •

Write about how you have been kind at least one time in one of these ways:

• Be friendly

• Give help

• Show appreciation

• Reach out to those with serious needs

_____

_____

# Train Your Mind

*Put up a roof of mindfulness and meditation to keep out the cold unkindness and keep in the warm kindness.*

Scientific findings: 5
Real-world examples: 31
Opportunities to apply what you are learning: 25

**Teachings from the World Religions**

Christianity: "But blessed are your eyes, for they see, and your ears, for they hear." (Matthew 13:16)

Buddhism: "Meditation brings wisdom; lack of meditation leaves ignorance. Know well what leads you forward and what holds you back, and choose the path that leads to wisdom."

Judaism: "Truly, you are where your mind is." —Baal Shem Tov

Sufism: "The moment you accept what troubles you've been given, the door will open." —Rumi

Taoism: "Be content with what you have; rejoice in the way things are. When you realize there is nothing lacking, the whole world belongs to you." —Lao

Native American: "When you are in doubt, be still and wait; when doubt no longer exists for you, then go forward with courage. So long as mists envelop you, be still. Be still until the sunlight pours through and dispels the mist—as it surely will." —Chief White Eagle, Ponca chief

## Chapter 5

# Train Your Mind with Meditation and the Three-Breath Method

*Meditation is like a gym in which you develop the powerful mental muscles of calm and insight.*                Ajahn Brahm

Consider how much better you think, feel, and act when you're calm. Given the growing levels of stress, anxiety, and depression in our time, calmness has a lot to offer. Calmness helps us build kind habits and dismantle unkind habits because we are better able to direct our attention when we are calm; as a result, we are able to direct our attention to what is important rather than being overwhelmed by distracting thoughts and emotions. This chapter and the next two describe how to train our mind to attend to what is important or meaningful in the moment. In one moment, finishing a report might be important. We can learn to attend fully to writing an excellent report. In another moment, calming down after an argument might be important. Or maybe cleaning up after a meal might be important. Training the mind to fully attend to our current activity—whether writing a report, calming down after an argument, cleaning up after a meal, or listening to music—is our gateway to lasting happiness. When you are stressed or anxious, how does it feel to write a report, clean up in the kitchen, or do some other task? When you are fully attentive to what you are doing, how do you feel?

### Mindful Listening

Find a piece of music you love and listen to it while reading a book and eating at the same time. Next, listen to the same piece of music, but without reading or eating. Close your eyes and focus deeply on the music.

Write on page 283 about how your awareness was affected when you directed all your attention to listening. Did you feel more connected to the music? Less distracted by thoughts and emotions unrelated to the music?

# Meditation

> **meditation**
>
> For a set length of time we focus our attention on our breath, an image, or a set of words. Repeatedly shifting our attention away from distractions back to our focus calms us.

### EXAMPLE

Wendy from Philadelphia, who struggles with overeating and its effect on her self-esteem, affirms the worth of meditation for everyday people:

*It wasn't until I realized that meditating could solve my binge eating that I decided to try it. I heard that willpower is like a muscle and could be strengthened through meditation. The first time I tried to meditate was a disaster. I would start meditating and within three seconds be thinking about what I was going to make for dinner. It took practice, but now I love it! Like a muscle, willpower can grow, but it can also be fatigued. If willpower is like a cell phone battery, meditation is what charges it back up.*[1]

◆ ◆ ◆

While mindfulness and meditation are closely linked, they are not the same thing. We meditate for a set length of time, ideally in a quiet setting. Mindfulness can occur under any condition and for any length of time. When being mindful, we simply direct our attention to whatever our intention might be at that moment. Wendy refers to willpower as being like a muscle we can strengthen. In fact, meditation is an intense workout of what we can do all day long with mindfulness—shift our attention away from distractions and direct it to our current intention.

The exercises in this chapter offer several ways to develop "mental muscles of calm" by focusing our attention as we practice a variety of meditation and breathing methods. As you try these methods, think about which ones best suit you. They are intended to bring you a sense of calm and quiet joy.

# Steps for Meditating

1. Select a place to meditate where you will not be distracted by outside noise and where you are not likely to be interrupted.

2. Sit in a manner that is comfortable and that you can easily maintain throughout the time you are meditating. Sit on a cushion on the floor or sit on a chair. Make sure to sit upright so your back makes a natural curve. To create this curve, you can sit on a cushion's edge on the floor or on the front part of a wedge-shaped cushion on a chair. Lift up your spine so that your breath flows freely; avoid slouching.

3. Close your eyes, relax your muscles, and take a few deep breaths, breathing in and out through your nostrils.

After you have begun to regularly practice meditation, the place you choose to meditate doesn't have to be silent; many find the noises in nature can enhance their state of meditation. If you choose a place in nature with sounds, you may decide to focus on those sounds.

**An indigenous youth leader describes how she feels nature flowing through her body while she meditates: "Before and while I meditate, I hear the wind around. It rustles the leaves on the branches. Then I feel the wind hit my body. I feel the moving blades of grass that hit my skin as the grass blows in the wind. I hear the sound of birds chirping in the sunny weather, and I feel the warmth of the sun entering my body and soul."**

Sometimes, we will have a hard time learning to meditate because of the seemingly constant self-talk going on in our minds. Although there are many types of mediation, we will begin with two kinds of meditation that help stop our self-talk, particularly our negative self-talk. These are Embracing Kindness Meditation and Guided Meditation.

# Embracing Kindness Meditation

### embracing kindness meditation*

A type of meditation in which we replace negative self-talk with positive self-talk. If all of our attention is directed to positive self-talk, there is no attention left over for negative self-talk.

The Embracing Kindness Meditation has two parts. In the first part, you embrace yourself with kindness. In the second part, you embrace someone close to you with kindness.

---

\* In Buddhism, this is known as Loving Kindness Meditation.

## *Part 1: Embrace Yourself with Kindness*

As you meditate, imagine you are breathing in love or kindness, then breathing out tension and unneeded feelings. Take deep slow breaths. As you breathe in, say to yourself one of the positive, reassuring phrases listed below. As you breathe out, visualize any tension, pain, or worry you may have leaving your body as new energy flows in. Repeat saying this phrase as you breathe in, then visualize breathing out tension and worry. If your attention drifts as you say the phrase to yourself, gently redirect it back to breathing in as you say the phrase and then breathing out your tension and worry. Do this for several minutes.

- May I be happy and safe.
- May I be healthy, peaceful, and strong.
- May I give and receive appreciation today.
- May I find joy in my day.
- May I feel connected to the world and people around me.
- *Or create a reassuring positive phrase of your own.*

After meditating for several minutes saying your phrase, take a few moments to notice how you are feeling. Some people describe a feeling of warmth, connectivity, and a letting go of troubles. Did you have any of these feelings?

PUT INTO PRACTICE **Journal**

### *Embracing Kindness Meditation, Part 1*

Practice Embracing Kindness Meditation for several days. Then on page 283, describe what went well and what did not go well. Also, describe your feelings when it went well.

## *Part 2: Embrace Someone Close to You with Kindness*

**After a few days of embracing yourself with kindness, add a second part: Embrace someone close to you with kindness.** First go through Part 1 for several minutes, where you embrace kindness for yourself. Then shift your focus to a friend or loved one. Select someone you are very close to, such as a partner, parent, sibling, best friend, or even a pet. Feel gratitude and love for them as you breathe in and say phrases such as those below. Then visualize breathing out any unhappiness they may have. Continue breathing in love and gratitude and breathing out unhappiness for several minutes. As you breathe in, say the phrases below or one of your own:

- May you be happy and safe.
- May you be healthy, peaceful, and strong.
- May you give and receive appreciation today.
- May you find joy in your day.

- May you find your place in the world.

Once you've held warm feelings toward a certain person for a little while, you can name other significant people from your life and repeat a kindness phrase for them, bringing them into your awareness one by one and envisioning them with perfect wellness and inner peace as you say the phrases while breathing in and then exhaling out their unhappiness or discomfort.

After each Embracing Kindness Meditation session has finished, open your eyes and take a few moments to see how you are feeling. If you have warm feelings generated from this meditation, you can revisit those feelings throughout the day by naming yourself or someone you care about and saying or feeling the phrases.

PUT INTO PRACTICE **Journal**

### Embracing Kindness Meditation, Part 2

Do the Embracing Kindness Meditation for yourself and for those close to you for 3 days. Then, on page 284, describe what went well and what did not go well. Tell how you felt when this practice went well.

#### EXAMPLE

A 21-year-old, who read an earlier version of this book, comments on adding positive thoughts into their meditation practice:

*I am so glad I got an introduction to positive-thought-generating meditation through this chapter. I have meditated in short intervals on and off for a few years but have never used positive self-talk in my practice. Just in my first brief attempt as I was reading through this chapter, I found it was much easier to focus deeply on the positivity as opposed to the nothingness that people often try to simulate with wordless meditation. I am starting with Embracing Kindness Meditation before going back into wordless meditation so I can work my way up to solely focusing on my breath.*

## Guided Meditation

Guided Meditation is a second type of meditation that can help us stop our self-talk by listening rather than speaking. During Guided Meditation, we listen to instructions that generate positive feelings rather than saying the positive Embracing Kindness phrases. In Guided Meditation, the voice of a guide (in person or from a recording) gives step-by-step instructions about where and how to direct our attention. Some people will find meditation easier with Embracing Kindness while others will be more comfortable meditating with a guide or in nature. Many videos on the internet provide free guided meditations, such as those found at the UCLA Mindful Awareness Research Center.*

---

* https://www.uclahealth.org/marc/mindful-meditations

**CAUTION—When Very Difficult Memories or Feelings Arise**  For some people, meditation brings painful feelings or memories to the surface. One of my prisoner pen pals experienced flashbacks to childhood abuse; another friend, who was coping with serious addiction and relationship issues, had bouts of intensified depression when beginning to practice meditation. If your meditation practice causes you psychological or emotional distress and these issues continue or become more serious, consider speaking with a pastor, elder, peer, trained therapist, counselor, or trusted adult.

# Wordless Meditation

Meditation practices that use words to generate positive thoughts, like the Embracing Kindness Meditation and Guided Meditation, are excellent ways to begin to learn how to meditate. Later, you might want to try a third type of meditation, Wordless Meditation, in which you do not use any words; you do not call up thoughts or engage in self-talk, not even positive self-talk.

In Wordless Meditation, we repeatedly return our attention to our focus. Our focus might be on any of these three things:

1.  Natural breathing. When you breathe in, feel the air coming in through your nostrils* and feel your belly and chest rise slightly. When you breathe out, let your belly and chest sink gently back down, and feel the air passing out through the nostrils. Direct all of your attention to the physical sensations of this movement. If thoughts come into your mind, do not focus on them; instead, just let them pass and return your attention to your breathing. If you focus wholeheartedly on these physical sensations, you do not have any attention left over for negative self-talk.

2.  An image; an object such as a candle flame or a branch blowing in the wind; or sound, such as chanting, humming, drumming, making a buzzing sound like a bee, or saying Oooommmm.

3.  Controlling our breathing. For example, inhaling to a count of four as you breathe in, holding for a count of four, then exhaling to a count of four, and holding for a count of four again. Repeat this cycle multiple times.

During Wordless Meditation, we become calm by repeatedly shifting our attention away from distractions to our focus. The value of Wordless Meditation is that we are training our mind to not attach to any set of sensations, thoughts, or emotions; we practice directing our attention away from negative self-talk in particular, which can be helpful all day long, not just when we are in meditation.

Wordless Meditation and Embracing Kindness Meditation are closely linked. If all of our attention is focused on saying and feeling positive phrases as we inhale and then breathe out tension and worry, we do not have any attention left over for negative self-talk. When we breathe in during Wordless Meditation, we focus on feeling the air coming in through the nostrils and feel our belly and chest rise slightly. When we breathe out, we let our belly and chest sink gently back down and feel the air passing out through the nostrils. By focusing wholeheartedly on these sensations, we do not have any attention left over for negative self-talk.

---

* If you breathe through your mouth, feel the air coming in and leaving your mouth.

PUT INTO PRACTICE **Journal**

### Wordless Meditation

Once you feel comfortable with your Embracing Kindness Meditation, try Wordless Meditation. It will be easy to start because you're already practicing mindful breathing and the Embracing Kindness Meditation. You will follow guidelines similar to those described for Embracing Kindness Meditation: find a quiet place, make a goal for how many minutes to meditate, sit up straight. Start small—5 minutes is good. Gradually increase the length of your meditation sessions over the coming days and weeks until you can sit for 10 or 20 minutes or longer in the morning (before checking messages or social media) and 10 minutes or longer in the evening, creating a "mindfulness sandwich" for your day. As you work to increase the duration of your meditation, take your time and don't bite off more than you can chew. *It is better to meditate for 5 minutes and keep up the practice daily than to meditate for 20 minutes for 3 days and then stop because you are too busy.*

After a week, write on page 284 about what went well with your meditation.

Feel free to mix Embracing Kindness Meditation with Wordless Meditation. Over time, meditation usually creates a sense of calm, connectivity to the world, and an increasing ability to direct our attention away from unkind and unhelpful thoughts and emotions.

### FROM THE OTHER SIDE

Roy Tester explains to Sergeant Eason what he experiences during meditation:

*I've been meditating a lot lately because the pain from this nerve damage has been redlining almost 24/7. No way was I aware Sergeant Eason was there. I was still in limbo with meditation, still "in," when I became aware she was at my cell door because of the perfume they apply by the pint, it seems, but I still hadn't opened my eyes. She said, "Tester, is you breathing when you do that meditation because I can't tell if you breathing."*

*"Yeah, Sarge, I'm breathing but just real shallow. The deeper I get the less breathing I do."*

*Then she asked, "How many times a week you do it?"*

*I told her every day, at least twice a day, sometimes three and four times a day, and at least 20 minutes at a time but usually a half hour or more. I told her the longer I meditate, the deeper I get. She said, "Well, then what?"*

*I said I try to get deep enough so I am you and you are me and we're no longer two but one energy, one with everyone and everything. She laughed and said, "OK, OK, that's enough Buddha for me for today."*

PUT INTO PRACTICE **Journal**

Choose one of the forms of meditation you have learned (such as Embracing Kindness, Guided, or Wordless Meditation) and continue your practice. Make a schedule for what time and for how long you meditate in the morning (and possibly in the evening as well). Use an app or paper and pencil to track how long you actually sit each time. After 5 days, describe on page 284 what went well and what did not go well. Also, describe how meditating made you feel.

# Three-Breath Method

After spending years studying meditation and talking with several meditation teachers, Doug adopted a well-established technique, the Three-Breath Method, to redirect attention away from distracting thoughts and emotions. This Three-Breath Method works not only during meditation but also in daily life.

> **three-breath method**
>
> The practice of redirecting attention away from distracting thoughts and emotions by taking three slow, deep breaths as we focus on the air entering and leaving the nostrils and the physical expansion and contraction of the abdomen and chest.

## Three-Breath Method During Meditation

During meditation, there will be times when our attention drifts away from our positive phrases or from other types of meditation not involving a focus on breaths. Use the Three-Breath Method to help regain focus. Doug describes his experience with the Three-Breath Method, "I have been meditating for over 40 years and still get caught up in some form of self-talk almost every time I meditate. When I become aware of the self-talk, I call on the Three-Breath Method."

PUT INTO PRACTICE **Journal**

*The Three-Breath Method*

For the next 3 times that you meditate, notice when you are distracted by self-talk and each time use the Three-Breath Method to regain your focus, taking three deeper, slower breaths. After using the Three-Breath Method for several days, describe on page 284 how you felt using the Three-Breath Method in your attempt to shift away from your distractions.

# Three-Breath Method Outside of Meditation

## — *Key Idea* —

Any time negative self-talk and emotions, such as anger or worry, arise during the day, you can engage the Three-Breath Method to calm yourself. For example, you are about to have a stressful meeting with your boss, your teacher, partner, or parents, and you start feeling very nervous. What sort of situations cause you to be nervous? How does that feel? If you've tried the Three-Breath Method, how has it helped to calm you down when you are nervous? Making this technique available to use when you are stressed and as part of your day-to-day mindfulness practice will be easier if you first get comfortable using it during meditation. However, even if you do not meditate, you can start using this technique in your daily life.

### FROM THE OTHER SIDE

Another of Roy's students, Cody, wrote about how he used the Three-Breath Method to calm himself when guards searched his cell:

*Afterwards, this dumb squad came in everyone's cell to check their lights. They were so rude and disrespectful. They threw my books all on the floor around my toilet where water was from the shower. I had a flash of anger run through my mind that I really never had before. I wanted to smack that Motherf—er up against the wall and tell him, "Don't take your anger out on me and my stuff. It ain't my fault you got to work." I took three deep breaths and asked them if they would like some candy and they did.*

✦ ✦ ✦

The Three-Breath Method allowed Cody to reflect. While the anger of the search initially led Cody to dark thoughts, he was able to calm himself and respond to a situation that was out of his control with a kind gesture. While this did not change the fact that he felt his space had been violated, Cody was able to reduce his negative emotions that could have gotten him into trouble. Have you ever responded with anger to what you consider acts of rudeness or disrespect? How did acting with anger feel?

Once you're comfortable using the Three-Breath Method to pull yourself back from distraction in meditation and mindfulness in daily life, you can start using it more proactively. For example, when you are walking in the park, you can use the Three-Breath Method to activate your mindfulness to more fully enjoy the sights, sounds, and physical sensations of your walk. Or maybe when you are with someone you care deeply about, you can use the Three-Breath Method to more fully feel how you love and cherish their company.

### FROM THE OTHER SIDE

Tad describes how proactively using the Three-Breath Method benefits him:

*This method is awesome for being totally absorbed into a moment, e.g., when I pace the floor of my small cell, listening to my radio, I listen to the lyrics of certain song. If the lyrics of that song are mentally, physically, and spiritually stimulating, I will stop walking, close my eyes, and allow the music to travel through me, taking in the lyrics, sound, vibrations, etc. as I breathe deeply, taking in every bit of the moment. An awesome song to do this to is "Humble and Kind" by Tim McGraw.*

## PUT INTO **Practice**

### *Three-Breath Method in Daily Life*

List three situations that you could make more pleasurable/meaningful or less stressful by using the Three-Breath Method. For example, when you are studying for an exam or working at your job, this method could improve your focus.

_____

_____

## — *Key Idea* —

Just as exercise prepares us for physical challenges that arise during the day, meditation and the Three-Breath Method prepare us for future mental challenges and to be able to maintain a balanced, positive mindset. Think of focusing your attention during meditation and practicing the Three-Breath Method as being similar to doing exercises to strengthen your biceps; the more often you do arm curls at the gym, the stronger your biceps become. Similarly, the more often you meditate and practice the Three-Breath Method, the better you will be able to be mindful outside of meditation. Training through yoga, running, and weight training can prevent us from pulling a muscle or becoming too fatigued when we are doing heavy work. Similarly, meditation and Three-Breath Method workouts can keep us from being swept away by negative self-talk and unkindness.

### EXAMPLE

In a *Huffington Post* blog post entitled "What I Know About Stress Now That I'm in My Twenties," Emma Gray, a reporter, talks about how the practice of intentional, slow deep breaths has helped her:

*Your 20s are defined by change and transition: new apartments, new cities, new jobs, new financial responsibilities, new friends, new loves—and lots of new things to stress about. Although I can't pretend to be an expert on eliminating these worries from your life, I have realized a few things over the last half a decade. "Just breathe" really is a helpful suggestion. When I feel overwhelmed by my list of to-dos, I've started putting both of my feet on the floor, closing my eyes, and breathing in and out for 10 seconds. Something that simple can reset your body chemistry and let you look at your day with a rational mind—instead of spiraling into a meltdown because you are physically unable.*[2]

### EXAMPLE

A college student uses intentional breathing combined with other techniques to deal with her anxiety attacks:

*I think that the Three-Breath Method can be incredibly applicable to calming down if someone feels an anxiety attack coming on. I have been doing a similar technique to the Three-Breath Method for my panic attacks for years, where I plant my (bare if possible) feet on the floor and take ten slow breaths, in through my nose and out through my mouth. If the attack has already started, I often sit on my own hands to still them, and this helps me focus on breathing. Overall, for most of my anxiety attacks this method has been incredibly helpful in stopping the spiral of anxiety and panic.*

PUT INTO PRACTICE **Journal**

### *The Three-Breath Method Outside Meditation*

Set a goal for how often you will use the Three-Breath Method during the day, outside meditation. Use an app or paper and pencil to count how many times you actually use the Three-Breath Method. At the end of 5 days, describe on page 285 what went well and what did not go well. Also, describe how using the Three-Breath Method made you feel.

# Wrapping Up

In Chapter 4 we read about pleasant kind habits that can bring joy, appreciation, and enrichment to our life, help sustain us during dark times, and buffer us against addictive behavior. This chapter gave suggestions for how to have more pleasant events and lasting happiness in our lives by meditating and using the Three-Breath Method. To be more specific, we've learned how mindfulness helps us become calm, which in turn helps us refrain from being unkind and makes it easier to be kind and present with ourselves and others. We have been introduced to three types of meditation: Embracing Kindness, Guided, and Wordless. A direct and efficient way to boost our mindfulness is through meditation, ideally twice a day, in the morning and the evening. At times, meditation will bring joy and contentment. The Three-Breath Method is useful during meditation and outside meditation; it can help us feel more connected, get out of unhappiness (reduce the self-talk). and increase happiness (by feeling more joy and gratitude).

## ☑ *Checking In*

Once in a while, it's a good idea to check back in to see how we're doing with the goals we set in previous chapters. Let's take another look at the Kindful Vow at the end of Chapter 2:

> *I will be more kindful to myself by . . .*
> *I will be more kindful in all my relationships by . . .*
> *I will extend the reach of my kindfulness by . . .*

Did you display the Kindful Vow in a place where you see it several times a day?

_____

Has your understanding of the Kindful Vow changed? If so, tell how.

_____

How have your actions over the past days or weeks fulfilled—or perhaps partially fulfilled or failed to fulfill—the vows you made when you took this pledge?

_____

Do you want to change the vows you made? If so, describe the change and again display your vow where you will see it several times a day.

_____

## Time for Reflection

For each kindful practice, mark one of the three boxes.

| | I'm not interested at this time. | I plan to begin. | I'm doing it. |
|---|---|---|---|
| I am being kind to myself by building a new pleasant kind habit. | ☐ | ☐ | ☐ |
| I have posted the Kindful Vow and read it on a regular basis. | ☐ | ☐ | ☐ |
| I will use the Three-Breath Method to pull myself back from distraction and negativity. | ☐ | ☐ | ☐ |
| I will follow my Daily Meditation and Mindfulness Plan as described in this chapter. | ☐ | ☐ | ☐ |
| I will use Embracing Kindness Meditation. | ☐ | ☐ | ☐ |
| I will use Wordless Meditation. | ☐ | ☐ | ☐ |

Write about how you have been kind at least one time in one of these ways:

- Be friendly
- Give help
- Show appreciation
- Reach out to those with serious needs

_____

_____

## Chapter 6

# Practicing Mindfulness with Sensations and Emotions

*Joy can be found in the smallest of things if you are open to seeing and experiencing them . . . . Use your five senses to identify things that bring you joy and cherish them.*

Nikki Bush

In Chapter 4, we read about pleasant kind habits that can bring joy, appreciation, and enrichment to our lives, help sustain us during dark times, and buffer us against addictive behavior. But we cannot engage in pleasant kind habits every minute of the day. So, what can we do during these other times to bring joy, appreciation, and enrichment to our lives, help sustain us during dark times, and buffer us against harmful, unkind habits? One answer to this question of how to sustain ourselves during difficult times is to practice mindfulness in all aspects of our lives: our physical bodies, our minds, and our feelings. How do you feel during difficult times in your life?

This chapter describes techniques for practicing mindfulness with sensations of the body and with our emotions.

### EXAMPLE

How one Indigenous youth uses sensations of the body to prepare himself for meditation:

*When I am getting ready to begin, I go into depth with how each of my muscles feels. Am I wearing socks or barefoot? Do I feel the thick braids of my meditation rug on my toes or the cool air between my toes? I make myself aware of how my buttocks take shape to the pillow beneath me, letting me sink in and take comfortable form. Are my shoulders open so that I can widen my chest cavity? Do I feel my pulse or any resonant energy in my fingertips if I focus hard enough?*

◆ ◆ ◆

Learning and incorporating mindfulness techniques in daily life gives us ways to be sensitive to our genuine needs and to the feelings and needs of those around us. The techniques also energize and calm us so we can not only be more kind to ourselves and others, but reduce our negative self-talk that can lead to unkind thoughts and actions.

We begin with two powerful mindfulness techniques having to do with our bodies: being mindful with sensations (sensing mindfulness), and using five grounding techniques. The chapter concludes by discussing why and how we can be mindful with our emotions.

## Mindfulness with Sensations (Sensing Mindfulness)

### sensing mindfulness

Sensing mindfulness, or the intentional noticing of sensations, is the wordless practice of focusing all our attention on one or more of our physical senses (touch, sight, smell, taste, and hearing).

When we are able to focus all of our attention on our senses, there is no attention left over for negative mind-wandering, such as negative self-talk. How does negative self-talk make you feel? When you are calm and open to your surroundings, do you feel more tuned in to your bodily sensations and better connected to your surroundings? How does such a connection feel?

Of course, we spend most of our time attending to our thoughts and emotions, so we are not in the habit of frequently tuning in to our bodily sensations unless called for by pain, work, a hobby, or a sport. But we can learn to attend to our senses at other times as well.

## — *Key Idea* —

Sensing mindfulness (intentional noticing of sensations) is one of the most important ways we can receive an energy boost and then experience quiet joy and calmness. Just like in meditation, sensing mindfulness can give our mind a rest by calming our body and creating a sense of connection with everything and everyone around us. Developing sensing mindfulness is like developing a muscle: All it takes is practice for it to grow.

### EXAMPLE

Let's say we're playing with our dog at the end of the day and finding ourselves thinking about what bothered us earlier in the day. We find ourselves starting to get more and more angry. We can shift our attention to our senses like this: Enjoy the grace of our dog's leap as he catches a Frisbee and brings it back. Look into our dog's eyes and hear his soft breath. Such interactions with a pet can calm us and help bothersome thoughts disappear. Engaging in calming activities at bedtime can help people who have trouble falling asleep. When we are in bed and not able to go to sleep, we can engage sensing mindfulness by feeling all the places where our body is in contact with the bed and feeling the rising and falling of our chest and abdomen as we breathe.

 PUT INTO PRACTICE **Journal**

Practicing sensing mindfulness during times of low stress prepares us to use sensing mindfulness when we are under stress. In this exercise you will pick one of the two practices below—sensing mindfulness while eating or sensing mindfulness while working out.

### Sensing Mindfulness While Eating

Try this the next time you are eating: First, eat several bites while you're engaged in another activity, like reading, listening to music, or talking to a friend. Then, eat in silence with closed eyes. Notice the variations in texture and how the food tastes more flavorful when your eyes are closed and your attention is directed toward what you are eating, with no distractions. Of course, the food hasn't changed—you're just noticing more.

### Sensing Mindfulness While Working Out

You can use sensing mindfulness to enhance your exercising. What physical activity do you enjoy? Shooting hoops? Golf? Jogging? Soccer? Walking? Riding a bike? Skateboarding? Yoga? Dancing? Canoeing? Weight training? Next time you are enjoying your exercise, do it with sensing mindfulness. For example, feel the texture and pressure of the basketball against your hands as you shoot, concentrate on the sensation of the road under your feet while jogging, or focus on the stretch of your muscles during yoga. When you notice mind-wandering, direct your attention back to the physical sensations coming from the skill you are practicing. Fully experiencing the sensations as you exercise without negative self-talk is often quite pleasant.

After completing one of the exercises above, find page 285 and write about your experience with the sensing mindfulness practice you chose to do.

The beauty of the sensing mindfulness practice is that we can do it anytime, anywhere. If we are getting more and more anxious about a test or job performance evaluation, we can shift our attention to our senses, for example, by feeling the wind blowing through our hair as we drive, looking intently at the sunrise, or noticing the rising and falling of our chest as we take three deep breaths.

### EXAMPLE

The practice of meditation and sensing mindfulness have positive payoffs if we have the patience to practice them over time. Tatiana Posada, a law student who practiced meditation and spent some time each morning in sensing mindfulness, wrote this about her experiences:

*I noticed the changes in my personal life first. Small things, like I was calmer while driving in heavy traffic. Instead of getting frustrated, I was rolling down my windows and enjoying the sunrise. My personal relationships grew and became healthier as I became more patient and less anxious. I also noticed a difference in my academics. I remember sitting for my first final, Civil Procedure I. When I opened the exam, I saw that the fact pattern was about seven pages long and involved confusing cases in Florida and Georgia. I could feel my anxiety rise, my heart rate elevate, my breathing intensify, and my body tense. So I closed my eyes, took several deep breaths and told myself I was ready: I did everything to prepare.*[1]

 PUT INTO PRACTICE **Journal**

Choose something that typically makes you nervous, such as competing in a gaming tournament, waiting to meet someone on a blind date, speaking in public, or talking to your parents about a difficult topic. The next time you are in that situation, practice sensing mindfulness (intentional noticing of sensations) just before you do the activity. Notice how much calmer you are if you stop thinking about the gaming or the blind date and instead look around you; focus on something beautiful or interesting in your surroundings, such as a sunrise, the way your cat stretches, or simply your breath as the air moves in and out of your body.

Find page 285 and write about if and how your feelings changed when you shifted your attention to noticing the world around you instead of thinking about the activity that makes you nervous.

Shifting to sensing mindfulness throughout the day is like taking a water station break while running a marathon. Every so often, runners grab some water to refresh themselves and prevent dehydration and fatigue. Similarly, sensing mindfulness refreshes us by relaxing our bodies and minds at various times throughout the day. For example, an excellent sensing mindfulness refresher is to listen to the sound of a small desktop fountain. At various times during the day stopping and listening to the sound of the moving water can be refreshing.

*EXAMPLE*

One youth comments on using sensing mindfulness to help create a serene personal space, even in the midst of busy places:

*Sometimes I just lazily let my eyes lose focus and kind of trance out, trying not to notice as all the objects in front of me become one, almost like crossing my eyes. I shut off my other senses a bit, calming me down, knowing that despite being out in the big wide world, walking alone, that there is my own little space around me and that the feet I see are my own and can take me wherever I want them to go.*

*Note:* If you have time to develop only one mindful habit while reading this book, make it sensing mindfulness and the related practices coming up in the next chapter on mindfulness with daily activities.

## Combining the Three-Breath Method and Sensing Mindfulness

Sensing mindfulness techniques can be combined with the Three-Breath Method.

*EXAMPLE*

A high school athlete talks about how she uses breathing to calm herself and prepare for javelin throwing in a track and field competition:

*I throw javelin. Essentially this event requires you to run sideways down a strip of track with a spear in your hand. A lot could go wrong. I was about to throw my first of three throws. The person before me was running up to throw her javelin and she tripped on the track and fell. It was very stressful to watch as she fell toward the ground. Luckily, her javelin had fallen away from her and nowhere near the danger zone. However, after this, I had to throw. I was a little panicked that this would happen to me. Taking my position at the start of the runway, I took three deep breaths and cleared my mind. I focused on my senses to distract from my thoughts. I felt the weight of the javelin in my hand, the warm sun on my shoulders, and listened to the wind in the nearby trees. This refocused my mind on the task at hand, and I ended up throwing a personal best!*

*EXAMPLE*

A Latinx community leader talks about coping with stress by using breathing and intentional noticing of sensations of the movement of her breaths moving through her body:

*When I worked as an executive director for a local nonprofit, I had to give public talks almost on a weekly basis, whether to a Rotary Club, a fundraising event, or a meeting with city councilors. I often felt nervous before I started speaking. Most of the time, the rooms had a majority of White people and hardly ever were there people of color with an accent like I have. I always took several deep, long breaths, making sure that the air went in slowly all the way to my stomach and then released through my mouth. This activity allowed me to stay calm and focused, and it worked almost every time.*

# Grounding Techniques

### grounding techniques

Specific, highly specialized techniques for making sensing mindfulness more intense.

While all forms of sensing mindfulness can make us calmer by resting our mind and freeing it from negative mind-wandering, the five grounding techniques described in this section can be particularly effective in quickly giving our mind a rest. Rest comes from fully focusing our attention in a particular way that requires considerable mental effort, which leaves little mental energy for mind-wandering. The five grounding techniques are soft-eyes, sharp-eyes, soft-ears, soft-contact, and soft-taste.

## *Soft-Eyes Grounding Technique*

### soft-eyes

The practice of relaxing our visual focus to take in not only what is in our direct line of sight, but also what's in our peripheral vision (the outer edge of our field of vision). Seeing what is in front of us and what is in our peripheral vision requires all our attention, which leaves no room for self-talk.

## — *Key Idea* —

During much of the day, we are not aware of most of what is coming in through our senses. For example, while walking home after working late, we might be thinking about how hungry we are and how long it will take to order at our favorite coffee shop. Or maybe we can't free ourselves from worrying about a difficult project at school or about a meeting with a supervisor at work that we are dreading. Soft-eyes is a different way of seeing that frees us from negative mind-wandering. How do you feel when you can't free your mind from worry? How attentive are you to your surroundings when you are caught up in negative self-talk?

With soft eyes, we give our full attention to not only what is in front of us, but also what is on both sides of us and what is above and below us. The effort to engage soft-eyes is particularly effective in commanding our full attention, crowding self-talk and everything else out of our mind.

Some martial arts incorporate soft-eyes into their awareness training. Several years ago, an Aikido master taught Doug what he called soft-eyes—widening the field of vision so that we are aware of all that is around us. Aikido practitioners use this technique to be aware of challengers approaching from any direction. It takes a lot of attention to maintain this broad, open awareness, so soft-eyes and its feeling of spaciousness also make it hard for us to engage in mind-wandering. Lots of activities engage this same practice of wide visual attention, from training horses to hip-hop dancing to rollerblading to playing quarterback in football.

Walking in a natural setting is an excellent environment for practicing soft-eyes. Walking on an easy trail with few obstacles requires little attention. Consequently, soft-eyes can open our awareness to the full range of sensations included in our peripheral vision, with no attention left over for mind-wandering.

Looking between 20 and 40 feet ahead on a well-groomed trail seems to be the right distance to engage soft-eyes while still feeling grounded and secure that the next step will be safe. After we feel safe, it's possible to feel a shift into a sense of deep calmness, trust, and spacious connection. However, gazing off in the distance beyond 40 feet is an invitation to fall. Obviously, some walks aren't suited for soft-eyes at all. When a trail is rocky and steep, don't try to keep a wide field of vision, but instead focus carefully on the path directly in front of you, using sharp-eyes, which is the grounding technique you will read about next.

### FROM THE OTHER SIDE

Tad, the artist who created the cover for the book *Saint Badass*, wrote about how soft-eyes keeps him out of trouble:

*In here, [soft-eyes] is a must. Always pay attention to your surroundings. Always! Early in my beginning of doing time I witnessed a man being beaten because someone scuffed the guy's shoes by not watching where he was going. Then I saw a man get his throat cut because he stepped in front of another man; in here, that is very disrespectful unless one says, "Excuse me."*

 PUT INTO PRACTICE **Journal**

### Soft-Eyes

Practice sensing mindfulness with soft-eyes next time you're taking an easy walk or sitting outdoors. Direct your vision to an object in front of you. Then expand your vision in both directions so you are including your peripheral vision. Notice how it requires all your attention to maintain this full field of vision.

Find page 286 and write about the experience (including your feelings). Note if you sense a feeling of being interwoven and connected with everything around you. If, however, you wear glasses and have problems with peripheral vision, soft-eyes might not work for you.

## Sharp-Eyes Grounding Technique

### sharp-eyes

The practice of focusing all our attention and vision on a specific object or part of an object.

With soft-eyes, our focus is very broad and includes our entire field of vision. Sharp-eyes is the opposite; it requires us to focus all our attention and vision on a specific object or part of an object.

We can use sharp-eyes during the day as a calming exercise, to enjoy, or to relieve stress. A famous meditation teacher would say, with great emphasis, "Just see the flower!" meaning not to think about it as a flower, not about color or shape, but rather to just experience the visual sensation of the flower instead of having thoughts or feelings about what you are seeing. Or try it with a pet. Stare into its eyes and focus on its face.

### Example

A youth who practiced tae kwon do describes how sharp-eyes is used in martial art training.

*I have done this practice before many times when tae kwon do was a large part of my life. I remember a few instances, one specifically while training in South Korea. My group and I were sitting in a line, each with a lit candle in front of us. We were told to focus on the flame, the way it dances, the way it moves with or against our deep breathing, and to try to determine if we could predict the flame's movements or not.*

 PUT INTO PRACTICE **Journal**

### Sharp-Eyes

Try engaging sharp-eyes in a variety of places or appropriate social situations, such as sitting on a bench or standing in line at a store. Direct your vision to a small object or part of an object. Focus on that object for a while. Switch from object to object.

Write about the experience on page 286, including what you focused on and the degree to which you experienced a slight energy boost, quiet joy, and calm. Did a sense of concentration, a feeling of connection, or other feelings arise when you used sharp-eyes? (You can also experiment with alternating sharp-eyes and soft-eyes).

## Soft-Ears Grounding Technique

### soft-ears

The practice of opening our attention to take in **all** of the surrounding sounds at the same time, without focusing on any specific sound. For example, we are waiting in line and the people around us are talking; with soft-ears we only hear a hum of sound. We do not hear the specific words of any of the conversations. We don't hear better because of soft-ears; we just hear differently.

With sensing mindfulness, we can direct our attention to whatever we are hearing, whether it is the sound of the fan running in our car, birds chirping, or a favorite song. With soft-ears we hear all these sounds at the same time: birds chirping, water running in the stream next to us, and the sound of wind blowing through the trees. The soft-ears grounding technique takes up all our attention, meaning we cannot attend to our self-talk.

For example, while sitting on a bench near a river, with soft-ears we might notice the sound of the water running over rocks, a breeze rustling the leaves in the trees, and the singing of birds, all without focusing our hearing on any one source. The mix of sounds rise and pass, as in all types of mindfulness practices. Consider being in a crowd where we might experience the sounds from multiple conversations blending together into a kind of low-key buzz or vibration. Listening to this buzz, we try not to hear or follow any single conversation.

Some individuals find it useful to practice sharp-ears. All of our attention focuses on the source of a single sound. We can heighten our focus by closing our eyes and not attending to any other physical sensations.

 PUT INTO PRACTICE **Journal**

### Soft-Ears

Experiment with soft-ears in a place where you are on your own but surrounded by people. You might try this while riding the bus, in the cafeteria at school, at a sporting event, or at a rock concert between songs. Open your attention to all the sounds and conversations around you.

Write about your experience on page 286, especially if you were able to just hear the hum/buzz from the conversations and not listen to any single conversation. Describe what you heard, felt in your body, and any times of contentment. Or make a drawing in the back of the workbook that represents the variations in your experience.

## Soft-Contact Grounding Technique

**soft-contact**

> The practice of opening our attention to take in tactile sensations from all the parts of our body, without focusing on any one source.

Think about how many sensations of contact we are experiencing at this moment—the surface of a chair supporting your body, the tension in a foot propped at an odd angle, a lock of hair brushing against your face, the temperature of the air on your skin. At any moment of any day, we can practice soft-contact by being aware, at the same time, of the multiple sensations from everything touching our skin. In soft-contact, we attend to whatever sensation attracts our attention. Soft-contact is closely related to a popular type of meditation called body-scan meditation, in which we systematically shift our attention from one part of our body to the next. In body-scan meditation, we lie on our back, directing our attention to each body part in turn to notice the presence of tension—and release it. Releasing our physical tensions can calm our body and mind. For a quick body scan, we can start releasing with our forehead, then eyebrows, cheeks, lips, chin, neck, shoulders, arms, elbows, forearms, wrists, palm of hands, top of hands, each finger, then go to the chest, and step by step move our attention until we reach our feet.

## PUT INTO PRACTICE **Journal**

### *Soft-Contact*

Try practicing soft-contact during different activities throughout the day. For example, when putting on our shoes we are aware of touching our shoes, the contact with the chair we are sitting on, and the leaning forward so we can touch our shoes. In pouring a glass of orange juice, we are aware of our contact with the container of orange juice, how our body is in contact with the floor or our chair, and the extension of our arm. We can relax any tension in our body as we tune in to these physical sensations. Write about the experience on page 286, including your feelings.

### *Soft-Taste Grounding Technique*

---

**soft-taste**

> The practice of focusing all our attention, as we eat, on the changing texture and taste of food and on the sensations from chewing and swallowing.

Taste involves multiple sensations, but we usually focus on the taste when the food first enters our mouth. Soft-taste is similar to some of the other soft grounding techniques in that we attend to multiple sources of taste at the same time, just as we listen to multiple sources of sound in soft-ears and see a range of people and things with soft-eyes. With soft-taste, we notice the initial texture and taste of the food we take in. As we chew, the taste of the food may change, while the texture usually also changes. For example, a soft caramel might stick to our teeth at first before melting in our mouth. Biting into an ear of sweet corn often leaves us with fibers stuck between our teeth. In contrast, many soups simply glide down our throat without the texture changing.

In chewing a bite of food, notice which side of your mouth does most of the chewing and where the pressure is on your teeth and jaws. Does the chewing switch from side to side? Listen to sounds the chewing creates. Chew each mouthful of food completely, then swallow. In initially learning to experience soft-taste, you might intentionally shift your attention from taste to texture to chewing and to swallowing. Eventually, these various sensations will arise and pass naturally as you eat.

PUT INTO PRACTICE **Journal**

### Soft-Taste

The following exercise not only supports mindfulness, but can also help us develop the healthy eating habit of not rushing through a meal. Begin by focusing completely on chewing your food and then on swallowing. Do not take the next bite until you finish swallowing the food in your mouth. After 3 days, write on page 287 about what you noticed when you intentionally shifted your attention from taste to texture as you chew and to swallow while eating two different foods.

## Combining Multiple Grounding Techniques

The more you use the grounding techniques, the more confident and competent you will become in your mindfulness practice. We can engage one grounding technique after another.

### EXAMPLE

A teenager named Finnian explains how he uses soft-touch (muscle relaxation and breathing) and sharp-eyes (imagery).

*I consider myself an overthinker. All day, every day, I battle with obsessive thoughts and I have to write stuff down or else I can't move forward. I have the hardest time when I lie down for bed. In the dark and quiet, my brain accelerates to a new pace. The speed of sound would be jealous! During these difficult times, I try to push my thoughts away, but I have found that to only cause more thoughts to bombard me. Instead, over a long time, I have developed two go-to strategies: progressive muscle relaxation with breathing and imagery. With progressive muscle relaxation, I turn all of my thoughts to focusing on one part of my body at a time. In time with my breath, I actively relax the part. This helps calm my mind and relax my body for sleep. For imagery, I think of sticky notes. When I have an obsessive thought, I imagine myself writing it on a sticky note. I then take this mental sticky note and fold it until I can't see the writing. I then imagine moving the note into a box. This stores the idea away and gives it a safe space to be. Basically, along the lines of "out of sight, out of mind."*

Meditation, breathing exercises, and sensing mindfulness can help prepare us to deal with difficult emotions, as shown in the Mind Body Awareness Project (MBA) used with troubled youth in California.* The project's mission is to "help at-risk populations transform their harmful behavior and live meaningful lives through mindfulness meditation and emotional awareness."

---

* For more information, visit https://www.mbaproject.org/about-mindfulness-3/youth-stories/

### EXAMPLES

Three troubled youth describe the benefits of their mind-body awareness practices:

Youth 1, Michael, participated in the MBA Project while incarcerated. He was released in fall 2014 and continues to practice meditation. He is heading to community college. *I was there when my brother got shot. It messes me up and I can't sleep. MBA has helped me be able to sleep faster. I used to just snap at people. MBA helped me with that.*

Youth 2: *Mindful meditation is a way to release from all the stress . . . . It's always like you can just take a break. It's like taking a break from life. It's like pausing. You got a remote control for life. You just hit pause and all the [stuff] that's going on around you doesn't matter right now; you're just doing you. It's all that is there in the moment.*

Youth 3: *Instead of reacting, I can just stop, think about it, feel me, you know, I can actually choose instead of reacting to it. It's [mindfulness] going to help me in a lot of ways: family issues, school, stuff at the house, camp (long-term juvenile detention) right now. And like knowing there's gonna be people you're gonna meet in the real world, it's gonna help me . . . build my character too.*

## PERSONAL CHALLENGE **Journal**

Let's expand our practice with exercises that will help you experience and develop your capacity for sensing mindfulness (intentional noticing of sensations). Choose two of the five grounding techniques (soft-eyes, sharp-eyes, soft-ears, soft-contact, and soft-taste) and alternate between them several times in a day. Do this for 3 days, then write about the experience of going back and forth from one technique to the other. Is using sensing mindfulness and grounding techniques calming you and making it easier to be kinder? Write about your thoughts on page 287.

> ### With Mindfulness, Positive Emotions Become More Intense and More Pleasurable
>
> Possibly the greatest benefit of sensing mindfulness is that by increasing our time being mindful, we will find positive emotions more intense and even more joyful. For example, mindfulness makes the pleasure from eating, physical and emotional intimacy, and friendship more intense and therefore more pleasurable and joyful. This greater pleasure and joy come as we repeatedly use sensing mindfulness and the grounding techniques. The mindful practices in daily life described in the next chapter also contribute to this increased pleasure and joy. They transform seemingly trivial chores, like making the bed and brushing our teeth, into calming and satisfying activities.

# Mindfulness with Emotions

Mindfulness with emotions refers to the state of mind in which we experience an emotion but are not distracted from our intention by the emotion. For example, imagine we are painting a portrait for a person who will pay us a lot of money and will recommend us to their friends. The person wants the portrait very soon. While we are painting, the postal carrier delivers the mail, and we open a letter and find out we have been accepted to attend our favorite college with a scholarship. We feel the emotion of being excited. We quickly call our parents and two of our best friends. Then, realizing our intention to get the portrait done, we take three breaths and get back to painting. We are mindful with the emotion. Our emotion of happiness has not distracted us from our intention. However, if we are so excited by the good news that we want to go out and celebrate and will not soon return to painting, we are being seriously distracted by the emotion.

# Low-Key Emotions

Some emotions may be pleasant and some slightly unpleasant. Some common examples of pleasant emotions are feeling joy, feeling satisfied, feeling proud, feeling strong, feeling grateful, and feeling relaxed. Some common unpleasant emotions are feeling annoyed, feeling bored, feeling ashamed, feeling confused, and feeling embarrassed.

An emotion is low key for us if the emotion does not interfere significantly with our intention. We can experience the emotion and continue with our intention, or we can name the emotion and then use some form of sensing mindfulness to not let the emotion distract us so we can return to our intention in a reasonable time.

### *Example*

Mike used the Three-Breath Method in response to his low-key emotion of annoyance:

*Mike was taking the bus when he received a call on his cell phone. When he tried to listen to the caller, he had difficulty because several young people on the bus were speaking and laughing. Mike said to himself, "I am annoyed." He quickly realized that the phone call was not important, and that the teenagers were just acting as normal teenagers. Mike took three breaths. After the third breath, he shifted his attention away from the thoughts that had fed his angry feelings, and his agitation was gone.*

✦ ✦ ✦

Interestingly, what is a low-key emotion for one person may not be low-key for another person. For example, John and Ben are reading books on a park bench when they hear loud barking from nearby dogs. Both feel the emotion of fear. They look up and see the dogs are not charging at them, but are playing with their owner. Ben says to himself, "I am afraid," and is able to stop feeling the fear and go back to reading his book, but John is so upset that he cannot read or calm down and tells Ben he wants to leave the park.

## PUT INTO **Practice**

Write about two of your most common low-key emotions:

One that is pleasant _____

One that is unpleasant _____

Indicate how you might use sensing mindfulness to keep this emotion from distracting you.

_____

_____

## Negative Emotional Disturbance

Low-key emotions are not a concern when we have the ability to quickly return to mindfulness. Sometimes, though, an emotion will activate a negative emotional disturbance.

**negative emotional disturbance**

> A negative emotional disturbance occurs when our attention is taken over by an emotion so upsetting that it significantly distracts us from our current intention. The negative emotional disturbance quickly captures our attention and holds it so we cannot easily return to our intention.

When a negative emotional disturbance occurs, we do the best we can to keep focused on our intention, possibly naming the emotion (for example, saying to yourself "I am angry" or "I am anxious"), and then calling on sensing mindfulness, grounding techniques, or the Three-Breath Method. But it is often not possible to return our focus to our intention because the emotional disturbance is so upsetting. This situation can lead us to try to escape from the uncomfortable emotion by adopting unkind habits, which can provide short-term relief.

Chapter 8, "Face Up to Your Unkind Habits," discusses some of the many unkind habits we may use to hide from our emotional disturbances. Here are a few unkind habits that we direct at ourselves to escape from our emotional disturbances: engaging in excessive digital media (internet, social media, and texting), substance abuse, unhealthy eating, procrastination (putting off what you need to do), and not meeting our own needs because of putting the needs of others above our own (called being a doormat). Unkind habits such as these may make us feel good at first, but over many months we are likely to become unhappy, and our unkind habits may bring unhappiness to others as well.

Here are examples of unkind habits we direct at others that we may adopt when being stressed by our emotional disturbances: explosive anger, frequent criticism of ourself or others, being disrespectful, frequent complaining, and aggressive rudeness. As mentioned earlier, the next part of the book helps us not only recognize our unkind habits but also break or at least weaken them.

PUT INTO **Practice**

Describe a situation in which you experienced a negative emotional disturbance and used an unkind habit to distract yourself from the negative emotion.

_____

_____

## Not Acting with Unkindness in Response to a Negative Emotional Disturbance

Neuroscientist Jill Bolte Taylor in her book *My Stroke of Insight*[2] described an important fact about the chemical responses in our body that responds to our negative emotional disturbance: When a strong negative emotion occurs, a surge of chemicals passes through our body and triggers our instinctual "fight, flight, or freeze" survival response. Think how your body feels when you are startled or witness an event that is very upsetting. You may feel your heart beating faster and a tightness across your torso, more rapid breathing, and you may even start to sweat. It takes about 90 seconds for those chemicals that cause these reactions to pass through our body. We do not want to respond during these 90 seconds because we are likely to make an unkind, possibly violent response that we will regret later. A strategy that will sometimes be effective for minimizing the effects of a strong negative emotional disturbance is to wait for about 90 seconds to allow our body and mind to calm down some, then use the Three-Breath Method.

### EXAMPLE

How do you feel when you think you've been treated unfairly? When we feel wronged by those close to us, such as our partner, we often lose control of our emotions because we are deeply hurt.

Mike's mother was making a special dinner for Mike and his girlfriend, Jenny. Mike's mother told them that dinner would be ready at 7 p.m. Mike arrived at 6:30 from work, but by 8 p.m., Jenny had not arrived or called to tell them she would be late. When Mike tried to call Jenny, the phone rang and rang without anybody answering. Mike could see his mother was upset. Jenny did not arrive until 9 p.m., and it was obvious that she had been drinking. Feeling betrayed by Jenny's inconsiderate behavior, but not wanting to upset his mother more, Mike said to himself, "I am furious," paused 90 seconds and used the Three-Breath Method and was able to control his instinctual response to yell at Jenny. However, for the next day and a half his emotions swirled between being agitated and being quite disturbed. Spending time around Jenny kept retriggering his anger. Naming the emotion, waiting 90 seconds after each emotional upheaval, and then using a grounding technique or taking three deep slow breaths helped somewhat, but not enough to free him from his distress. Using his Wise Warrior, he refrained from being overly aggressive with his partner, and a few days later was able to discuss how her actions had upset him, using a technique we will go over in Chapter 10: "Responding to the Unkind Habits of Others."

✦ ✦ ✦

To keep from causing harm during the 90 seconds, we can call on our Wise Warrior to name our emotion, engage in a grounding technique or sensing mindfulness, possibly by humming a song we really like or using sharp-eyes to focus on a plant or flower. If those practices are not enough to calm us, the Wise Warrior will need us to do something more powerful, possibly inhaling deeply as we draw our shoulder blades together. Naming the emotion and taking a 90-second pause may not free us from being upset and distracted, but it can at least help us from doing harm and possibly even soften the impact of the emotional disturbance.

 PUT INTO **Practice**

Describe a time you reacted with an unkind behavior to a negative emotional disturbance.

_____

How could you have used naming the emotion and then engaging sensing mindfulness or the 90-second pause to respond in a more constructive manner?

_____

_____

## Reviewing Your Kindness Plan: Making Habits Stick

Let's stop for a minute and switch our focus back to the kindness plan you created in Chapter 4, "Increase Your Kindness."

If you are having difficulty making progress with your kindness plan, the advice of habit-change specialists Dr. B. J. Fogg of Stanford University, author of *Tiny* Habits,[3] and James Clear, author of *Atomic Habits*,[4] might be helpful. Their suggestions can be organized into four steps for making habits stick:

- Start with a "tiny habit," something so easy it's almost impossible to fail—such as exercising or meditating for just one minute every day.

- Set aside a specific time you'll actually do it.

- If you have trouble sticking with the habit, try to figure out exactly what is holding you back.

- Celebrate or reward yourself immediately for every success, even if the reward is as little as telling yourself, "Good job!"

 PUT INTO PRACTICE **Journal**

### *Reviewing Your Kindness Plan*

Turn again to your Kindness Plan that you created on pages 280–281 and read it over. Then go to page 282 and answer the questions about your plan.

# Mindfulness: Anyplace, Anytime

Setting aside certain times of our day to practice something like the guitar or skateboarding stunts will most likely lead to improvement. But mindfulness with sensations and emotions is different. It's not just for certain activities or particular times of the day. We can use mindfulness in all aspects of our life and at any time during the day or night.

## PUT INTO PRACTICE **Journal**

Think about ways you can take a sensing mindfulness break for one minute or less during the day. For example, in addition to the grounding techniques, you might try rolling your neck and shoulders, breathing in through your nose and blowing out through your mouth, or feeling the vibration in your lips while you hum a "mmmm" sound. Think about where and when you might be able to incorporate sensing mindfulness into your day. In the shower? Riding the bus to school or work? Waiting in line? Before you eat?

Start by taking a short sensing mindfulness break at least once a day. If possible, work up to doing it multiple times a day for 3 days. Then write about the experiences on page 287, including feelings such as one of connection and/or spaciousness.

## ━━━━━━━ Wrapping Up ━━━━━━━

Sensing mindfulness, the five grounding techniques (soft-eyes, sharp-eyes, soft-ears, soft-contact, and soft-taste), and the Three-Breath Method can help take us out of our self-centered thoughts and emotions and connect us to the people and earth around us. These practices benefit us in two ways: they allow us to savor moments of joy and contentment by bringing us to mindfulness, and they shift our attention away from negative emotional disturbances. These two benefits help us dismantle unkind habits and provide the opportunity to build kind habits, which are key steps toward lasting happiness.

## PUT INTO PRACTICE **Journal**

Meditating regularly is more important than how long you meditate. Choose one of the forms of meditation you learned about in Chapter 5: Embracing Kindness, Guided, or Wordless Meditation. Make a schedule for what time and for how long you will meditate in the morning (and possibly in the evening as well). Use an app or paper and pencil to indicate how long you actually sit each time. After 5 days, on page 287 describe what went well and what did not go well. Also describe how meditating made you feel.

# Time for Reflection

On a scale of 0 through 4, how are you feeling about these practices?
0 = I don't do this; 1 = Strongly disagree; 2 = Disagree; 3 = Agree; 4 = Strongly agree

_____ I find sensing mindfulness (intentional noticing of sensations) and the five grounding techniques helpful and will continue to use them.

_____ I find meditating to be helpful.

_____ I like the practice of strengthening one of my kind habits.

_____ I find it helpful to do activities I find on my list of pleasant kind habits.

_____ I think it is worthwhile to use the kind conversation habits.

_____ I believe it is helpful to be friendly, offer help, show appreciation, and reach out to those in need.

• • •

Think about each of these statements and then circle Yes or No.

| | | |
|---|---|---|
| I feel grateful for the people and pets I care about. | Yes | No |
| I feel grateful for something that went well today. | Yes | No |
| I feel grateful for what I can do with my body and mind. | Yes | No |
| I feel grateful for the people who help me and others. | Yes | No |
| I feel grateful for my beliefs that give me purpose and meaning. | Yes | No |
| I feel grateful for having fun and laughter. | Yes | No |
| I feel grateful for the earth and universe. | Yes | No |

• • •

Write about how you have been kind at least one time in one of these ways:

• Be friendly

• Give help

• Show appreciation

• Reach out to those with serious needs

• Give back to the earth

_____

_____

Chapter 7

# Mindfulness with Daily Activities and Thoughts

*Sometimes the smallest things take up the most room in our heart.*

Winnie The Pooh

Life tends to go better when we are mindful throughout the day. When our body is calm and our mind is at rest and able to focus, we are more able to be content in the moment and respond thoughtfully and kindly, rather than reacting impulsively. In fact, humans tend to be instinctively kind, but often lose touch with that inherent impulse. The more we can reduce our negative self-talk, the more opportunities we will have to act with kindness. Each moment of kindfulness can bring small pleasures and, at times, great pleasures. Over time, increasingly pleasant, life-sustaining moments are possible as we learn how to eliminate or at least substantially weaken unkind habits that keep us from the benefits of kindfulness.

## Mindful Micropractices

In the two previous chapters we described mindfulness with our senses and grounding techniques such as soft-eyes. This third and final chapter of the Train Your Mind step explains how to be mindful when doing chores or what seem to be life's least important activities. Chores do not seem to offer a way to train our mind, but in fact they can be a powerful opportunity to practice mindfulness. We can, for example, deliberately engage sensing mindfulness while we walk the dog, fold laundry, organize our binders for a report, wait in line at a drive-through, take a coffee break at work, take care of a sibling, help prepare food, turn out lights, or take a shower. When we do these activities with mindfulness, we call them *mindful micropractices.*

## mindful micropractice

A familiar, daily activity or chore that is performed as an exercise in mindfulness. Brushing our teeth is a daily chore, but brushing while listening to music is not a mindful micropractice. However, brushing our teeth with mindfulness is a mindful micropractice because we are totally focused on our intention, brushing our teeth.

*— Key Idea —*

Mindful micropractices have these benefits:

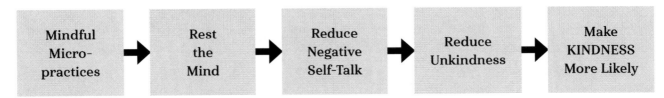

Throughout our lives, we are faced with doing daily chores. Some of us often engage in negative self-talk while doing these daily activities; for example, we might feel angry that no one is helping us or fixate on how much time we feel is being wasted doing chores. Our negative self-talk can drive us to rush through and resent our chores. This chapter focuses on how to reduce negative feelings as we perform necessary routines/chores and discusses how doing these chores mindfully can create a reservoir of calm and joy in our lives. There are many opportunities to do mindful micropractices during the day. For example:

- We can make scanning the supermarket shelves for our purchase a micropractice by paying close attention to the varied colors and smells of the vegetables or the expressions on the faces of other customers, as well as the sensation of our feet coming into contact with the ground as we push our cart.

- We can make waiting for the bus a mindful micropractice by listening with soft-ears to the hum of conversations or other sounds, such as the rumble of cars and horns, and using sharp-eyes to notice shapes and colors of cars or plants or people's clothing.

- We can make dressing a mindful micropractice by feeling the sensations from our hands as we button our clothing or tie our shoes.

**EXAMPLE**

One youth comments on the chore of sweeping as a mindful activity:

*Whenever I have to sweep, I turn it into a meditative practice by sometimes counting the number of motions I complete. I try to take deep breaths while matching the sweeping movements.*

**EXAMPLE**

A Native American youth finds himself consumed with boredom on his rural reservation. He starts using mindful micropractices to transform his feeling of boredom into gratitude and feelings of abundance. He begins to focus on nature and sensations as he walks around town. To be more present during traditional gatherings, he notices the smells of the food, sounds of the drums, and connection between all people.

Some of the benefits of giving your mind a rest by turning daily tasks into micropractices include less time for negative self-talk, completing a chore with a sense of satisfaction rather than resentment or boredom, and having more energy for dealing with difficult situations. How can we increase our sense of joy? What does joy feel like? The more rested our mind, the more joy we will be able to experience and the more willing we will be to act with kindness. In addition, we will develop the ability to notice unkind habits and work on weakening them.

 PUT INTO **Practice**

Write down two daily chores you could turn into mindful micropractices.

_____

_____

## Transforming Chores and Everyday Activities into Mindful Micropractices

Below are five common activities/chores that can be done mindfully, which transforms them into mindful micropractices: doing work around the house/apartment, attending to personal hygiene, making and following a schedule, organizing our surroundings, and moving quietly.

Following each explanation of an activity is an exercise. After you finish reading about the five activities, a Put into Practice assignment will ask you to do two of these five exercises for at least several days.

### Doing Work Around the House/Apartment

When making our bed, we can use sensing mindfulness by directing our attention to the colors of our bedding, the feel of the texture of the bedding, the sensation of spreading the sheet into place, and the feel of the weight of our pillow. Other daily micropractices around the house include: changing the oil in a car, washing dishes, replacing batteries, putting tools away, sharpening knives, feeding animals, washing the car, and putting dishes away.

 MICROPRACTICE EXERCISE 1 **Journal**

Use sensing mindfulness (smell, sound, touch, taste, sight) on a specific household chore 3 days in a row. On page 288, answer the questions about using sensing mindfulness.

## Attending to Personal Hygiene

Washing, toothbrushing, flossing, brushing hair, putting on lotion, putting on makeup, and shaving can all be mindful micropractices. While showering, we can engage sensing mindfulness by focusing on the sensations of beads of water striking our face and eyelids, the relaxing scalp massage as we rub in the shampoo, and the feel of our hands on our skin as we soap up and rinse.

 MICROPRACTICE EXERCISE 2 **Journal**

Use sensing mindfulness when brushing your teeth (or a similar personal hygiene activity such as washing your hands). Pay careful attention to the sensations of holding the brush, the taste of the toothpaste, the feel of the brush on your teeth, etc. Did using sensing mindfulness during these personal hygiene activities give your mind a rest? On page 288, describe your feelings.

## Organizing Your Surroundings

Creating a clean and well-organized environment is a kind habit for ourselves and those who are around us. Not cleaning up our messes can contribute to other unkind habits, such as being irresponsible and putting off what we are supposed to do (procrastinating). Leaving a messy work space can negatively affect the people we work with. Leaving a messy kitchen, dining room, or bedroom can irritate and anger the people we live with.

Converting clutter into order is a mindful micropractice. Cleaning up clutter is an act of kindness not just to ourselves but to others we live with, who are often much happier when they don't have to live with or clean up our messes. An added bonus for organizing our surroundings is that we can replace negative self-talk with feelings of appreciation and gratitude for being able to create a supportive environment for ourselves and the others in our life.

 MICROPRACTICE EXERCISE 3 **Journal**

Take a few minutes to look—really look—around where you live or work. Are there messes or piles that often distract you or might agitate others? Is there too much stuff left undone for "later"? Choose something to organize. While organizing, pay attention to how you feel. Maybe you are picking up dirty clothes that need to go to the laundry. As in other practices, pay attention to your senses. How do the clothes smell before you wash them? Do they smell fresh after laundering them? What does the space look like once your clothes are folded and put away in your drawers and hung in your closet?

On page 288, describe how you feel once you organized your surroundings.

If you are still attending school, consider organizing your schoolwork, electronically or by creating folders with sections for each subject area. Put your notes in order so they become easier to study. Create a task list for all of your assignments so you know when your due dates and tests are. How do you feel as your work becomes more organized? Does the organization reduce your stress? How does it feel to know when things are due? Does being organized in advance reduce procrastination and increase your sense of calm?

On page 288, describe how you organized your schoolwork and how it made you feel.

## Making and Following a Schedule

In addition to sensing mindfulness with vision, taste, touch, sound, and smell, we also sense time. For example, we often experience stress if we try to multitask because we feel rushed. In fact, many of us find ourselves squeezing an activity into a schedule that is already full. Adding in another nonurgent activity when we don't have time is a form of greed. How does it feel when you add multiple activities because you don't want to miss anything? Does it increase your sense of pleasure or does it cause tension? Most likely multitasking causes us stress and may inconvenience others when we are late or make mistakes because we were in a hurry to do it all.

The cure for the stress that comes from running late and rushing is like that for any unkind habit. Our first step is realizing and acknowledging the harm our unkind habit is doing to ourself and others. We need to take a moment to experience that unpleasant feeling of stress as a motivator to plan our time more carefully, to slow down and stop squeezing in too many activities. This unpleasant feeling of stress can remind us to make and follow a realistic schedule.

In making a schedule, we need to think of priorities, focusing on what is really important and making sure we have adequate time to do important things. We also need to set aside some time for some fun along with time to decompress and recharge. Remember, time for self-care is a priority.

### EXAMPLE

Twenty-one-year-old Isabel schedules time for self-care:

*I've often received advice to schedule in time for self-care and that it should be one of the nonnegotiable activities. We often jam-pack our schedules, but with a designated time to refresh and refocus, meditate, etc. it can help us be more effective in the rest of the day (or in the next day if we choose to put our self-care at the end of the day). It could be anything: napping, playing or listening to music, meditation, food prep, reading a book, watching an episode of our favorite TV show—whatever makes us feel able to relax and then continue our day with intention. It wouldn't necessarily have to be every day, that's what the "Take Three Breaths" write-ins are for. But having some designated time a few days each week to do whatever I may feel like doing in the moment has been very helpful for me.*

## MICROPRACTICE EXERCISE 4 **Journal**

Put your weekly activities and appointments on a calendar. (A calendar you might use is located online at https://bit.ly/LH_Calendar.

You can think of this as your to-do list. The schedule/list could include assignments for school or work, meetings to attend, cultural events, gym workouts, self-care, and chores. It can also include reminders to call people you want to keep in touch with. After making your schedule, examine it to see if it is too tightly packed. If so, where can you change the schedule to eliminate a nonurgent activity?

In addition, look for or create open spaces in your schedule and write "Take Three Breaths" as a reminder to be mindful. Post this calendar with dates and times where you can see it each day. Or put the activities on your phone calendar or your reminder app. Crossing off each completed task can be very satisfying.

On page 289, describe what happens and how you feel as a consequence of making and following a realistic schedule and to-do list.

## *Moving Quietly/Gracefully Through the World*

When we are being mindful, we think about how our actions affect others. One major way our actions can affect others is through the noise we make. Think about noise on a scale of one to ten, with ten being the loudest. Is the noise we create in the high range? Do we add unnecessary intentional noise without thinking about the impacts first? For example, do we shout at someone in another room instead of walking to where they are to say something? Do we turn up the television to high volume even if others are trying to do something else in the same room? Many of us are not bothered by our own noise. It is as if we don't hear the noise coming from the plates that clatter as we set them down or the doors we slam or our own loud talking. With those actions, we are not being mindful of how our noisy actions can upset others and can distract us from having moments of calm.

Out of kindness to ourselves and respect to others nearby, we can refrain from voluntarily causing disruptive noise. Creating quiet by refraining from being noisy is a mindful micropractice. When we notice a time when we might make disturbing noise, such as putting away dishes and silverware in the kitchen, we can use sensing mindfulness to put down the objects gently to reduce the noise. Think proactively: We do not need to turn on the radio, TV, or other device unless it is going to be the focus of our attention. If we need to talk to someone in the house, instead of shouting, we can walk to where they are to speak to them. Silence, or at least doing things quietly, is often a support for mindfulness and for resting our mind, and thus is a kindness for us. Not imposing noise on others is also a kindness.

We should be aware that some people purposely create a noisy environment to distract them from their negative self-talk.

Tad wrote: *Some in here seem to fear silence because then they have to listen to their own mind and they'd rather get into loud radio/TV, yelling, etc. just to keep their mind distracted.*

An Indigenous youth leader pointed out that there are times when loud sounds can be used to enhance a meditative, mindful, or connective state. One example is the practice of synchronized drumming. The loud boom of the drums fills a longhouse or gathering place. The beat is a symbol of the heartbeat of all of us and our relation to each other. In these cases, the sound refreshes us and helps the process of connecting to the earth and each other. The key is to ensure that loud activities are enjoyed by those around you without causing unreasonable disruptions to others.

 MICROPRACTICE EXERCISE 5 **Journal**

Think about a way you are often noisy and try instead to be as quiet as possible. It can be something as simple as entering a room quietly and closing the door as soundlessly as possible. Or setting the table for dinner by quietly setting down the plates and glasses. Practice the quiet activity for 3 days, then on page 289 write responses to these questions: How did it feel to be quiet? Was your quiet noticed or appreciated by others? Or draw a picture of how it felt to be quiet. Consider colors or symbols that depict your sense of quiet.

# Mindfulness with Thoughts

### mindfulness with thoughts

The practice of keeping our attention on what we are intending to think about. Being mindful with thoughts is a kind habit.

Mindfulness with thoughts refers to the practice of keeping our thoughts focused on what we are intending to think about. When we become distracted, we are able to quickly return our attention back to what we are intending to do or think about. Being mindful with thoughts is a kind habit because, by being able to keep our attention on what we are intending to do or think about, we are likely to achieve our intentions and experience the emotion of satisfaction. Also, when we are mindful with thoughts, we are less likely to experience negative self-talk.

Since we spend most of our waking hours thinking about or doing one thing or another, we can be grateful that mindfulness with thoughts brings us moments of joy and calmness many times during the day.

On the other hand, failing to be mindful with thoughts can cause problems such as performing poorly at school or at work.

*EXAMPLE*

Nathan almost lost his job because he did not do an adequate job on an assignment for work. He accepted the assignment, which was due in a week. Nathan knew he would have to do a good deal of research on the internet. Not being mindful with thoughts got him in trouble because as he searched for information for his assignment, he would get distracted, spending hours surfing the web reading articles about sports teams he rooted for. Finally, on Friday, he quickly put together the inadequate amount of information and turned in his report. His supervisor read the report and told Nathan she was disappointed. She would give him another chance, but she expected him to do a better job.

◆ ◆ ◆

Not being mindful with thoughts is an unkind habit that can cause unhappiness. The unhappiness comes from not getting either what we want (praise for doing a good job) or getting what we do not want (reprimand for doing a poor job). When we realize that being unmindful with thoughts is causing a problem, we become motivated to become more mindful with our thoughts. We can use the tools we've learned to halt the distracting thoughts; the Three-Breath Method, sensing mindfulness, and grounding techniques help us return to mindfulness when thoughts are distracting us from our intention.

*EXAMPLE*

When Jason did his assignments for class, he would spend hours longer than necessary because he kept thinking about wanting to get texts from his friends. So he interrupted his work every few minutes to check his cell phone and text. As a result, he started to fall behind on his school project. Jason got so far behind that he decided to assume the role of a Wise Warrior and used the Three-Breath Method when he felt the impulse to use his phone. Also, to help him stay mindful while working on his project, he would take a quick sensing mindfulness break or use a grounding technique each time he had the urge to turn to his phone. For the next few days, he spent additional time mindfully thinking about his project and was able to finish it on schedule.

 PUT INTO **Practice**

Think about a time you were doing something important and became distracted and did not accomplish your intention. How did that failed intention feel? Describe what happened and think what you could have done differently.

_____

_____

## Low-key mind-wandering

The state of mind that drifts away from our current intention and instead attends to distracting thoughts, which may be pleasant or somewhat unpleasant.

Being mindful with our thoughts is important, but should we expect to be mindful with our thoughts every moment? Of course not. Throughout our day, we will frequently take breaks from being mindful with thoughts. We can refer to these breaks as mind-wandering. We all know what that feels like. Sometimes letting our thoughts drift along with the clouds can feel quite pleasant. This kind of low-key mind-wandering is not unkind.

## — *Key Idea* —

In low-key mind-wandering, we may be distracted by either pleasant or unpleasant thoughts. For example, we might realize in the middle of doing an assignment that we forgot our lunch or phone at home (unpleasant), or while writing a report, we might daydream about an upcoming vacation (pleasant); both are forms of low-key mind-wandering. These thoughts may be distractions, but they don't necessarily indicate an unkind habit unless they distract us from accomplishing our intention. If we can return to what we were thinking about without major interruption, our low-key mind-wandering is not a problem. In fact, sometimes low-key mind-wandering helps us remember important tasks or boosts our creativity with a sudden brainstorm. Low-key mind-wandering in nature can be very calming. Letting your mind notice the trees blowing, birds flying, and light filtering through leaves can greatly contribute to a positive state of mind.

### EXAMPLE

How a young person of color and his friends enjoy each other's company while in low-key mind-wandering.

*No matter which group of friends I hang out with, we can respect one another in conversation while doing other things. My pre-med friends have a habit of looking at our phones during conversation, but we always pay attention to what is being said and provide specific responses. At times, the use of our devices helps us continue the conversation, like sharing memes or funny videos we scroll past. My working friends and I will have discussions about a video as we watch it while also catching up on each other's lives, but we never miss anything and always enjoy the company. I even have friends where company is all we enjoy, we do our own things but just being side by side is enough. Showing our care for others has many forms, and love language is not universal. It is all about finding what dynamic works best for you with different people.*

### EXAMPLE

Low-key mind-wandering as a group of young Indigenous youth go for a walk:

While they talk about life and their plans for the day, they also notice things in nature. One friend points out an eagle flying above them. Later one of the others stops to pick up a special rock in the middle of their conversations. Although it may seem to be an interruption, with the like-minded friends this low-key mind-wandering is encouraged, accepted, and appreciated when it occurs. The friends get right back to their conversations or they drift fluidly to something else triggered by the natural world around them. This low-key mind-wandering in nature can enforce appreciation and mindfulness of the natural gifts around us.

✦ ✦ ✦

However, there are times when low-key mind-wandering is harmful. On these occasions, we should stop the low-key mind-wandering and return to mindfulness. Think of a kayaker paddling through a long stretch of difficult rapids. She directs her attention to the current, the whitewater, and the exposed boulders in front of her as she approaches a dangerous waterfall. Suddenly, she sees a group of children on the shore and wonders how they got there. Her low-key mind-wandering could be disastrous.

### EXAMPLE

Low-key mind-wandering at times can be unkind:

You are talking with a friend who is upset and have only a few minutes to catch up after not seeing each other for a long time. Listening with full attention would make your friend feel special, heard, and important, and this would strengthen your relationship. But, if you're in low-key mind-wandering, distracted by worries about school or work, or daydreaming about the date you have planned for that evening, your friend will likely notice your lack of attention to the conversation and feel that you are disconnected, even if you continue to smile and nod. In fact, your low-key mind-wandering shows you are being unkind, even though you probably do not recognize it.

### EXAMPLE

In extreme cases, low-key mind-wandering can cause a disaster:

In 2008, the engineer of a passenger train was engaged in low-key mind-wandering (sending and receiving text messages) and consequently failed to see a red light signaling him to stop the train, which caused a fatal train wreck.

 PUT INTO **Practice**

Write about one of your most common low-key mind-wandering **pleasant** thoughts.

_____

Write about one of your most common low-key mind-wandering **unpleasant** thoughts.

_____

# Negative Mind-Wandering

**negative mind-wandering**

We are distracted from our intended thoughts and caught up in almost constant agitated or disturbing thoughts.

While low-key mind-wandering is often harmless, negative mind-wandering is different. Negative mind-wandering does more than just take us away from our current intention—it also causes unhappiness. Studies have found that the more time spent with negative mind-wandering, the more unhappy people are likely to be. Spending less time with negative mind-wandering, which frees people to nurture their relationships, is actually more closely tied to people's happiness than how much money they make.

Here are several examples of negative mind-wandering:

- Negative self-talk: obsessive constant thinking about our inadequacies

  **Example:** Evan had been criticized frequently as he grew up. Nothing he did seemed to satisfy his parents. As he went through school and grew into adulthood, he was constantly being told that he was not working up to his potential. His problem was that he never got things done on time. When he had reports or projects to do, he would start thinking that his work would not be acceptable and of the criticism he would receive when he handed in the project. He rarely handed in his work on time and, even worse, would not respond to calls from his supervisors asking about the project. His negative self-talk resulted in him frequently losing jobs.

- Frequently thinking about things we can do nothing about, for example, worrying about things that happened in the past that cannot be changed

  **Example:** Joan was the star player on her basketball team. With only one second left in the championship game and her team behind by one point, she took what should have been an easy shot at the basket and missed. Her team lost. Joan could not get over her sadness at having missed the last shot. She blamed herself for the team's loss. She starting thinking about how the other players must be mad at her. She started to miss some practices and came late to other practices. She had trouble falling asleep as she thought constantly about missing the shot and what would have happened if she made the shot.

- Frequent judgmental thinking, such as blaming others

  **Example:** Margaret spends a lot of time thinking how things are not her fault. She makes excuses or blames other people for her mistakes and unhappiness. When she fails a test, she blames the teacher for creating an unfair test. When she gets a poor work appraisal at her part-time job, she blames her boss for being unfair. She spends a great deal of time in negative mind-wandering, thinking about who is to blame for her problems. The time she spends in negative mind-wandering not only makes her upset, but also hurts her relations with her friends, who get tired of her complaining.

Negative mind-wandering can and does at times lead us to develop unkind habits we use to distract ourselves or escape from our unhappiness. The next step of this book, titled "Deal with Unkind Habits," is where we will learn to identify our unkind habits and how to break or at least weaken them. We will also learn how to respond to the unkind habits of others.

# Wrapping Up

Daily activities, including doing work around the house/apartment, attending to personal hygiene, making and following a schedule, organizing our surroundings, and moving quietly are examples of chores that can be transformed into mindful micropractices that relax and calm our mind. The more we can calm our mind, the easier it will be to spend time being mindful. When we are mindful, we can avoid negative mind-wandering and identify and break unkind habits while building kind habits. This chapter on micropractices concludes our description of mindfulness practices to train our mind: meditation, mindfulness with sensations, and grounding techniques. Overall, mindful micropractices and other wordless practices can dramatically reduce our negative self-talk, which opens us to opportunities to act mindfully with our instinctual kindness and kindness engenders a feeling of joy and connection to others and to ourselves.

## Time for Reflection

On a scale of 0 through 4, how are you feeling about these practices?
0 = I don't do this; 1 = Strongly disagree; 2 = Disagree; 3 = Agree; 4 = Strongly agree

_____ I find sensing mindfulness and the five grounding techniques helpful and will continue to try using them.

_____ The Three-Breath Method reduces my stress and makes sense of my activities more meaningful or pleasurable.

_____ I am trying some of the meditation practices that I found helpful.

_____ I like these practices for strengthening my kind habits: be friendly, offer help, show appreciation, and reach out to those in need.

_____ I find it helpful to refer to my list of pleasant kind habits and pick activities from it to do.

_____ The kind conversation habits make it easier to get along with other people.

• • •

Do you think this mindful micropractice might be helpful for you? Circle Yes or No.

Doing Work Around the House/Apartment                                    Yes    No

Attending to Personal Hygiene                                            Yes    No

| | | |
|---|---|---|
| Making and Following a Schedule | Yes | No |
| Organizing Our Surroundings | Yes | No |
| Moving Quietly Through the World | Yes | No |

Write down other micropractices that might be helpful to you: _____

_____

• • •

Write about how you have been kind at least one time in one of these ways:

- Be friendly
- Offer help
- Show appreciation
- Reach out to those in need

_____

_____

# Deal with Unkind Habits

*Install electrical circuits that conduct positive energy but prevent the flow of negative, unkind energy.*

Scientific findings: 15

Real-world examples: 36

Opportunities to apply what you are learning: 31

**Teachings from the World Religions**

Christianity: "Do not judge, and you will not be judged. Do not condemn, and you will not be condemned. Forgive, and you will be forgiven." (MSG: Jesus, Luke 6:37)

Sufism: "You must empty out the dirty water before you fill the pitcher with clean." —Idries Shah.

Buddhism: "All wrongdoing arises because of mind. If mind is transformed can wrongdoing remain?"

Islam: Allah said, "Descend from Paradise, for it is not for you to be arrogant therein. So get out; indeed, you are of the debased." (Quran 7:13)

Native American: "Be tolerant of those who are lost on their path. Ignorance, conceit, anger, jealousy, and greed stem from a lost soul. Pray that they will find guidance." (Lakota code of ethics)

## Chapter 8

# Face Up to Your Unkind Habits

*You can't let your failures define you. You have to let your failures teach you.*

Barack Obama

**Before beginning this chapter, for one minute meditate in the way that works best for you.**

**W**e've all experienced times when we rushed to get somewhere on time or became frantic over meeting a deadline. Sometimes we ignore the needs of others in order to meet our goal. Often the person in a hurry doesn't even notice their unpleasant behavior. It's as though other people don't count when we are feeling in a hurry. If such rudeness goes unchecked, it can become a habit, an unkind one.

As we become more mindful, we will be able to find more opportunities to be kind. But increasing these opportunities depends on us being able to recognize and remove our unkind habits that create obstacles to kindness. Some of the best known and oldest spiritual guides (the Christian Ten Commandments, the Jewish mitzvahs, the Buddhist precepts, and the Five Pillars of Islam) specify unkind habits to avoid, such as killing, stealing, lying, being misled by personal desires, not helping the poor, and gossiping about others.

But here's good news! The fact that you are reading this workbook suggests you recognize an important change that needs to be made in your life. You're ready to take the first step: looking honestly at yourself and admitting you have habits that are creating challenges and discomfort. After learning to face up to your unkind habits in this chapter, you will develop ways to weaken those unkind habits in the next chapter.

 PUT INTO **Practice**

Changing our unkind habits isn't easy. Think of one you have failed to change. Describe the failure and tell how thinking of that failure makes you feel.

_____

_____

## — Key Idea —

Unkind habits make us unhappy, make our life more difficult, and get in the way of forming and maintaining close, caring relationships with others, ourselves, and the earth.

To change our unkind habits, we need to have a growth mindset, take responsibility for making the necessary effort, and be patient. Consequently, we're not likely to make that effort unless we're motivated. And we're not likely to be motivated unless we experience the harm our unkind habits cause ourselves and others.

Some people, like Tad, develop unkind habits because of the trauma in their personal histories. Tad experienced the harm those unkind habits caused and came to find the motivation to change them.

### FROM THE OTHER SIDE

Tad experienced traumatic unkindness in his life, both in the abuse he had endured and in the harm he had caused. Doug asked Tad about what motivated him to face up to his most unkind habit. Tad replied:

*My hatred toward my stepfather. This was my greatest unkind habit. What made it deadly was the fact that I realized just how toxic it was for me. Eating me from the inside out. This man is a monster. The true meaning of evil, if one believes in such. The shit he did to me and my brothers and sisters is unforgettable. But I've, through years of practice, learned to forgive him. How? Every time I was reminded of the past, I would tell myself, "His past abuse is my strength today." My intention was to stop the self-destruction from within that caused external pain. Not just for myself, but those I would intentionally hurt. Just so they would feel my pain and hatred! The realization of this need for change was the* beginning . . . . *Through each step on this journey, new doors are being opened to other unkind habits to overcome.*

Extreme unkindness, such as what Tad describes in his relationship with his stepfather, can result in violence. More often, small, everyday unkind habits can slowly chip away at our happiness and sense of well-being. However, before we can get rid of our unkind habits, which is explained in detail in the next chapter, we first have to recognize them.

Our unkind habits arise in two places:

- Thinking habits that take place inside us, in our mental world
- Action habits that take place outside of us, in our physical world

Most unkind habits are a combination of harmful internal mental thinking and damaging external actions in the physical world.

# Unkind Action Habits

**unkind action habits**

Unkind habits that take place primarily in the physical world and cause harm whether directed toward others or toward ourselves.

## Unkind Action Habits Directed at Others

By studying failed marriages, psychologist John Gottman and his research team identified four unkind habits that are toxic to relationships: criticism, contempt (lack of respect for a partner), defensiveness, and stonewalling (refusing to talk about a problem).[1] These four unkind habits cause unhappiness to both people in the relationship.

The sentences below illustrate the four toxic unkind habits: Let's say that one person in a relationship says, "We need to talk. I feel you are angry with me, but I don't know why." The partner responds:

Criticism: "You always want to talk about feelings."

Contempt: "I don't have any feelings for you, not even anger."

Defensiveness: "You are the one who is angry all the time."

Stonewalling: "It upsets me to talk about it."

Examples of these four unkind action habits and nine additional unkind action habits directed at others are illustrated in Table 8.1 on the next page. Others can see us carry out these unkind action habits because they take place in the physical world. They do not take place in our minds and our mental world.

Our unkind action habits are usually visible to those around us, but we may not see them in ourselves; that is, we are blind to the unkind habits we direct at other people. To see our own unkind habits, we need to take a moment to think about all the people we typically come into contact with over the course of our daily life: family, friends, classmates, co-workers, and those in marginalized groups such as those who are homeless, discriminated against because of their skin color or language, were once incarcerated, are low income, or are bullied at home or school

The unkind action habits in the examples that follow show displaying hostility, being inconsiderate in blaming, and discriminating against marginalized persons.

### EXAMPLE

A high school counselor talks about a boy who learned to reflect on how his unkind actions affected others:

*Nick, who was 16 years old, ended up in my Options to Anger class in high school. One day I called on him to do a role-play and show me the skills we had been discussing in class. I asked him why he never spoke to anyone and appeared to look angry all the time. He said no one liked him, including teachers, so why should he talk to anyone. I started the conversation about facial expressions and body language and asked him if he knew what message he was giving. He did not have a clue. I started to give him feedback from my perspective, and students hesitantly chimed in, in a caring way. He started looking more alert, even teared up a bit, and said he had no idea that was the message he was giving off. Over the course of the semester, he stopped wearing his hood and gave more eye contact in class. We checked in with him each week to see how he was doing. He reported small successes with other teachers and a few students outside of this class by the end of the semester.*

### EXAMPLE

A young adult recognizes his unkind action in blaming a coworker in front of a group:

*I sent out a group message to whoever closed the previous night to put things away in a cleaner manner. I knew the coworker who did the closing that night, but by sending out a group text I seemed to have hurt my coworker by singling him out to everyone else instead of sending it to him alone. My intention was to make it seem like this was something the group should know, but by being unmindful at that very moment, I carelessly ended up hurting my coworker/friend's feelings.*

### EXAMPLE

A Latinx community leader reflects on how earlier in her life she discriminated against Indigenous people and how later in her life North Americans discriminated against her:

*Having been raised in a middle-class family in Mexico, I was somewhat aware that I was being raised in a very classist society that heavily discriminated against Indigenous peoples. I noticed the often unkind treatment that was given to Indigenous housekeepers, gardeners, construction workers, or really any person that was under someone else's social class. While our opinions had value, theirs did not. When I*

**TABLE 8.1**    *Unkind Action Habits*

| Habit | Definition | Example |
|---|---|---|
| Contempt | Showing someone in a hostile way that you do not respect them. | Frequently saying in response to a friend's statement or action, "How could you be so stupid?" |
| Defensiveness | Constantly making excuses for your actions or explaining why something that happened isn't your fault instead of taking responsibility for it. | "What do you mean I'm not cleaning up my messes? I had things to do and didn't have time to wash my dishes." |
| Aggression | A hostile or violent attitude or behavior directed at another. | "If you talk to my girlfriend again, you are going to have a problem with me." |
| Stonewalling | A persistent refusal to communicate or express emotions. | You do not respond to someone making a comment or criticism, but instead just roll your eyes or remain quiet. |
| Explosive Anger | A type of aggression that happens fast and comes on strong. | You refuse to loan someone your car and they swear at you and shove you into the wall. |
| Arrogance | Believing you are better than others. | "You don't know the first thing about skateboarding. Let me show you the right way to do it." |
| Frequent Criticism | Frequently criticizing the actions of a person and giving them a negative label about what kind of person they are. | "Ugh, you always leave your dirty dishes in the sink. You're such an inconsiderate slob." |
| Being Disrespectful | Showing a person that you don't think they are worth much. | "You are such a fat head. No wonder you dropped out of college." |
| Irresponsible | Doing what you like and not caring about what happens afterward. | You say you will give your friend a ride to work but show up 45 minutes late, causing them to be late to work. |
| Frequent Complaining | Frequently expressing unhappiness or dissatisfaction about another person or a situation. | You often make these types of comments to others: "I don't know why you are fixing pasta again. Can't you come up with something new to cook?" |
| Rudeness | Acting in a way that offends the people you are with. It comes from cluelessness, being inconsiderate, not thinking it through, or simply not imagining that somebody could be offended by something. | "Get your stinking ugly clothes out of my closet." |
| Being Untrustworthy | Being a person who often does not keep their commitments. | "You said you would pay me back, but now you say you won't be able to." |
| Being Selfish | Being concerned excessively or exclusively for oneself or for one's own advantage, pleasure, or welfare, regardless of others. | Taking so much food during dinner that the last person served will not have enough to eat. |

*came to the States, I started experiencing this type of mean-spirited behavior directed toward me. Only then did I become aware of things I had done in the past that insulted and humiliated others. At this point, I was able to realize how systems of oppression and exclusion work, and it helped me enormously to change my behavior. This realization and change eventually made me a much better and more loving person who is able to meaningfully interact with a much wider range of people, no matter what their background may be.*

## PUT INTO **Practice**

Describe an unkind action habit you direct at others.

_____

How has it caused hurt?

_____

How did that make you feel?

_____

If you can, be brave and take on the role of Wise Warrior. Ask those close to you to describe ways you have been unkind.

Write a checkmark in front of this Put into Practice item because we will return to it later.

### Ignoring the Opportunity to Be Kind to Others

While most unkind action habits directed at others are obvious, some are not. Ignoring the opportunity to be kind to others is an often unrecognized unkind action habit. Ignoring the opportunity to act with kindness—either by not showing appreciation (for example, not listening carefully to the other person), not being friendly, not offering to help, or not reaching out to those with serious needs—is an unkind habit. The cause of this unkind habit can be that we are too wrapped up with negative self-talk about regrets or traumatic events from our past, our current responsibilities, or worries about the future. Or possibly we are so angry, resentful, or prejudiced against others that we do not want to be kind to them. Regardless of the cause of this unkind habit, we can decide to make an effort to break the habit of ignoring opportunities to be kind to others. Ignoring the opportunity to be kind keeps us from receiving the benefits of the mindful kindness cycle. When we are kind, we experience the feel-good chemicals in our body, which lead us to be more kind.

> *While most unkind habits directed at others are obvious, some are not. Ignoring the opportunity to be kind to others is an often unrecognized unkind habit.*

Do you have the unkind habit of missing opportunities to be kind? If so, what do you think causes you to miss the opportunities to be kind?

_____

_____

Pick an unkind habit you would like to change because it causes you to miss opportunities to be kind. Describe that habit and how it makes you feel.

_____

_____

## Unkind Action Habits Directed at Ourselves

We direct unkind action habits at ourselves and at others. Examples of unkind action habits directed primarily toward ourselves include engaging in too much digital media (internet, social media, and texting), substance abuse, unhealthy eating, procrastination (putting off what we need to do), and not meeting our own needs because of putting the needs of others above our own (called being a doormat). Unkind action habits such as these may make us feel good at first, but over many months we are likely to become unhappy and our unkind habits may bring unhappiness to others as well. The unkind action habits we direct at ourselves take place in our outside world, the physical world. Other people can see our substance abuse, unhealthy eating, and more.

PUT INTO **Practice**

Being honest with yourself about your unkind habits can be challenging. Take the time you need to identify the ways you are unkind to yourself. Describe in writing one unkind action habit directed toward yourself that causes you pain and suffering.

_____

_____

Write about how this habit makes you feel and how it affects your life and perhaps the lives of those around you as well. (If you are uncertain about the unkind habits you direct at yourself, ask someone close to you.)

_____

_____

Write a checkmark in front of this Put into Practice item. We will return to it later.

# Unkind Mental/Thinking Habits

Our unkind mental/thinking habits take place inside us. Other people cannot see us carrying out our unkind mental/thinking habits. In our unkind thinking (mental) habits, we talk to ourselves in negative, unkind ways. Some unkind mental habits are easy to recognize. For example, we might have a mental habit of jealousy, thinking to ourself that a person who seems to do everything right is just a show-off. We might have a mental anger habit, for example, fantasizing about destroying the neighbor's electric guitar when she's practicing late at night. Much of the time, our unkind mental/thinking habits are not about someone else. They are about us! For example, the unkind mental habit of feeling inadequate: "Why did I eat that whole banana split? I have no self-control." "I'm not surprised he didn't text back; who would want to spend time with someone like me?" For some of us, unkind self-talk has become so normal, we don't even recognize it as unkind.[2]

 PUT INTO **Practice**

Do you have unkind thoughts about yourself? Name one that you hope to change.

_____

_____

## Two Levels of Intensity

We can think of unkind mental habits as negative mind-wandering (also called intrusive thoughts). We briefly described the negative feelings unkind mental habits can cause. Now we will look more closely at those negative feelings by describing two levels of intensity linked to those feelings: Level 1—agitating and Level 2—deeply disturbing.

### *Agitating Negative Mind-Wandering*

> **agitating negative mind-wandering**
>
> Negative self-talk that upsets us but does not sink us into depression, self-hatred, or self-harm.

We deal with many experiences in our lives that are sources of frustration. These experiences can become barriers to mindful kindness when they lead to negative mind-wandering habits that agitate us. We might, for example, complain to ourselves about our partner's insensitive behavior, a real or perceived insult by a friend, an inability to find anything to do with our free time, or even how badly we sleep at night.

*EXAMPLE*

An 18-year old comments on recognizing the negative habit of being worried about what others think:

*As an anxious teen I remember constantly worrying about what others thought of me or said about me behind my back, and my feelings got hurt, especially by girls my own age. But even today I can get wrapped up in my thoughts, worrying about why my best friend didn't get back to me after I texted her. I often question myself, asking if I did something wrong. I suffered quite often with these negative thoughts. As I am learning to face my unkind habit of almost always blaming myself, I'm learning to talk things out with friends to find out what they really think rather than making up stuff about what they are thinking. Talking things out makes me less anxious about what others might be thinking.*

*EXAMPLE*

A young adult in recovery recognizes the harm caused by his habit of negative self-talk:

*I think about how I feel lonely, pathetic, or down on myself for not having a partner. Because I feel emotionally weakened, I don't end up going for a daily run. Because I don't do that, I don't get some personal meditation time to heal and recharge my spiritual energy and willpower.*

 PUT INTO **Practice**

Describe one thing that causes you agitating negative mind-wandering, such as complaining about something to yourself and never verbalizing it.

_____

How does the agitation feel?

_____

Has it led you to overlook the needs of others and miss an opportunity to be kind? Tell how.

_____

Put a checkmark next to this Put into Practice item because you will be asked about it at the end of this chapter.

> **CAUTION**  If we allow unkind agitating mental habits to go unchecked, they can take up more and more of our time and eventually become deeply disturbing. The next chapter will focus on getting rid of our unkind habits and putting into place practices that can keep our agitating mental habits from becoming disturbing.

## *Deeply Disturbing Negative Mind-Wandering*

---

**deeply disturbing negative mind-wandering**

Negative self-talk that is more intense than agitating and leads us to becoming consumed by dark, negative thoughts and emotions; we are deeply disturbed.

Feeling deeply disturbed, we are self-absorbed and may feel cut off from everyone and everything around us, or closed in, as if we are in a tiny room from which we cannot escape. These feelings can cause us to distract ourselves by overdoing it with alcohol, unhealthy social media use, or other substance abuse. Feeling deeply disturbed creates barriers to mindful kindness that are much stronger than the barriers caused by agitation. Agitation is somewhat unpleasant, but being deeply disturbed is extremely unpleasant and can lead to dangerous unkind habits.

*EXAMPLE*

A 16-year-old Indigenous youth who works very hard full time and goes to school copes with stress by drinking with friends every night. She feels drinking relieves her stress from working so hard all the time and dealing with stress from her mom. She feels like she is being treated unfairly and like a child by her mom and feels she deserves to be treated more like an adult since she works so hard. She copes with this feeling by asserting her independence by drinking and partaking in risky activity with her friends. The stress from working full time, going to school, and being treated poorly by her mother is too much. Her excessive drinking and partaking in risky behaviors are endangering her future.

✦ ✦ ✦

Taking on the role of the Diligent Detective, Wise Warrior, and Kindful Practitioner can keep us from falling from agitation into the despair of being deeply disturbed. Of course, an even better course of action is to take on these roles to keep us from becoming agitated in the first place. We will learn how to get through times of agitation and being disturbed in the chapters that follow.

**WARNING**

If you are contemplating harming yourself, using illicit substances, or contemplating suicide, seek help immediately. You can call the National Suicide Prevention Hotline: 1-800-273-8255 and Crisis Text Line: text TALK to 741-741.

## ☑ *Checking for Understanding*

For each of the four items below, write an **A** for agitating negative mind-wandering or write a **DD** for deeply disturbing negative mind-wandering.

_____  I'm impatient when I have to wait for my manager to finish his presentations. He should hurry up so I can get back to work.

_____  I'm going to drop out of school if that teacher keeps giving me Ds. I can't even sleep because he is picking on me all the time. I know he doesn't like me.

_____  I need to watch my favorite Netflix movie, but my father won't let me. He's ruining my evening just because of a stupid hockey game he's watching.

_____  I'm so afraid I'm going to be fired that I can't concentrate on my work and get it done. Without this job, I won't have enough money to pay my rent. I'll be living on the street in the winter. I never thought this could happen to me.

## PUT INTO **Practice**

Describe a time you experienced agitating mind-wandering.

_____

Describe a time you experienced deeply disturbing mind-wandering.

_____

Put a checkmark in front of this Put into Practice item because you will return to it later.

## PERSONAL **Challenge**

Table 8.2 on the next page includes a list of unkind mental habits. Do any of the unkind mental habits in the table lead you to negative mind-wandering? If so, indicate how intense the negative mind-wandering is by marking one of these four boxes for each unkind habit: disturbing negative mind-wandering, agitating mind-wandering, a little negative mind-wandering, or none at all. For example, the first habit is about complaining to yourself. If your complaining is causing some negative mind-wandering, make a mark in the box under agitating, which is some negative mind-wandering. There are also two blank places at the bottom of the table where you can write in your own unkind habits that do not appear in the table.

**TABLE 8.2**    *Unkind Mental/Thinking Habits*

| Unkind Mental Habits | Intensity of Mind-Wandering | | | |
|---|---|---|---|---|
| | A great deal (Disturbing) | Some (Agitating) | A little | None at all |
| Blaming yourself for not being able to stop your bad habits, which can range from addictions to merely overdoing it with food, alcohol, vaping, smoking, or gaming. | | | | |
| Complaining to yourself about things you don't like. | | | | |
| Negative self-talk about others because of their appearance, education level, economic status (for example, waiters and clerks), religion, gender identity, accent and English fluency, sexual orientation, political beliefs, or skin color. | | | | |
| Negative self-talk about your anger toward certain people. | | | | |
| Blaming yourself for being isolated and lonely. | | | | |
| Negative self-talk about being not good enough and a failure. | | | | |
| Often wishing you did not feel so discouraged. | | | | |
| Worrying about things you can do nothing about. | | | | |
| Being hard on yourself for not having a purpose. | | | | |
| Worrying that you are failing to make important changes in your life. | | | | |
| Being hard on yourself over mistakes you made and opportunities you missed. | | | | |
| Complaining to yourself about how often you feel anxious. | | | | |
| Frequently thinking about things you can do nothing about. | | | | |
| Constantly thinking about what might go wrong in the future. | | | | |
| Worrying about not knowing how to communicate with your loved ones and friends. | | | | |
| Being hard on yourself because of your feelings of guilt and shame. | | | | |
| Wishing you did not have so many angry feelings and thoughts at home, at school, at work, or in other places. | | | | |
| Going over and over in your mind about your feelings of resentment over not receiving the attention you deserve at school, work, or home. | | | | |
| Blaming others for being responsible for your problems. | | | | |
| Feeling less than others because of your race, sexuality, personal, or generational identity. | | | | |
| | | | | |
| | | | | |

PUT INTO **Practice**

First, circle each unkind mental habit in the table that you are motivated to change. Next, look at all the circled habits. Pick the one you would most like to change. Make a checkmark in front of it and write it below.

_____

_____

Describe how the unkind mental habit you selected affects your life and why you want to change it.

_____

_____

In the next chapter, we will discuss what you can do to decrease or eliminate the unkind habits you indicated as being agitating or disturbing.

## A Major Cause of Negative Mind-Wandering

One major cause of negative mind-wandering comes from treating our preferences, what we would like to be doing or like to have, as something we feel we must be doing or must have. So, when we don't get what we want, we often complain to ourselves with internal self-talk. This negative mind-wandering can be an agitating or even deeply disturbing unkind mental habit.

When we are overly self-centered, we think of our desires as having greater importance than others' desires and expect others to meet our desires:

Imagine that we are planning to play video games with our friend Friday night. On Thursday night, the plan to play video games on Friday is canceled. We react with agitation. Rather than thinking we prefer to play video games with our friends on Friday night, we feel we must play. When "I'd like to play video games" becomes "I need to play video games," we might feel insulted by our friends not paying enough attention to what we perceive as our important need. So, we might drop into agitating negative mind-wandering by complaining to ourselves about our friends. In contrast, if we see playing the video game as something we would like to do (but do not need to do), we might avoid falling into agitating negative mind-wandering.

## Learning from Our Unkind Habits

Here is how to tell if we are ready to learn from our unkind habits: We do something unkind and then we feel guilt, remorse, regret, angry or disappointed with ourselves, and sadness. These feelings are teaching us that we have acted with unkindness. And the feelings are unpleasant; we don't want to feel guilt, regret, and the rest. To be more specific, guilt can be an excellent teacher because it motivates us to stop an unkind habit that is making us unhappy. That unpleasant feeling of guilt comes from different chemicals our body makes when we act with unkindness. Because guilt is such an unpleasant feeling, we want to stop the unkind habit that is causing the feeling of guilt. A table on unkind action habits and a table of unkind mental/thinking habits appeared earlier in this chapter.

### EXAMPLE FROM AN AUTHOR

Doug experienced guilt caused by his unkind habit of anger:

*I lashed out, sometimes swearing or slamming a door, such as the time I accidentally knocked over a carton of dog food, spilling the dry dog food all over the floor. In this case, seeing the mess filled me with rage at my own carelessness. I swore and slammed the cabinet door shut. Then I kicked the carton, which of course only made the situation worse—and made me even angrier. I felt guilty when I noticed the fear on my wife's and children's faces during this sudden display of anger. The guilt motivated me to seriously work on breaking my habit of anger.*

### EXAMPLE

A hostile response alerts Jason to his insensitive behavior.

Jason texted a coworker asking for immediate help with his project and became impatient when his coworker didn't quickly respond to his text. When his coworker did text him somewhat later, agreeing to help, Jason answered as if he had been insulted, asking why his coworker always took so long to respond to his requests. Upon receiving the text, his coworker wrote back withdrawing the offer to help. It's not surprising that his coworker expressed irritation toward Jason. Jason's arrogant action not only resulted in his coworker withdrawing their offer to help, but also hurt Jason's relationship with his coworker.

Jason's first reaction was anger toward his coworker, but then he remembered the fight he had with his roommate, who told Jason that he was selfish and did not think about other people's feelings. The roommate told Jason he needed to learn to care more about other people's feelings. So Jason had begun to learn about mindful kindness. He realized that his coworker could have been in a meeting or under pressure because of a deadline. Recognizing his insensitivity and feeling guilt for being too demanding was the first step in changing Jason's unkind habit of being unaware and insensitive to the feelings of others. Once that habit is broken, relationships can improve. For example, instead of criticizing how long it took the coworker to respond, Jason could have been patient and responded with appreciation when he received his coworker's delayed offer of help.

✦ ✦ ✦

Of course, we can distract ourselves to cover up the unpleasant feelings that are caused by our unkind habits; for example, we could become impatient and blame someone else, as Jason did, or lash out with anger the way Doug did when he spilled the dog food. There are many other distractions we can use, such as overdoing it with food, drugs, or vaping. Distractions can keep us from feeling bad, at least for a while. We must be very careful, though. The distractions we use to cover up our feeling of guilt can lead to very damaging unkind habits.

PUT INTO **Practice**

Do you have an unkind habit that has caused or is still causing someone close to you pain and unhappiness? Describe the habit and how this habit makes you feel.

_____

_____

Are you motivated to change it? _____

# Causes of Our Unkind Habits: Instinctual, Societal, and Personal

You have finished reading the parts of this book titled "Build Kind Habits" and "Train Your Mind" and have begun to learn about unkind habits. But consistently being mindfully kind and breaking unkind habits will probably be challenging for most of us. Why is it so hard? We might become less discouraged once we come to understand the personal, instinctual, and societal obstacles that actually support our unkind habits and stand in the way of increasing our kindness. This section will describe these three obstacles: our instincts, society's values, and our personal history.

## Our Instincts

We have four basic instincts: to survive, reproduce, succeed, and be kind.* These basic instincts cause us to have both positive and negative thoughts and emotions. These thoughts/feelings often arise suddenly and can pass just as quickly. Problems can arise when our basic instincts lead to feelings/thoughts that are unkind and we act on those negative feelings. If we act on those negative feelings/thoughts over and over, they become unkind habits. Because the prisoners Doug corresponds with were abused as children, their survival instinct activated their anger over and over, setting the stage for them to develop anger and violence as unkind habits.

As teens and young adults, your brains are still developing. The prefrontal cortex, which regulates behavior and self-control, will not be fully developed until you are around 25, which makes it more challenging during the teen and young adult years to control emotions set off by negative instincts.

---

* There are many theories about human instinct. We are working from Professor Robert Winston's book and BBC program: *Human Instinct: How our primeval impulses shape our modern world* (2002, Bantam Press). The four episodes on the BBC program were to survive, reproduce, succeed, and act with kindness. (https://www.bbc.co.uk/programmes/b00pfrv4/episodes/guide).

*EXAMPLE*

A Latinx community leader explains how people of color have a challenge in not reacting instinctively in a defensive manner when hearing a discriminatory remark:

*It is completely understandable that people of color would be very reactive since they have experienced countless discriminatory acts. But as an individual person of color, if we eventually want to be happier, we need to decide not to react instinctively to other people's remarks that may or may not have been intentionally discriminatory. Our goal is to not allow inconsiderate remarks to take us away from our ability to be calm and happy. Instead, if possible, we want to see if we can help the other person realize their behavior is harmful.*

## Inherited Discriminatory Unkind Habits

According to Resmaa Menakem, in his book *My Grandmother's Hands: Racialized Trauma and the Pathway to Mending Our Hearts and Bodies,*[3] some of the unkind habits of white people directed at persons-of-color groups have been inherited, passed down from generation to generation.

*EXAMPLE*

An Indigenous youth leader copes with inherited unkind habits of White people:

*I was in a really bad head space for a whole year after I went to Standing Rock to stand peacefully against the Dakota Access Pipeline. The acts of violence I witnessed and followed on social media activated much intergenerational trauma for me and many others, including my ancestors who continue to be with us. The events activated feelings of being worthless and unworthy of the natural resources given to us by our earth. The oppression by the police and oil companies made me feel like my people did not matter, and that our land and lives could be sacrificed so easily for the greed of powerful people and companies. I found myself in a dark place, facing the realities that the genocide my ancestors faced was remaining still to this day in different ways. The events at Standing Rock made me have unkind habits toward myself as well as resentment and unkindness toward others, mostly White people. I finally realized that I would not be able to heal and progress if I continue the unkind habits resulting from the treatment of my ancestors in the past and of my community today. To address these feelings when they arise I try to refocus myself in the present, and direct my thoughts to the strength I have today because of my ancestors' hardships.*

◆ ◆ ◆

In Chapter 12: "Extend the Reach of Our Kindfulness," we will learn about Menakem's work and some of his suggestions for how White people can become aware of and weaken these inherited unkind habits.

# Some of Society's Values

Social media, TV, and magazines relentlessly project values that reinforce the unkind habits of materialism (being excessively concerned with money and material possessions) and self-centered individualism (being absorbed with our own well-being, with little concern for the well-being of others). The almost constant barrage of these values on television and on social media makes it difficult for us to be mindfully kind, in part because the messages encourage unkind thinking and action habits of self-centered individualism and materialistic thinking.

Many selfish habits grow out of self-centered individualism (focusing on what makes me happy, not what makes other people happy) and materialistic thinking (wearing fashionable clothes, driving the 'right' car, and owning the best sound system). These selfish and materialistic habits often take the form of believing that getting what we want, regardless of how we go about getting it, will make us happy.

*Note on materialistic thinking:* Researchers did a study among people with different family incomes. The researchers found that while low incomes caused stress, as a family's income increased to $90,000 a year their happiness increased. However, earning very high incomes, even earning a billion dollars, did not automatically make people happier. People were happier when the money they earned was used to support relationships with or help other people.*

### EXAMPLE

The thrill of personal social popularity (individualism) can stand in the way of being mindfully kind.

Trevor, a high school junior and varsity football player, often felt the personal thrill of approval from peers when he agreed to skip class with them. His thrilling thoughts about skipping class and being popular lasted until he saw Ds on his midterm report card. He finally realized that if his skipping continued, his poor grades might interfere with his eligibility to play football during his senior year; he was harming himself and was about to let down his teammates. This realization motivated him to make a change for the better by going to class and studying. This change would also increase the likelihood that he could work on being mindfully kind.

## Dangers of Social Media

Spending time interacting with digital media is enticing and can be addictive. But spending more time online also means more exposure to advertisements that play off the insecurities of teens and young adults by making them feel that an advertised product or service will improve their lives; for example, the advertising suggests that buying certain clothes, sneakers, cosmetics, and even a car will make it possible to join a desirable social circle or hang out with an attractive person. Advertisements fill our minds with thoughts about popularity, fashion, alcohol, and sex. These thoughts block our efforts to train our minds and to be more kind to ourselves and others.

Moreover, recent studies have shown that too much digital media (internet, social media, texting) can be highly destructive. Happiness and life satisfaction among U.S. adolescents has declined. Our society's increased use of digital media is correlated with increased depression, suicidal thoughts, and self-harm among young people.[4]

---

\* Spending money to have experiences, buying time, and giving money away to help others all reliably raise happiness. "The key factor connecting all those approaches is other people. If you buy an experience, whether it be a vacation or just a dinner out, you can raise your happiness if you share it with someone you love. Friends and family are two key ingredients in well-being, and fun experiences with these people give us sweet memories we can enjoy for the rest of our lives—unlike the designer shoes that will wear out or go out of style." These findings were replicated across three very different cultures: Canada, Uganda, and India. From Aknin, L. B., Barrington-Leigh, C. P., Dunn, E. W., Helliwell, J. F., Burns, J., Biswas-Diener, R., Kemeza, I., Nyende, P., Ashton-James, C. E., & Norton, M. I. (2013). Prosocial spending and well-being: Cross-cultural evidence for a psychological universal. *Journal of Personality and Social Psychology, 104*(4), 635–652. Retrieved from https://psycnet.apa.org/record/2013-04859-001

The disturbing emotional effects of social media is a global issue as well: "The smartphone brought about a planetary rewiring of human interaction. As smartphones became common, they transformed peer relationships, family relationships, and the texture of daily life for everyone—even those who don't own a phone or don't have an Instagram account. It's harder to strike up a casual conversation in the cafeteria or after class when everyone is staring down at their phones. It's harder to have a deep conversation when each party is interrupted randomly by buzzing, vibrating notifications."[5]

The Netflix documentary *The Social Dilemma* explains how social media companies such as Facebook and Google have manipulated us into spending more time online and pulled us away from more face-to-face social interactions that are associated with happiness. These face-to-face activities include attending religious services, participating in outdoor activities, volunteering, going with friends to dances and amusement parks, attending arts and crafts classes, and other activities that involve interacting face to face with friends and others. Too much time online reduces our face-to-face social interactions and seems to increase mental health problems; for example, too much social media often leads to a sense of inadequacy. In one study of the top five social media platforms, only YouTube had an overall positive rating (Twitter came in second, followed by Facebook and then Snapchat, with Instagram bringing up the rear, with all four of these rated as increasing anxiety and depression).[6]

Anxiety, depression, and increased loneliness are most prevalent among females, who feel they must live up to a quantified measure of acceptance based on the number of likes given to their Instagram postings: "By 2012, as the world now knows, the major platforms had created an outrage machine that made life online far uglier, faster, more polarized, and more likely to incite performative shaming. In addition, as Instagram grew in popularity over the next decade, it had particularly strong effects on girls and young women, inviting them to 'compare and despair.'"[7]

In short, some of us are being manipulated to spend too much time online, which makes us unhappy, and too little time offline. With less time offline, we are not able to engage as much in the person-to-person activities that can increase our happiness and kindness. Social media companies seem to sacrifice our happiness, well-being, and capacity for kindness.

A Beatles song[8] put it this way:

> "I don't know why nobody told you how to unfold your love
>
> I don't know how someone controlled you
>
> They bought and sold you . . ."

In contrast, training to become a Kindful Practitioner helps us become genuinely happy by learning to care for ourselves in healthy ways and to cultivate close, caring relationships.

## Our Personal History

We all have our own unique personal history. It is in the past and we cannot go back and change what happened. Obviously, what happened to us in the past contributes to our current outlook on the world and the kind and unkind habits we have developed.

There are unfortunately many unkind habits that we may learn when we are young. For example, if a child grows up with frequent criticism, the child may develop a sense of inadequacy. If a child grows up in a home with frequent, emotional racist remarks, that child may grow up with the unkind thinking habit that persons of color have serious faults. If a child saw one of their parents frequently making excuses for not keeping promises or carrying out their responsibilities, the child may grow up making excuses, thinking it is not important to be responsible and keep their promises.

*There are unfortunately many unkind habits that we may learn when we are young.*

### EXAMPLE

Shannon had a difficult childhood, being subject to abuse both physically and mentally. She came from a big family and felt unloved. In high school, she hung around with other kids who were angry and felt lost. She eventually started hanging around with kids who described themselves as skinheads. She was comfortable with them because they accepted her and were like her in being angry at the world. She kept up her involvement with the hate group for a number of years until she moved in with a family who were kind people. The exposure to the kindness made her think about her involvement with the hate group. Over the next months she used her Wise Warrior to leave the hate group and begin a new chapter in her life.

### EXAMPLE

A young adult comments on how being in recovery increased his motivation to be kind:

*With all the time and energy saved by deleting alcohol out of my life entirely, I now have this reserve of kindness that I wish to share.*

The survival instinct activated anger and violence in the men Doug corresponds with in prison. Their personal experience was to use anger and violence to get what they wanted and to distract themselves from the memories of how they grew up and how they harmed others when they were older. However, with a great deal of effort, many of these prisoners have been able to be Kindful Practitioners by, for the most part, breaking their trauma-induced mental/thinking and action habits of anger and violence.

PUT INTO **Practice**

Describe how one of your unkind habits may have resulted from one or more of these three influences: your instincts, personal experiences, and/or society's values.

_____

_____

# Wrapping Up

Kind habits create happiness primarily by supporting caring relationships with others and enabling us to take better care of ourselves; on the other hand, unkind habits prevent or damage the relationships that can bring happiness to ourselves and others. Before we can change our unkind habits, we have to first admit we have them. Unkind habits come in many forms:

- Unkind mental/thinking habits (internal, inside our mind): Negative mind-wandering can be agitating or deeply disturbing.

- Unkind action habits (external, in the physical world) can be directed at ourselves or others.

Mindfulness appears in exercises in every chapter because it is a critical tool in learning to break our unkind habits. Mindfulness makes us sensitive to the harm these habits cause, which motivates us to break the unkind habits. Mindfulness also allows us to recognize our unkind habits so that we know what changes we need to make. The next chapters are devoted to ways to use mindfulness and meditation to break our unkind habits.

 PUT INTO **Practice**

Most of us have so many unwanted, unkind habits that we need to decide which ones we most want to change. As you've worked through this chapter, you made checkmarks to identify both unkind internal mental habits and unkind physical action habits. Now you are ready to set your priorities. Go back through the chapter and find those checkmarks. You are going to fill in the table that follows by writing a brief description of each unkind habit you marked. The table has two columns: Easier and Harder. If you think an unkind habit of yours is easier to break, write the name of that habit in the Easier column. If you think the unkind habit is harder to break, write that habit in the Harder column.

**Easier**                                    **Harder**

_____          _____

_____          _____

_____          _____

_____          _____

_____          _____

Pick one unkind easier-to-break habit and one unkind harder-to-break habit. For each habit, answer the following questions.

**The Easier-to-Break Unkind Habit I Selected**

What is the easier-to-bread unkind habit you selected?

_____

Is the unkind habit a negative mental habit or an action habit?

_____

If it is an unkind action habit, is it directed at yourself or others? If directed at others, who are they?

_____

What activates this unkind habit?

_____

What is the effect of your unkindness on you and/or anybody else who is involved?

_____

_____

**Harder-to-Break Unkind Habit**

What is harder-to-break habit you selected?

_____

Is the unkind habit a negative mental habit or an action habit?

_____

If it is an unkind action habit, is it directed at yourself or others? If directed at others, who or what are they?

_____

What activates this unkind habit?

_____

What is the effect of your unkindness on you and/or anybody else who is involved?

_____

_____

# Time for Reflection

Take a few moments to reflect on the degree to which the practices below are benefiting you. On a scale of 0 through 4, how are you feeling about these practices? 0 = I haven't tried it yet; 1 = Hasn't worked yet; 2 = Often doesn't work; 3 = Sometimes works; 4 = Working well

_____ Mindful breathing when feeling upset.

_____ Meditating on a regular basis.

_____ Naming at least one thing I am grateful for.

_____ Performing at least one act of kindness by showing appreciation, offering to help, being friendly, or reaching out to those in need.

_____ Remembering to review my list of pleasant kind habits and acting on some of those habits.

_____ Using the kind conversation skills.

Look again at the six practices listed above. Then circle the practice that is most helpful to you.

• • •

Think about each statement and then circle Yes or No.

| | | |
|---|---|---|
| I feel grateful for people and pets I care about. | Yes | No |
| I feel grateful for something that went well today. | Yes | No |
| I feel grateful for what I can do with my body and mind. | Yes | No |
| I feel grateful for people who help me and others. | Yes | No |
| I feel grateful for my beliefs that give me purpose and meaning. | Yes | No |
| I feel grateful for having fun and laughter. | Yes | No |
| I feel thankful for the earth and universe. | Yes | No |

• • •

Write about how you have been kind recently in one of these ways and how you felt:

- Be friendly
- Show appreciation
- Offer help
- Reach out to those in need

How did you feel when you behaved kindly in the specific circumstances you noted above?

_____

_____

Chapter 9

# Get Your Unkind Habits Out of the Way

*I think if you stop bad habits, and you stop long enough, you develop good habits.*

Jordan Knight

**Before beginning this chapter, for one minute meditate in the way that works best for you.**

Everybody has unkind habits. Our experiences have taught us that unkind habits are not easy to break. Consider how hard it is for many of us to turn off our cell phone, even when we are with someone else or are tired and want to go to sleep. Think about how hard it is for us to eat healthy snacks if we have the habit of buying candy when we pass vending machines because we are constantly in a rush. In the same way, it's hard to become a better listener if we have the habit of interrupting.

## Our Mindfulness Practices Help Us Break Our Unkind Habits

Chapter 8 illustrated how mindfulness allows us to recognize and experience the harm caused by our unkind habits. This chapter describes how our mindfulness practices help us break or weaken our unkind habits.

## Building Kind Habits Requires Breaking Unkind Habits

### — *Key Idea* —

To build kind habits, it's crucial to break or at least significantly weaken our serious unkind habits. Our unkind habits keep us from being kind.

### *EXAMPLE*

> Jessica has a habit of interrupting the person she is talking to and talking about herself. The interruptions and talking about herself get in the way of her keeping friends. Her friends get tired of her interruptions and don't want to be around her. Once she weakens the unkind habit of interrupting, she will find it easier to make friends using the kind conversation habits described in Chapter 4: giving feedback in the form of asking to hear more, agreeing verbally, making an encouraging comment, offering interesting and relevant information, and responding in a kind, supportive manner.

◆ ◆ ◆

Completely eliminating longstanding unkind habits takes consistent, persistent effort. For example, many people who have had problems with alcohol or drugs stay in recovery for years by attending weekly support meetings.

Doug, one of the authors of this workbook, admits, "I personally have not yet been successful in completely eliminating my unkind habits of acting with anger, being controlling, and blaming others. However, I have greatly weakened these unkind habits. While unkind thoughts arise, I almost never act on them. But when I do act with unkindness, the guilt I feel motivates me to work harder on my mindful kindness practices."

As Doug noted, awareness of the harm caused by our unkind habits motivates us to put in the needed effort to weaken those unkind habits.

*FROM THE OTHER SIDE*

Roy wrote about how seeing a tree frog gave him the opportunity to weaken his anger habit activated by his chronic, debilitating pain:

*Wasn't really "Lettin Go" of anger till a few days ago. I noticed the tenseness, the constrictions in my body. I had nearly been consumed by anger at the [health services clinic]. I started to just fkn breathe, slowly but smoothly, visualizing the anger, the tenseness leaving my body, allowing my body to slowly become calmness. I realized I was causing myself a lot of fkn pain and discomfort. Anger was influencing my thinking and intentions, my character.*

*Then I saw a tiny tree frog stuck on my window. I got closer and closer so I could "sit" with him and be part of his [meditation group]. I watched him just "BE," just breathe and be, being in the moment. Moment by moment. All the anger in me was slowly released with every beat of his heart. I just couldn't fathom how much pain and suffering I was causing myself. I realized I could "Let Go" of my anger and that in turn would lessen my self-inflicted pain and suffering. It's like flipping a light switch. I was feeling my body react in a positive way, a relaxed looseness. Anger is not only a stupid waste of time and energy, it causes pain and suffering; everything about it is negative.*

Roy's extreme unkind habit of anger stemmed from a childhood of abuse and his current relentless pain. In contrast to Roy's extreme unkindness, some of our unkind habits will seem mild. However, these unkind habits can have a major effect on our lives, getting in the way of forming close relationships for lasting happiness.

## PUT INTO **Practice**

In Chapter 8, you prioritized unkind habits that you wanted to eliminate or weaken. Turn back to that list on page 146 and select an unkind habit you want to break or weaken.

Write the unkind habit and tell about how you feel when you engage in that unkind habit.

_____

_____

Now think about an unkind habit you have already broken or nearly broken. Describe that habit and tell how it feels to have weakened that habit.

_____

_____

# Working on Our Unkind Habits

Choosing to be mindfully kind while developing our skills of character sets the stage for making a systematic plan to intentionally weaken our unkind habits.

Initially, we need to call on our Diligent Detective to suggest a specific plan for stopping the unkind habit and tap into our Wise Warrior to stick to the plan. We must also be humble, realizing that we need to be realistic and patient in carrying out our plan. After all, great change does not happen overnight.

This chapter describes a six-step plan for weakening or breaking unkind habits:

- Step 1: Strengthen your mindfulness practices so you can experience a moment of freedom.
- Step 2: Select an unkind habit to work on.
- Step 3: Diagnose whether to focus first on your mental world or your physical world.
- Step 4. Identify the activators for the unkind habit.
- Step 5: Prevent the unkind habit by acting early.
- Step 6: If you cannot prevent the unkind habit from starting, stop it or turn it into something neutral or positive.

## Step 1: Strengthen Your Mindfulness Practices So You Can Experience a Moment of Freedom

**moment of freedom**

> Awareness of the moment just before you engage in an unkind habit. This awareness gives us the opportunity to not carry out the unkind habit.

### EXAMPLE FROM AN AUTHOR

Fifty-plus years ago, Doug had the unkind mental habit of believing he had the right to control what his wife said.

*I was so controlling that when Linda said something I disagreed with in front of other people, I would respond with ridicule or scorn. When I realized how much I was hurting her, I felt pain and shame, and this motivated me to never again ridicule her.*

*Fortunately, I did not have to rely on my resolve alone to break this unkind action habit of ridiculing the woman I love. She would not tolerate the ridicule. It was clear to me that if I wanted to continue our relationship, I would have to stop this socially embarrassing and controlling behavior. I was able to recognize when I was about to say something hurtful about her. This recognition gave me a moment of freedom before acting on the habit. In that moment of freedom, I actually felt the pain and suffering the ridicule would cause. In addition, I felt the fear of losing her because of my arrogance. Had I not broken that habit, we would not have been married these 51 years. It was the moment of freedom, the awareness of the need to be mindful, that gave me the opportunity to break that unkind habit and not say something hurtful.*

✦ ✦ ✦

Another way to look at a moment of freedom is to see it as a sacred pause. According to a *Harvard Business Review* article, "When we experience the sacred pause, we become less compelled by what simply makes us feel better; we feel less compelled to attack, run away, or give in to what makes us feel bad."[1] In short, taking a moment of freedom or a sacred pause makes us less likely to be unkind to ourselves or someone else. In fact, this moment of freedom is the key to breaking our unkind habits.

Moments of freedom, or sacred pauses, provide us the opportunity to catch unkind habits before they start. If we understand the extent of the harm our unkind habits cause and reflect on the hurt they can cause others and ourselves, we are more likely to pause before putting them into action. At such times we feel a sense of freedom.

 PUT INTO **Practice**

Have you ever felt a moment of freedom enabling you to stop before you did something unkind? How did that moment feel?

---

## Preparing Ourself for Moments of Freedom

We prepare ourselves for these moments of freedom by strengthening our mindful kindness practices in the morning, during the day, and in the evening. Regardless of our particular unkind habits, we will be better able to break them if we have well-established mindful kindness practices, such as:

- Kind habits directed to ourselves and others
- Meditation
- The Three-Breath Method
- Mindfulness with thoughts, emotions, and sensations
- Grounding techniques
- Time in and respect for nature
- Micropractices

In addition, we need to practice our self-care habits, such as getting the right amount of sleep, exercise, and healthy food, and obtaining the education and skills needed for our work.

These practices reduce our negative mind-wandering and prepare us to experience the moments of freedom that allow us to not carry out our unkind habit. The more often these mindful kindness practices give us those moments of freedom, the greater our confidence that we can continue to weaken our unkind habits in the future.

 PUT INTO **Practice**

Decide, then list, which mindfulness practices would be most helpful in enabling you to have a moment of freedom that will help you to not carry out an unkind habit. The sample schedule below will give you some ideas for making your list and putting your practices into action.

**Sample Daily Schedule**

- *Morning:* Meditate for 10 minutes, turn a daily activity (such as brushing your teeth) into a micropractice, enjoy being outside, and name one thing you are grateful for.

- *Daytime:* Intentionally be kind 2 or 3 times and use one or 2 of these mindfulness practices: Three-Breath Method; mindfulness with thoughts, emotions, and sensations; grounding techniques; or micropractices.

- *Evening:* Meditate for 10 minutes, use a micropractice with a daily activity, reflect on a kindness and mindfulness practice you have been doing, and name one thing you are grateful for. How do you feel when you reflect on your acts of kindness?

Now, write your own daily schedule to strengthen your mindful kindness practice. Include only those practices that fit into your life and you are ready to work on:

Morning: _____

_____

Daytime: _____

_____

Evening: _____

_____

## Step 2: Select an Unkind Habit to Work On

You need to select an unkind habit to work on. There are two factors to consider when selecting the unkind habit: the importance to you to weaken or eliminate that unkind habit, and the likelihood you will be successful in your efforts to weaken the unkind habit.

PUT INTO **Practice**

Write an unkind habit to weaken or break. It can be the one you selected from Chapter 8 for the Put into Practice exercise on page 159. Or you can pick another of your unkind habits to work on. Consider picking an unkind habit that is troublesome while at the same time one you are likely to have success eliminating, transforming into a kind habit, or at least weakening.

_____

_____

## Step 3: Diagnose Whether to Focus First on Your Mental World or Your Physical World

Use the Skill of Diagnosis to determine if the unkind habit requires you to act primarily in your mental world or in your physical world. Remember that to weaken many unkind action habits, we need to start with our unkind mental habits.

### Focus on Changing Your Mental World

All our unkind mental habits involve negative mind-wandering. The emotions and thoughts stemming from our unkind mental habits harm us, but do not directly affect others and are usually not observable to others. Of course, side effects of the unkind mental habits may be observable; for example, if we are very worried about something, our friends might notice that we are nervous. How do you feel when someone tries to be helpful when they notice that you are upset?

We've learned a number of mindfulness practices that we can use to reduce our negative mind-wandering. These include the Three-Breath Method, meditating, mindfulness, sensing mindfulness, grounding techniques, and micropractices.

Sometimes, these mindfulness practices will be successful in weakening our unkind mental habits. Other times, we will need help from a friend, counselor, teacher, or spiritual/religious leader.

#### EXAMPLE

Rafael, a high school senior, was finishing his applications to college. There was one college that Rafael really wanted to attend. After Rafael sent off his application to this college, he found himself extremely worried about his application. He fixated obsessively about how he could have written a better essay or provided better recommendations. He could not sleep at night. He kept talking about his concern to his friends, who were becoming annoyed with constantly hearing about his college applications.

Eventually, Rafael used his Wise Warrior and accepted his parents' advice to see a counselor. The counselor helped Rafael recognize that his worrying and anxiety would not help him achieve his goal of college acceptance. The counselor also helped him to recognize how his worrying was isolating him from his friends and, quite importantly, helped him understand he had a good chance of being accepted at a good college.

✦ ✦ ✦

Sometimes worry and anxiety are tied to grief from the loss of someone close to us. This grief can be so deep that we find ourselves depressed and shut off from communication with others. This isolation can make us feel hopeless. Grieving is natural and causes great sadness, but if the sadness becomes depression and goes on for too long a time, it can become an unkind habit of feeling depressed. In times like this we can change our mental world by meeting with a supportive adult, peer, or counselor. Have you felt a relief from isolation when someone you trusted offered you the support you needed when you were grieving or upset for some other reason?

### EXAMPLE

J.D. decided to focus on his unkind mental habit of feeling sad for too long a time. He learned that helping others weakened his habit of feeling depressed.

J.D. remembers how he struggled with his unkind habit of depression over the suicide of a friend in high school. A counselor helped him learn strategies for coping with his distress. One way that was very effective involved volunteering at a local elementary school.

PUT INTO **Practice**

### *A New Breathing Exercise*

Breaking unkind habits can be stressful. Give yourself a break by trying this new breathing exercise: Inhale through your mouth. Exhale through your nose.

1. Put your tongue on your bottom lip.
2. Breathe in through your mouth.
3. Swallow the breath and hold it for 4 seconds
4. Exhale through your nose.

Repeat the four steps ten times.

Write about your experience with this breathing exercise.

---

## Focus on Changing Your Physical World

When we determine that the need to act is primarily in our physical world, we can take on the role of our Diligent Detective to determine how to weaken the unkind habit and then take on the role of the Wise Warrior to carry out the plan. Unkind action habits directed toward others include, for example, consistently being rude, arrogant, disrespectful, or inconsiderate, as well as frequent instinctive reactions to events such as becoming extremely mad when cut off by another car in traffic or being very aggressive when bumped by another person on a bus.

Here are some examples of people using their Diligent Detective to learn how to change an unkind habit in their physical world.

- A person with the habit of not listening to others and constantly interrupting can take action in the physical world by getting help from a peer, elder, counselor, online articles, an app, or class that teaches and provides role-playing practice with healthy communication skills, such as the kind communication habits described in Chapter 4.

- A supervisor who recognizes that she often acts in an unpleasant manner can take action in the physical world by reading books or watching YouTube videos on being a supportive supervisor or on changing how we interact with people we supervise.

 PUT INTO **Practice**

For the unkind habit you selected in Step 2 to weaken or break, will you focus first on your mental world or your physical world? Explain why you selected your mental or physical world.

## Step 4: Identify the Activators for the Unkind Habit

**activator**

An event that activates an unkind habit.

Each of us has our own set of activators that cause us to unleash an unkind habit. And many of our unkind action habits in the physical world are activated by our unkind mental habits. The activators in the earlier examples include Rafael's excessive worrying being activated by thinking about his college application and J.D.'s depression being activated by thinking about his high school friend who died by suicide. Here are some examples of activators that may set off unkind mental habits:

- Washing your face can activate anxiety about your looks.

- Eating dessert can activate being hard on yourself about not stopping your bad habit of overindulging in sweets.

- Thinking of a conversation as boring can activate complaining to yourself about things you don't like and places you'd rather be.

- Contempt and resentment can be activated by contact with other people because of appearance, education level, economic status (for example waiters and clerks), religion, gender identity, accent and use of other languages, sexual orientation, political beliefs, or skin color.

- Watching the news can activate negative mind-wandering about your anger towards certain people and organizations such as government, police, other countries, or hate groups.

- Driving by a park and seeing a young couple walking and holding hands can activate thinking about being isolated and lonely.

- Listening to a conversation about your cousin doing well in school can activate negative self-talk about being inadequate and a failure.

- Seeing a well-dressed, attractive person can activate envy.

- Having the person you have been seeing tell you that they cannot go out with you this weekend can activate believing that you are unwanted.

- Watching a documentary about how surgeons save lives can activate being hard on yourself for not having a purpose in life yet.

- Listening to your parents arguing can activate your thinking about other things you can do nothing about besides stopping your parents from arguing.

- Seeing a TV show about climate change can activate worry about what might go wrong in the future.

- Not knowing what to say when your friend tells you about a serious personal challenge can activate negative mind-wandering about not knowing how to communicate with your loved ones and friends.

- Seeing your ex-partner with a new partner may activate your feelings of inadequacy.

- Your teacher not being able to help you after school can activate negative mind-wandering about your feelings of resentment over not receiving the attention you deserve at school, work, or home.

Here are some examples of activators that may set off unkind physical habits:

- Your partner criticizing you in front of your friends makes you feel bad and can cause you to yell at your partner.

- Following slow drivers can activate anger, either mentally to yourself or physically through screaming at or threatening the other driver.

- Being with friends celebrating a classmate's move to a new job overseas can activate harsh feelings over mistakes you made and opportunities you missed and cause you to drink excessively.

- Washing dishes can activate resentment about why others don't take their turns and activate complaining to your roommates.

- When playing basketball, a member of the other team knocks you over. You feel angry and may start to attack the other player.

- Seeing a homeless person activates your disrespectful self-talk about the homeless and can result in you insulting the person.

The next step explains the importance of being able to determine what event or events activate our unkind habits.

## PUT INTO **Practice**

What activates the unkind habit you selected to weaken or break? Explain your answer.

_____

_____

## Step 5: Stop the Unkind Habit by Acting Early

A direct and powerful way of stopping an unkind habit is to recognize an activator and promptly take action in our moment of freedom to keep the unkind behavior from occurring. Earlier we heard about how Rafael and his counselor made a plan (in Rafael's mental world) that he would apply in his physical world. First, whenever he started thinking about his college application (his activator) and felt the worry and anxiety returning in his mind, he would use his moment of freedom to take three deep breaths and return his focus to what he was doing at that moment. Second, during the day he would use some grounding techniques and micropractices to relax so that he would be more able to create his moment of freedom. Finally, he would try to fill his day with more activities that keep him from worrying, like playing basketball and tutoring young students.

J.D. implemented his plan for the physical world soon after he met with the counselor. Going each day to help younger children greatly reduced the time he thought about his friend who died by suicide. When those thoughts were coming into his mind, he would, whenever possible, engage the moment of freedom with sensing mindfulness that prevented the depression from arising. Moreover, the work with children brought him hope and peace from the traumatic loss. Guiding the children gave him a sense of purpose, which was a way to heal and become a healthier, more helpful, and kind person.

Often, it's not just one event but a chain of events that activates our unkind habit. With mindfulness, we can be aware of feelings, thoughts, and behaviors that occur very early in the process leading up to us carrying out the unkind behavior.

We're likely to be more successful at weakening habits when we can stop a behavior early in the process. For example, if we eat too much junk food, we can take an action to weaken the habit when we are shopping by not buying or picking up junk food. If the junk food is not in our possession, we cannot eat it. If we spend too much time on unhealthy digital media activities, we can turn our phone off before dinner and leave it off until morning. For many of us this will take our Wise Warrior to accomplish. Changing a difficult-to-change unkind habit may have to wait until we have had success with some easier-to-break unkind habits.

### EXAMPLE

Using a moment of freedom to stop an unkind habit by engaging grounding techniques:

Waiting can activate our unkind mental habits of impatience and frustration. We may feel frustration when waiting at a stoplight, for the bus, in a line at the store, for a table at a restaurant, or even waiting to grow up. Our agitation is often greater when we consider the wait needlessly long—think about how quickly we become frustrated when we have to take a number at the DMV (Division of Motor Vehicles) and have 20 people ahead of us while waiting to take a driver's test.

Rather than glare at the people being called before us and allowing our anger to increase, we might take advantage of a moment of freedom and engage in a combination of soft-ears, soft-eyes, and soft-touch. With soft-ears, we hear the hum of conversation of other people and with soft-eyes view the scenery or the motion of cars out the DMV window, or watch employees typing on their computers. With soft-touch, we notice our feet resting on the ground and the feel of our arms hanging relaxed at our side. Before long, waiting in line can become a micropractice that rests the mind and opens us up to act with kindness rather than impatience. Waiting can be transformed from an annoyance into an opportunity to be mindful, to get grounded, and to connect with our surroundings or other people.

### EXAMPLE FROM AN AUTHOR

Using a moment of freedom to stop an unkind habit by engaging mindfulness with emotions:

*By my early 30s, mindfulness training allowed me to fully feel how my displays of anger frightened Linda and my daughters, which motivated me to notice my rising feelings of anger as an activator leading to a physical act of anger. Here is an example of how I changed:*

*In the past when I made a mess, like spilling a box of dry dog food, I would kick the box, which made the mess worse. After practicing mindful kindness when I felt the beginning of my anger over spilling the dog food, I was able to shift my attention away from my feelings of anger to a moment of freedom, allowing the stirred-up emotions to settle. The power of the moment of freedom was driven home to me when I once again spilled dog food and found myself looking down on a mess of my own making. This time, knowing that kicking the carton half full of dry dog food would only make things worse, I engaged in a moment of freedom. Instead of angrily spreading the dry dog food with another kick, I cleaned up the mess. As I cleaned up, I actually felt relief from not experiencing the stress of throwing a tantrum.*

### EXAMPLE

Using a moment of freedom to engage the Three-Breath Method:

A high school student found himself increasingly frustrated because he was not saving enough money to buy a video game he wanted. Instead, he had been spending his money daily on donuts and soda at a neighborhood store. Whenever he came near the store, he used his moment of freedom to take three mindful breaths. This allowed him to control his impulse to enter the store. Each day, he put the money he would have spent at the store in an envelope, and after 2 months he had enough money to buy the video game.

PUT INTO **Practice**

For the unkind habit you selected to weaken or break, describe how you can stop that behavior from occurring by acting mindfully early.

_____

_____

## Step 6: When You Cannot Prevent the Unkind Habit from Starting, Stop it or Turn it into Something Neutral or Positive

When we are having difficulty trying to stop an unkind habit, we can link the activator to a replacement neutral or kind behavior. Think of a clerk who transforms the habit of reaching for candy on their break into the habit of reaching for a carrot stick instead. Likewise, if we are in the habit of gossiping, when we feel the impulse to speak unkindly about someone else, we can acknowledge the impulse but instead of saying something negative, we can say something positive, neutral, or nothing at all. If we are impatient when we have to wait in line, we can replace our impatience with grounding techniques such as soft-eyes, sharp-eyes, or soft-ears.

The following examples illustrate these replacement habits: transforming frustration into a game while driving, replacing retreating from socializing with new people to reaching out to connect with others, replacing negative self-talk with a kind and calm music playlist, replacing doormat behavior with an assertive behavior, and replacing feeling badly with productive behaviors.

### EXAMPLE

One teacher caught up routinely in city traffic uses her moment of freedom to replace her irritation with her own private "Be Nice" game:

_I like to tell people about a little game I play. It's called "Be Nice." My goal is to be as nice as possible to the most unexpected people. For example, in traffic, I try to let in as many people as possible when merging, changing lanes, and at traffic signals that allow for my extra "be nice" attitude and actions. When possible, I stop and let people waiting to cross the street do so. In turn, doing this actually makes my day better and less stressed. I have found an immediate correlation with my "Be Nice" game and my personal level of happiness. I'm secretly hoping that if I tell others of my private game that they will be inspired to do the same._

### EXAMPLE

Tasha, a young woman who had the unkind habit of using her cell phone to withdraw from people because of her feelings of inadequacy, now recognizes that when she's feeling nervous in a social situation, she need not withdraw. With mindfulness, she can use her anxiety, the activator for the unkind habit, as a reminder to do something positive. When she feels this impulse to escape, she uses her moment of freedom to engage her replacement habits, such as turning to someone near her and starting a conversation or simply sitting still with a friendly smile to people-watch. Whatever it is, mindfulness can help her recognize when her old habit is being activated and to substitute a new kind habit instead.

These types of changes in Tasha's physical world can also lead to changes in her mental world. As she becomes less lonely and happier through connection with others, feelings of inadequacy in her mental world will most likely diminish. She is now in the mindful-kind cycle.

### EXAMPLE

College student Chad, a poetic young man, describes how he transformed his habit of negative mind-wandering with unkind thoughts into a form of kindness to himself and others through developing musical playlists.*

*While my weeks are filled with thoughts about what shoes I should wear to match my top and which route I should take to class, it would be dishonest to gloss over the rather consistent drone of an orchestra of negative self-speak looming within. It is the sound of a person I know well. It is my voice, filtered to lose any semblance of kindness. With the help of my headphones, I have learned to build worlds through playlists, erecting spaces furnished with the utilities I believe constitute kindness. Though I also curate listening experiences for specific people in my life, more often than not, these spaces act as coordinates for reminding myself how to be kind unto the figure in the mirror and those around me. Through songs, I find the words to use to calm myself, the strains of feeling to aim for when looking to affirm others. I guess, behind the armor of poetic writing, what I am trying to say is that I turn to playlist-making to construct hope. These digital love letters are the lighthouses I can rely on to guide the way when the storms of life reduce visibility to only the thoughts in my head.*

### EXAMPLE

Jenny, a high school senior, had been worried that she was drinking too much and, after several months, had made progress in getting her drinking mostly in check. But when she was with her group of friends who drank often, her fear that she would make her friends angry by refusing to join them resulted in her giving in to their requests to drink with them. Jenny's inability to refuse to drink with these friends is an example of her mental unkind habit of feeling that she needed to give in to peer pressure; she did not make her own decisions but let others make her decisions for her. She started by being a Diligent Detective to figure out how to change her mental world. When she began seeing a counselor, she saw that standing up for herself would not cause her friends to reject her, and she learned how she could be more assertive in a friendly way. She rehearsed in her mind how to tell her friends she did not want to drink. Using the mind of the Wise Warrior, in her moment of freedom she kindly said no to drinking with them, in effect replacing alcohol with a soda. She also saw how she could use a new assertive mindset in other situations, such as when her date was being too sexual. She would firmly tell them to stop (and maybe even express that their behavior was inappropriate) rather than submitting to their unwanted advances.

---

* Sample playlist, Happy Songs: https://open.spotify.com/playlist/4AnAUkQNrLKlJCInZGSXRO

*EXAMPLE*

Raven has had a very difficult relationship with his parents due in part to their excessive drinking. He has been waiting to turn 18 so he can move out of his parents' home. His parents constantly make him feel unloved, stupid, and unwelcome. To avoid feeling like a failure in life, Raven spends most of his time in his room. Raven knows he still has a year until he is 18, so he uses his moments of freedom to replace negative self-talk with learning new hobbies on the internet, listening to music to tune the negativity out, and planning for his future.

PUT INTO **Practice**

For the unkind habit you selected to weaken or break, describe how you will use a mindfulness practice to create your moment of freedom and put in place a positive replacement habit.

_____

_____

_____

# Revisiting the Challenges to Learning to Be Mindfully Kind

Chapter 8 described how unkind habits can be caused by these three challenges:

- Society's values of materialistic thinking and self-centered individualism
- Instincts other than kindness (survival, reproduction and success)
- Our personal history that we cannot go back and change

Now that we have a plan for addressing our unkind habits, let's see what the implications are for how to address unkind habits that result in part from these three challenges.

## Society's Values of Materialistic Thinking and Self-Centered Individualism

Step 2 in the plan for breaking an unkind habit is identifying the unkind habit and acknowledging that you have it. Mindfulness can help us become aware that an unkind habit is caused by self-centered or materialistic ways of thinking. Some of these self-centered thoughts include being controlling, being overly competitive, needing to be special, and being arrogant.

### EXAMPLE

Jean was working with a team to redesign the student recreation area. During meetings, she would dominate the conversation by interrupting others and disagreeing in a disrespectful manner. She did not respond to her teammate's comments with interest, rarely asking questions about ideas different from hers, and often ridiculed others' suggestions and comments. Eventually, several teammates asked to leave the team.

After she began her work on mindfulness, Jean recognized her arrogance. She learned that a suggestion she didn't agree with activated her unkind habit of ridiculing the suggestion. She had to learn to use her moment of freedom before she interrupted or disagreed in a disrespectful manner. She did this by taking three breaths immediately when a teammate was making a suggestion. This helped calm her and keep from immediately being disrespectful. By not interrupting, she came to realize that the other members were knowledgeable, and when she listened more carefully, asked questions in a respectful manner, and got others involved, the team could be more successful. Jean took on the role of the Wise Warrior to change her behaviors so she could become a constructive, contributing member of the team.

### EXAMPLE

All the guys Sam hung out with had either Lebron X EXT-QS Hazelnut Men's shoes costing $325.90 or Adidas Kanye-designed Yeezy Boots 350 V2 for around $220. They often bragged about how great it was to have those shoes. Sam felt great pressure to get one of those pairs of shoes. He began to think about shoplifting a pair. Soon he realized that these thoughts of greed could land him in jail. Whenever the thought of shoplifting came into his mind, he would use his moment of freedom to engage sensing mindfulness or a grounding technique to calm himself and then visualize his mother getting a phone call that he was arrested. Sam also realized that his friends' focus on having expensive shoes was activating his greed. He gradually spent less time with those guys as he found friends who were not so caught up in the kind of shoes they wore and other types of materialistic thinking.

◆ ◆ ◆

Chapter 8 described how the self-centered thoughts and feelings coming from individualism and materialism can also lead to the often unrecognized unkind habit of ignoring the opportunity to act with kindness. Because both Jean and Sam learned about their unkind habits and used mindfulness to break those habits, they will be less likely to pass up opportunities to act with kindness. However, actually doing something when they notice an opportunity to act with kindness will not come automatically just because they have lessened their arrogance and greed; they will need to engage the Diligent Detective and Wise Warrior to do more kind acts and spend more of their time as a Kindful Practitioner.

We will discuss what we might do to change the influence of social values on us in Chapter 14: "Do You Want to Be a Kindness Ambassador?"

PUT INTO **Practice**

Identify an unkind habit you have that is caused by society's values of materialistic thinking or self-centered individualism.

_____

Describe how thinking and acting in that way makes you feel and how it might make others feel.

_____

Describe how you will begin to address this unkind habit.

_____


# Instincts Other Than Kindness (Survival, Reproduction, and Success)

Some of our most simple daily chores and activities can be activators for unkind habits. For example, looking in the mirror as we brush our hair can make us feel anxious about not being attractive enough, or looking at our friends' names on the honor roll at school can make us feel unsuccessful. The challenge is much greater when an activity activates an extreme unkind habit, such as forming very unhealthy eating habits because of how we perceive our appearance.

Everyday distractions, stress, and negative mind-wandering are common for us all. While our brain is still developing, risky, impulsive behavior is more likely; for example, we might become aggressive when a person insults us, a behavior based on the situation activating our survival instinct. Until around the age of 25 we need to be particularly wary of impulsive, instinctual behavior.

Doug's work with about 20 prisoners convicted of murder revealed that most of the murders were impulsive acts. The ability to access a moment of freedom could have prevented at least some of those murders.

Learning to tune in to the present moment through mindful practices and engaging the moment of freedom can prevent impulsive, reactive mistakes. Consider the difference between Respond and React. Respond means you think first and then act. React means you do not think first but act out of habit or instinct. When we are threatened, we are likely to react without thinking, especially when we are young. With mindfulness, we learn to be able to respond—thinking before acting. We will begin reacting without thinking less often. One of Doug's martial arts teachers said the goal of learning the martial art is so that we can respond rather than react to an attack.

### EXAMPLE

A teen uses a moment of freedom to reflect and decides not to react with anger:

_Now I think twice about something. If somebody called me something, instead of swinging, I . . . think about consequences I might get. It [mindfulness] makes you think about, "Are you sure you want to do this?" or "You want to react that way?" It just helps me a lot._[2]

The ability to respond rather than react can keep us out of trouble, as Doug has learned from his friends in prison,[3] most of whom reacted out of impulse in their youth and will now remain in prison for the rest of their lives.

## PUT INTO **Practice**

Describe a situation in which you reacted without thinking rather than responded after thinking.

_____

Describe how your behavior made you feel and how it probably made others feel.

_____

Describe how you might address this unkind habit in the future.

_____

## Our Personal History That We Cannot Go Back and Change

Our personal history is the third challenge we face in weakening our unkind habits. We all have our own unique personal history. It is in the past and we cannot go back and change what led to the unkind thinking and action habits we have now. How do we meet the challenge of stopping or weakening the unkind habits that have formed because of our past personal experiences?

We use our Diligent Detective to identify what happened in the past that led to our unkind habits. If we made mistakes, we make plans so that we will not make the same mistakes again. Then we act as the Wise Warrior to implement our plan to weaken or break the unkind habit. In implementing the plan, we rely on our growth mindset, believing we can change. We take responsibility for our thoughts and actions as we work to make change, and remember to be patient and humble.

In Chapter 8, we read about Shannon. Being rejected by her family led her to develop the unkind habits of insecurity and anger, which in turn led eventually to her joining a hate group. She became motivated to confront her unkind habit of anger after she went to live with a family who practiced kindness in all their relationships, including their relationships with her. The motivation led her to use her Diligent Detective to understand why she had joined the hate group. With this understanding, she was able to confront her anger and insecurity and use her Wise Warrior to disengage from the hate group.

## PUT INTO **Practice**

Identify an unkind habit you have that stems from your personal experiences.

_____

Describe how acting in that way makes you feel and how it makes others feel.

Describe how you might work on this unkind habit.

 PERSONAL **Challenge**

Use the six steps presented in this chapter to make a plan to weaken or break an unkind habit different than the one you wrote about in the earlier Put into Practice exercises. Write what you would do for each of the six steps to break the unkind habit.

| Step 1 | Strengthen your mindfulness practices so you are ready to experience a moment of freedom. | |
|---|---|---|
| Step 2 | Select and describe an unkind habit to work on | |
| Step 3 | Diagnose whether to focus first on your mental world or your physical world. | |
| Step 4 | Identify the activators for the unkind habit. | |
| Step 5 | Stop the unkind habit by acting early. | |
| Step 6 | If you cannot prevent the unkind habit from starting, stop it or turn it into something neutral or positive. | |

# Wrapping Up

Unkind habits, like anger, can consume our attention for hours at a time and even leave us hungover, as we regret later what we might have said or done in our time of anger. Our unkind habits not only harm us and other people, but also take up time and effort that could be used for kindness to ourselves, the earth, and others. Moreover, our unkind habits often stand in the way of building kind habits. A downward unmindful-unkind cycle is likely to continue until we use mindfulness to break our most destructive unkind habits. The key to breaking our unkind habits is to have a strong set of mindful kindness practices. The six steps to break or weaken an unkind habit are listed in the preceding Personal Challenge exercise.

Remember, when selecting an unkind habit to work on, consider which may be the easiest to break and which is the most important to break. You may want to delay work on the most important habit until you've had success with some easier-to-break habits, or you might be motivated to work right away on your most important unkind habit to break.

# Time for Reflection

How are you doing with these practices? For each statement below, circle the best word(s) that fits your feeling, or add one of your own.

1.  How do you feel when you practice a pleasant kind habit?

    Happier, Calmer, Satisfied, Joyful, _____

2.  Have you used a gentle way to tell someone about something that has been irritating you rather than keeping it bottled up inside?   Yes   No

    If yes, how did you feel when you did it?

    Relieved, Vulnerable, Scared, Calmer, Powerful, _____

3.  How do you feel when you carry out an unkind habit directed toward yourself, the earth, or others?

    Upset, Confused, Sorry, Happy, Calm, _____

4.  How do you feel when you carry out a kind habit directed toward others?

    Upset, Confused, Sorry, Happy, Calm, _____

5.  How does it feel to use the kind conversation skills?

    Enjoyable, Vulnerable, Challenging, Calming, _____

6.  Have any of these micropractices been helpful for you?

    | | | |
    |---|---|---|
    | Doing Work around the House/Apartment | Yes | No |
    | Attending to Personal Hygiene | Yes | No |
    | Making and Following a Schedule | Yes | No |
    | Organizing Your Surroundings | Yes | No |
    | Moving Quietly through the World | Yes | No |
    | Picking up Others' Trash When You Come across It | Yes | No |

● ● ●

Write about how you have been kind recently in one of these ways and how you felt:

- Be friendly
- Show appreciation
- Offer help
- Reach out to those in need

_____

_____

Chapter 10

# Responding to the Unkind Habits of Others

*Be kind to unkind people. They need it the most.*

Dalai Lama

**Before beginning this chapter, for one minute meditate in the way that works best for you.**

Not only do we deal in our personal lives with our own unkind habits, we are also negatively affected by the unkind habits of others. This chapter describes how to cope with unkindness from other people, either through direct contact with them or through social media. Before we discuss how to deal with the unkind habits of others, let's look at three ways we might be affected.

- **Another person's unkind habits can teach us to be unkind.** For example, if in childhood we are consistently around people with unkind, violent habits, we may begin to use these harmful habits as models for our own behaviors. Tad and the other incarcerated men Doug mentors developed their unkind habits during childhoods filled with violence and abuse. Sometimes children learn unkind habits from their parents even when there is no physical abuse. Doug learned his habit of anger from his dad's frequent outbursts of verbal anger, which resulted from his father's World War 2 post-traumatic stress disorder (PTSD). His father tried to cope with his PTSD, for example, by secretly destroying all his World War 2 medals in an attempt to rid himself of his traumatic memories.

- **A person's unkind habit makes us unhappy.** For example, when a close friend or our partner is continually critical of us, our sadness can lead to depression. In other situations, we may become anxious and fearful when being frequently harmed, whether in person or over social media. Has someone else's unkindness made you unhappy? How did that feel?

- **A person's unkind habit puts us in an unpleasant or dangerous situation.** For example, if a friend who drives us to work drives very fast while texting on their cell phone, we are being put in danger. Or when a coworker at a fast food restaurant constantly leaves work early, which in turn makes us work late, it feels very unpleasant. Or if a coworker posts racist and threatening posts on social media about Native Americans or targets other groups, it can cause fear at work.

PUT INTO **Practice**

Write about your experience with one of the three ways the unkind habits of another person can cause harm:

1.  How it might lead us to learn an unkind habit,

2.  How it might make us feel unhappy, or

3.  How it might put us in dangerous or unpleasant situations.

Describe the circumstance, how it made you feel, and how you reacted or wish you had reacted to change the situation.

_____

_____

_____

# Preparing to Deal with the Unkind Habits of Others

As we discussed in the last chapter, it's important to strengthen our kindful practices to be able to break our own unkind habits. We also need to strengthen our kindfulness habits to help us cope with the unkind habits of others. By strengthening our mindfulness practices (meditation; the Three-Breath Method; mindfulness with thoughts, emotions, and sensations; grounding techniques; and micropractices), we will have more capacity to handle the unkind habits of others. Self-care is also important in preparing ourselves to deal with the stress from the unkind habits of others. Obtaining the education and skills needed for work, weakening the unkind habits we direct at ourselves, and getting the right amount of sleep, exercise, and healthy food will all help prepare us to deal with unkind habits of others.

## PUT INTO **Practice**

As we prepare to learn how to handle the unkind habits of others, let's see how you are strengthening your kindful practices. Take a moment to write about how you are progressing with each of these mindfulness practices:

1. Meditation: _____

_____

2. The Three-Breath Method: _____

_____

3. Mindfulness (thoughts, emotions, sensations): _____

_____

4. Grounding techniques: _____

_____

5. Micropractices: _____

_____

6. Self-care: _____

_____

# Responding to the Unkind Habits of Others

We run into the unkind habits of others in various forms in our daily lives. Let's begin by describing options for how we can respond to unkind habits that are directed toward us.

- The first option is to respond to the unkindness with kindness.

- The second option is to try to speak with the person whose unkind habits are affecting us and see if we can get them to stop their unkind habit.

- The third option is to simply avoid the person or group.

- The fourth option is to change our mental world to decrease the damage that their unkind habit can cause us, even if the unkind habit comes from a certain group's cultural beliefs, for example, hate groups.

## Option One: Respond with Kindness When Confronted with Unkindness

Unkindness directed at us from another person can often show up when the other person is dealing with a difficult situation themselves. If a friend who is usually kind suddenly acts unkindly, we might assume something is stressing our friend and that this is an unintended unkind action. Because the unkindness is not common, we engage our Diligent Detective to determine the "why" behind the unkind behavior. We see if we can help our friend deal with the situation that is causing the stress. In contrast, if we respond to our friend's unkindness with more unkindness, the situation can lead to an unmindful-unkind cycle for our friendship.

Sometimes people who do not know us can be intentionally mean, yet it is usually best to start by responding with kindness. Our kindness might surprise them, and they may choose to respond to our kindness with kindness, or at least decrease the intensity of their unkindness. However, our Diligent Detective must be alert. If the unkindness is repeated, we are probably better off trying one of the other options discussed below.

### EXAMPLE FROM AN AUTHOR

In Doug's teaching kindness to prisoners, some of them would lie to him, for example, his prisoner friend Robert lied so he could get money:

*I told Robert that I would not contact him for 3 months as a way to give him time to use his Diligent Detective to determine why he lied and to use his Wise Warrior to not lie again. After this period of time, I reconnected with him and found he had returned to his mindful kindness practices. There is no guarantee that Robert will not lie to me again in the future. Similarly, my prisoner friends were sometimes lied to by other prisoners in order to get food, stamps, or money. Once my friends discovered the dishonesty, they stayed away from those prisoners.*

## Option Two: Come to an Agreement with the Person about Stopping their Unkind Habit

Sometimes, the person with the unkind habit may not be aware of how their habit is hurting us. When we explain how the person's unkind habit is affecting us, the person may be willing to stop the unkind habit. Also, if we can help the person break the unkind habit, we are actually acting with kindness.

Below is a series of six steps to take if you think there is a possibility a person might be willing and able to work on their unkind habit.*

1. **Choose a suitable time and setting for a conversation.** Pick a time to talk to the person when you are relatively calm. Try not to have the conversation when you or the other person is upset and angry.

2. **Analyze the problem.** Before meeting with the person, use the skills of the Diligent Detective to understand what is bothering you and what could be possible solutions. Use this time to also reflect on how your own actions could be a part of the problem.

3. **Begin an honest and open conversation.** Find a private or safe place to meet and start with an open-ended question related to your need that is not being met. An open-ended question is a question that does not call for a yes, no, or maybe answer, but is designed to encourage the person to give a longer response. As you go through the rest of the steps, listen very carefully and paraphrase back to the person what you believe they have said. When you paraphrase, you are saying in your own words what you think the person meant to say. By the other person confirming your paraphrase, you both know you are working from the same information.

4. **Explain how the habit makes you feel and acknowledge your part in causing the problem.** Include one or two details that make clear what is bothering you while being careful not to be angry or insulting. If you have played a part in creating the unkind situation, let the other person know that you are also responsible for the problem. This will help the other person understand that you are looking to improve the situation with them.

5. **Suggest or work together to develop a solution.** Request that the unkind habit stop and present or brainstorm together a solution that meets both of your needs. Be mindful of the words you use; try not to use blaming words such as "you always" or "you never." The other person will feel better toward you and likely be more willing to accept what you say if you avoid a negative confrontation. In fact, make positive statements, if possible, about your relationship as a friend or coworker. Positive statements can reassure them that they are valued. And of course you will want to find a solution that works for both you and the other person.

6. **Revisit and revise (if needed).** If things don't change after making an agreement, you may want to have a "do-over." In other words, give it another try.

Below is an example of the six steps.

*EXAMPLE*

Isabel had just begun her first job after graduating. She was upset because her coworker Sam kept bothering her. Isabel came home every night and complained about Sam to her sister. What irritated her was how Sam interrupted her when she was trying to write her reports. Sam would walk over to her desk and spend a great deal of time telling personal stories and distracting her from her work. As a result, Isabel often had to stay late to finish her work. Isabel decided to talk with Sam to see if they could reach an agreement. The purpose of the agreement would be to break Sam's

---

* These steps are adapted from Susan and Peter Glaser's book *Be Quiet, Be Heard* (5th ed., 2013, Communication Solutions Publishing) to consider using when trying to come to agreement with the person whose unkind habit is harming you.

unkind habit of interrupting and also allow Isabel to deal with her own unkind habits of complaining and getting angry at home.

Let's look more closely at the six steps as Isabel uses them to reach an agreement with Sam.

1.  **Choose a suitable time and setting:** First Isabel finds a time she can be relatively calm because the other steps will not go smoothly if she is agitated.

2.  **Analyze the problem:** Isabel realizes she never let Sam know how disruptive the conversations are to her work. As a Diligent Detective, she felt that by talking with him they could come up with a solution together.

3.  **Begin an honest and open conversation:** To have a conversation with Sam, Isabel selects a private place that doesn't draw the attention of others in the office. Isabel might ask to go for a short walk with Sam or find a space for a private conversation. When asking an open-ended question, Isabel might say, "It seems like you come over to my desk quite often to talk when I'm working. Do you have any particular reason for doing this?" Isabel listens very carefully and paraphrases what she hears. For example, Sam might say to Isabel, "Hey, I just like to talk to you to give me a break. It gets so tedious sitting at a desk all day long." In response, Isabel might paraphrase by saying, "So you're using our conversations for a positive break during the day when you're tired of sitting so long at your desk?"

4.  **Explain how the habit makes you feel and acknowledge your part in causing the problem:** Isabel might say, "When you come to my desk when I'm working, I usually stop what I'm doing and listen and talk with you." Then she might give just one or two examples of the problem (more than two examples could overwhelm Sam), "Usually, this goes on too long. Yesterday I was trying to get this monthly report on safety checks done when you came over and started talking about where you and your family were hoping to go on vacation. This went on for about 15 minutes. By the time I got back to my report, it was nearly time to go home, but I had to stay almost an extra half hour to finish the report and some other work. I missed my bus and got home more than an hour late." Then Isabel might take responsibility for her part of the problem, saying, "I've never let you know that the time I spend in these conversations often causes me to have to work late." Isabel tells how this makes her feel. "Getting home late bothers me because I have to help my sister with her kids."

5.  **Suggest or work together to develop a solution:** Next, Isabel asks Sam to ask her permission before starting a conversation and interrupting her work. "If you were to ask me if I have time to talk, that would be helpful. Should we try that?" Sam responds with, "Sure, I can try not to interrupt you without asking your permission first. Thanks for letting me know." Isabel's efforts can help Sam break the unkind habit of interrupting other people when they are busy. In breaking this unkind habit Sam might begin to learn the kind habit of being more considerate of the needs of other people.

6.  **Revisit and revise (if needed):** Clearly, if things do not improve with Sam's interruptions, Isabel can try one more time to communicate how serious a problem this is. If Isabel chooses to try again, i.e., have a "do-over," she might say something like, "I'm not sure I got my point across when we talked the other day. I want to give it another try."

A young adult in recovery found these steps very useful: "Sometimes people do not realize that they have hurt you, and the best way to build a stronger relationship is to communicate how their words or actions caused you harm or discomfort." By communicating with each other in an open way you can build a more healthy relationship. Have you had the experience of opening the way to a better relationship by communicating clearly what caused you harm or discomfort? How did it feel to communicate?

More disturbing yet, a person may be intentionally targeting you with their unkind habit. In the next example, James shows his unkind habit of arrogance by the way he harasses Ernesto.

## EXAMPLE

Ernesto enjoyed his Spanish class and was making good progress. He often stayed after class and practiced conversing in Spanish with his teacher. A classmate, James, who had high grades in Spanish as well as in other classes, began to ridicule Ernesto during lunch time when they sat together with their other friends. James called Ernesto the teacher's pet and said no matter how much Ernesto tried to butter up the teacher, he would never be as good in Spanish as him. Ernesto felt very uncomfortable with James's arrogant behavior, but did not want to change lunch tables because he enjoyed the company of his other friends.

✦ ✦ ✦

Ernesto might try to come to an agreement with James by following the six steps to make an agreement. However, if Ernesto knows that James acts this way in many situations, Ernesto will not bother to try to make an agreement with James.* Research shows that having a student talk about their feelings with an unkind student typically strengthens the unkind habit. Below are the steps Ernesto could take if he believes there is a chance that James will change.

Step 1. Ernesto felt that first thing in the morning would be a time when they could have a low-key conversation.

Step 2. Ernesto analyzed the problem and felt James was just teasing, not intending to be cruel. So, Ernesto thought if he was direct with James, there was a chance that James might stop the habit. Ernesto was not sure, but figured he had nothing to lose. He asked James if they could talk together before school. He wanted to talk when their friends were not around.

Step 3. Ernesto told James that it might look like he was trying to be the teacher's pet, but that was not why he spent the extra time with the teacher. Ernesto explained that he really wanted to learn Spanish so he could talk with members of his family who were from Central America. He also told James that he needed to do well in the class because he needed good grades so he could afford to go to college.

Step 4. Ernesto said that James's teasing him during lunch was humiliating and hurting his relationship with his friends sitting at the lunch table.

Step 5. Ernesto asked James to please not call him the teacher's pet and not tease him in other ways he often does in the cafeteria.

Step 6. If James continues with his habit, Ernesto might ask another friend who James also teases to join him in asking if James would stop the teasing.

---

* Here is where you can learn about the aggressive bully, the taunting bully, and the emotional bully: https://www.wikihow.com/Deal-With-Bullies (Styzek, K. [2021, October 31]. How to deal with bullies. *WikiHow*).

## — *Key Idea* —

The "making an agreement" strategy is something you can use not only with coworkers and friends, but also with your own family members. In addition, you can apply the strategy to a variety of situations in which you are being harmed by another person's unkind habit, such as anger, ridicule, contempt, jealousy, defensiveness, arrogance, rudeness, resentment, blaming, or impatience.

 PUT INTO **Practice**

### Come to an Agreement with the Person to Stop the Unkind Habit

Is there someone with an unkind habit directed at you? Will you try to make an agreement with that person to stop their unkind habit? If no one is directing an unkind habit at you, imagine that someone has an unkind habit such as interrupting you whenever you are on the phone. Using the six steps above, write a plan to show how you could make an agreement to reduce the harm caused by that person's unkind habit. First describe the unkind habit directed at you, then describe what you could do for each of the six steps in the table.

Describe the unkind habit directed at you by another person.

_____

_____

### Making an Agreement with Person Directing Unkind Behavior at You to Stop

| | |
|---|---|
| 1. Choose a suitable time and setting. | |
| 2. Analyze the problem. | |
| 3. Begin an honest and open conversation. | |
| 4. Explain how the habit makes you feel and acknowledge your part in causing the problem. | |
| 5. Suggest or work together to develop a solution. | |
| 6. Revisit and revise (if needed). | |

# Option Three: Stay Away from the Unkindness If You Can

If we cannot come to an agreement with another person about weakening their unkind habit directed at us, the next option can be to simply stay away from that person. The harm caused by another person's unkind habit is often obvious. Some unkind habits of others, such as drinking and driving, can put us at risk. If a person who has been drinking is the one who we are supposed to ride home with after a party, we can refuse to ride with that person. Other unkind actions directed at us may not be dangerous but do bring unpleasantness into our life, for example, someone's disrespect toward others makes us feel uncomfortable. To take care of ourselves, we may choose to not be around a person whose unkind habit is dangerous or unpleasant.

### EXAMPLE

Jesse and Dennis had been acquaintances for years. However, Jesse became increasingly aware that Dennis was always complaining and gossiping about others: sometimes about the stupidity of their friends, sometimes about not having enough money, sometimes about not having enough time to do what he wanted. Jesse tried to encourage Dennis to be more positive, but Dennis ignored the advice. Jesse began spending less and less time with Dennis. It was too much negativity to bear.

### EXAMPLE

Jenny met Thomas at work and they started dating. They had a good time going to the movies and going for walks. After a while, Jenny noticed that when they were around other people, Thomas would be rude to others. For example, when they were eating at restaurants, Thomas would be disrespectful to the food servers. If the restaurant was crowded and the waiter had not yet taken their order, Thomas would reach out and grab the waiter's arm. If the food took a long time to be delivered, Thomas would scold the waiter. On several occasions, Jenny asked Thomas to stop being rude and disrespectful, but Thomas did not change. Jenny decided to no longer go out with Thomas.

 PUT INTO **Practice**

Write about someone you stopped spending time with because of their unkind actions. What could you have done, if anything, to help that person work to become aware of and break their unkind habit? Or write about someone you are thinking about not spending time with because of their unkind habit. Write about why you want to stop spending time with that person and what you will do to stay away from that person.

_____

_____

_____

_____

## Option Four: Change Your Mental World

Sometimes, there will be situations in which we cannot stop the unkind actions of another person directed toward us, nor can we avoid contact with the person. When we cannot change our physical world to avoid the unkind habits of others, we must work to change our mental world to limit the damage done to us. In these situations, we will be more likely to be successful if we have been practicing our mindfulness practices: meditation, the Three-Breath Method, sensing mindfulness, grounding techniques, mindfulness with thoughts and emotions, and micropractices.

### FROM THE OTHER SIDE

In prison, the primary option for dealing with the unkind habits of others is to change your mental world. Roy described how strongly he was affected when he changed his mental world:

*I became blessed because I was suddenly aware that I was now experiencing a peace of mind, a freedom in the mind, that I had never come close to on the streets, where I had had plenty of money to buy whatever I wanted.*

✦ ✦ ✦

Although changing his mental state of mind through kindfulness can lead to a positive experience, as seen in Roy's example, it's not always so easy. We might, however, be in a job with an unkind supervisor or in school with an unkind teacher or at home with unkind parents. In this case, we can use mindfulness practices to limit our anger, agitation, and depression.

When possible, we can call on the Diligent Detective to come up with a plan for how to be kindful in an unkind situation. Then we can call on the Wise Warrior to support us in carrying out the plan. That is what Roy did when he and Doug created the mindful kindness partnership, in which he acted with kindness in many different ways to various other prisoners. So we can change our mental world to limit our negative emotions, but also we can try to make and follow a plan to be kindful in that difficult situation.

 PUT INTO **Practice**

Were you ever in a situation in which you were being harmed by the unkind habits of another and could neither stop the unkind actions nor avoid contact with the person? If so, describe the situation, how it made you feel, and how you changed or could have changed your mental world to deal with that situation by limiting negative emotions and possibly by trying to be kindful.

_____

_____

_____

_____

If you have not been in such a situation, have you seen another person in that kind of situation? Describe what that person could have done to deal with that situation.

_____

_____

# Intervening When Unkind Habits Are Directed at Another Person

In some situations, we are not the target of an unkind act, but we observe someone being treated in an unkind manner. This unkind act may come in several forms:

- **Verbal unkindness:** saying mean or threatening things to another person because of the color of their skin, their religion, their language, their immigration status, their sexual orientation, their political preferences, their limited income, or because of a real or perceived disability or a perceived inferiority. This can occur in person or online.

- **Social unkindness:** hurting someone's reputation or relationships.

- **Physical unkindness:** hurting a person or damaging their possessions.

Many of us want to do something in these situations, but are not sure what to do. Because awareness of the harm these unkind habits can cause is increasing, many organizations are offering training on how to intervene. A commonly used procedure is the Four Ds of Bystander Intervention: Direct, Distract, Delegate, Delay.[1]

## The Four Ds of Bystander Intervention

1. **Direct:** Step in and address the situation directly. This might look like saying, "That's not cool. Please stop" or "Hey, leave them alone." This technique tends to work better when the person who you're trying to stop knows and trusts you. It does not work well when drugs or alcohol are being used—the person is more likely to become defensive.

2. **Distract:** Distract either person in the situation in order to intervene. This might look like saying, "Hey, aren't you in my Spanish class?" or "Who wants to go get pizza?" This technique is especially useful when drugs or alcohol are involved because people under the influence can be harder to reason with than when they are sober.

3. **Delegate:** Find others who can help you intervene in the situation. This might look like asking a friend to distract one person in the situation while you distract the other, asking someone to go sit with you in order to talk, or going and starting a dance party right in the middle of their conversation. If you didn't know either person in the situation, you could also ask around to see if someone else does and can intervene.

4. **Delay:** For many reasons, you may not be able to do something in the moment. For example, if you're feeling unsafe or if you're unsure whether or not someone in the situation is feeling unsafe, you may first want to check in with the person. In this case, you can combine a distraction technique such as asking the person to use the bathroom with you or go get a drink with you to separate them from the person being unkind. You could approach the person and quietly ask them, "Are you OK?" or "How can I help you get out of this situation?"

*Note:* If you are interested in learning more about the 4Ds, enter the words "bystander intervention training in the four Ds" in the search engine of your computer to find training opportunities near you.

# A More In-Depth Plan for Weakening Our Unkind Habits

 PERSONAL **Challenge**

We have presented four options for dealing with the unkind habits of others. However taking responsibility for breaking our own unkind habits is far more important than responding to the unkind habits of others. Because of the difficulty in breaking some of our deep-seated unkind habits, we are going spend the rest of this chapter looking at how to build a more powerful plan to change our deep-seated unkind habits.

Below is a more in-depth procedure built on the five steps you learned in the last chapter to break an unkind habit. In this in-depth procedure, we will go into more detail as we plan each step.

Before making your own in-depth plan, read through the sample plan a young person of color made to break an unkind habit directed at his mom.

### A SAMPLE PLAN FOR WEAKENING AN UNKIND HABIT

1. **Select and describe the unkind habit.**

   - What is the unkind habit I chose to work on?

     *I frequently ignore my mom when I'm tired.*

   - How do I feel after I carry out the unkind habit?

     *I feel guilty because I've denied her an opportunity to talk/spend time together, which is important since life is short and I know I'm all she has.*

   - Who is harmed by my unkind habit?

     *I am harmed because ignoring others is selfish and rude, and my mom is harmed because I make her feel lonely and sad.*

2. **Diagnose whether to focus first on your mental world or your physical world:**

   - What goes on in my mental world that is linked to this habit?

     *I think that because I'm mentally and physically drained I just want to avoid others.*

   - How does the habit show itself in the physical world?

     *When I finish school and work, I close my door and curl up in bed and sleep before my mom comes home from work. If I haven't fallen asleep before she comes home, I stay quiet when she opens my door.*

3. **Describe the activator for the unkind habit. Is it in your mental world or physical world?**

   *The activator for ignoring my mom is in my mental world. I'm more introverted and don't like interacting with other people often, so after spending all day talking to people at school and work, I think that I want to be alone.*

4. **Describe how to prevent the unkind habit by acting early.**

   - What Diligent Detective work (gathering of information, research) do I need to do?

     *I will pay attention to how many and what days I tend to ignore my mom the most.*

   - What foundational skills of character (growth mindset, responsible, patient, and humble) will I need most?

     *I will need to be more considerate of my mom's feelings and desires for social interaction. I need to use my growth mindset knowing that I can change my habit.*

   - Who will I ask for support, if anyone?

     *I will ask my best friend to ask me how I am doing with this important change in my behavior. I will also ask my mom's friends to call her and go out with her on weekends more so that she doesn't feel like I'm the only person she can talk to.*

   - What action will I take to stop the unkind habit in my mental world?

     *I will consider how hurtful my actions are. I will also remind myself that I thought I would have many years to spend time with my grandma, so I called/visited her less often during the COVID-19 pandemic, but since she died I can never spend time with her again. I will remind myself that even if someone seems healthy, unexpected things can take them away from us and it is important for me to show right now how much I care about my mom.*

   - What action will I take in my physical world?

     *I will wake up earlier to meditate and recharge my social battery with time to myself before starting my day. I will also go to the gym between classes and work to give myself a break from talking to others, instead of going to the gym before classes.*

5.  **If you cannot stop the unkind habit, what is something neutral or positive you can do?**

    *I can leave notes for my mom to read when she comes home, or text her throughout the day so she feels valued.*

**FOLLOW-UP ON PLAN TO CHANGE AN UNKIND HABIT**

After you began putting the plan into action:

1.  **What happened as you tried to implement your plan to break an unkind habit?**

    *I noticed that I tend to ignore my mom and go to sleep earlier on Tuesdays, Wednesdays, and Thursdays, because those are my busiest days at work. To compensate for the days when I was exhausted, I made or bought dinner for us to eat together on Fridays and watched movies with my mom on Saturdays.*

2.  **What adjustment, if any, did you make in your plan?**

    *Instead of talking when she came home, I called her on my drive home. I also talked to her about how tired I am some days, and that on those days I would like to be alone for a while. Her friends were also able to ask her out more often.*

3.  **How did you feel as you implemented your plan?**

    *I felt better knowing my mom isn't as lonely because I set specific times for us to do things together, and her friends are talking to her more.*

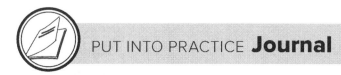

PUT INTO PRACTICE **Journal**

### *Creating Your Own In-Depth Plan for Weakening An Unkind Habit*

Now create your own plan. You can revise the plan to weaken an unkind habit you created in Chapter 9, or you can create a new plan. To revise your plan or create a new one to weaken an unkind habit, write your answers to the questions on page 290 of your journal.

One week after you put your plan into action, answer the questions on page 291 about how effective your plan has been and changes that may be necessary.

Although there are only three follow-up questions, you will probably spend more time answering them than you did writing the plan itself. It often takes many steps, missteps, and corrections before we can change something and make it stick. If you feel your plan is not going well, in the role of the Diligent Detective review the section near the end of Chapter 6 titled "Reviewing Your Kindness Plan: Making Habits Stick." If you try those steps with the mindset of the Wise Warrior and still feel frustrated, you might want to create a new plan.

# Wrapping Up

We have control over the way we work to break our own unkind habits. In contrast, we don't have control over the unkind habits of others. However, we can prepare to cope with the unkind habits of others. There are four options for dealing with the unkind habits of others: treat their unkindness with kindness, come to an agreement with the other person about stopping the unkind habit, stay away from the person with the unkind habit, and change our mental world. These are the six steps for coming to an agreement to stop an unkind habit:

1. Choose a suitable time and setting.
2. Analyze the problem.
3. Begin an honest and open conversation.
4. Explain how the habit makes you feel and acknowledge your part in causing the problem.
5. Suggest or work together to develop a solution.
6. Revisit and revise (if needed).

Finally we learned about some ways to intervene when an unkind habit is directed at another person.

 PUT INTO **Practice**

Below are two examples of others being unkind. Compare how you might respond to these two challenging situations with both kindness and unkindness.

1. Imagine you open your car door and it strikes the car next to yours. The person in that car yells, "Hey, watch what you're doing!" How could you respond, mentally and physically, in a kind way and in an unkind way?

   a. A kind response would be:

   _____

   b. An unkind response would be:

   _____

2. What about when someone cuts in front of you in a supermarket line? Again, how could you respond, mentally and physically, in a kind way and in an unkind way?

   a. A kind response would be:

   _____

   b. An unkind response would be:

   _____

## ☑ *Checking In*

Are you using any of these practices to prepare yourself to be ready to stop an unkind habit?

| | | |
|---|---|---|
| The Three-Breath Method | Yes | No |
| Sensing mindfulness | Yes | No |
| Grounding techniques | Yes | No |
| Micropractices | Yes | No |
| Kind conversation skills | Yes | No |

# Time for Reflection

Circle Yes or No. I feel grateful for:

| | | |
|---|---|---|
| People I care about | Yes | No |
| Pets I care about | Yes | No |
| Something that went well today | Yes | No |
| What I can do with my body and mind | Yes | No |
| People who help me and others | Yes | No |
| My beliefs that give me purpose and meaning | Yes | No |
| Having fun and laughing | Yes | No |
| Being able to meditate on a regular basis | Yes | No |
| Being able to practice mindfulness throughout my day | Yes | No |
| Being in nature and connected to the earth | Yes | No |
| Being part of my community | Yes | No |

• • •

Write about how you have been kind recently in one of these ways and how you felt:

- Be friendly
- Show appreciation
- Offer help
- Reach out to those in need

_____

_____

# Take the Final Steps to Lasting Happiness

*Add finishing touches that show all are welcome.*

---

---

Scientific findings: 34
Real-world examples: 41
Opportunities to apply what you are learning: 49

**Teachings from the World Religions**

Christianity: "And let us consider how to stir up one another to love and good works, not neglecting to meet together, as is the habit of some, but encouraging one another." (Hebrews 10:24-25)

Judaism: "When a stranger sojourns with you in your land, you shall not do him wrong. The stranger who sojourns with you shall be to you as the native among you, and you shall love him as yourself." (Leviticus 19:33-34)

Buddhism: "Silence the angry man with love. Silence the ill-natured man with kindness. Silence the miser with generosity. Silence the liar with truth."

Islam: "Do not let the hatred of people prevent you from being just. Be just; that is nearer to righteousness." (Quran 5:8)

Baha'i : "The obstacle to human happiness is racial or religious prejudice, the competitive struggle for existence, and inhumanity toward each other." —Abdu'l-Baha, *The Promulgation of Universal Peace*

## Chapter 11

# Kindful Options for Hard Times

*Although the world is full of suffering, it is also full of the overcoming of it.*

Helen Keller

**Before beginning this chapter, for one minute meditate in the way that works best for you.**

We all face hard times, whether it's when we have difficulty with a colleague at work, with a teacher at school, or with a parent or friend. However, at some point our difficulties could be more serious, such as when we feel trauma due to the loss of a loved one, get in trouble with the law, or sustain an injury that severely restricts our physical activity. Under these circumstances, we may become deeply distressed with intense feelings of sadness, loneliness, or even anger that extends over a period of time. This chapter does not focus on the cause of our hard times, but instead on what we can do when we are having a hard time.

One way to cope with hard times is through meditation. Meditation is an anchor helping to ground us during hard times.

### EXAMPLE FROM AN AUTHOR

Linda's lifelong friend Nancy was diagnosed with rheumatoid arthritis in midlife, a condition that eventually resulted in the amputation of her left leg below the knee. Later, she couldn't resist smiling as she told us about what happened in her aerobics dance class when her prosthetic leg fell off mid-workout, causing her to crash to the floor. Without missing a beat, the instructor called out, "Dancer down, dancer down!" Friends helped collect her prosthetic, Nancy reattached it, and the class continued. After spending time with her and Linda, I asked Nancy how she was able to maintain such a positive attitude in the face of her decades-long pain and disability. She said her secret was meditating for half an hour each day. If she missed even one day of meditation, she said, her thoughts turned negative.

## Using the Diligent Detective and the Wise Warrior to Cope with Hard Times

In dealing with a hard time, first our Diligent Detective uses the skill of diagnosis to determine whether to focus first on our mental world or on our physical world. After taking on the role of the Diligent Detective to determine where to start and how to select a kindful option, we take on the role of the Wise Warrior to implement the kindful option we choose.

### kindful option

Kindful actions we can choose to take in our mental and physical world to help us cope with difficult times.

### EXAMPLE

A teenager calls on her Diligent Detective to use the skill of diagnosis and select the kindful options of breathing and gratitude (writing about her thoughts). She then calls on her Wise Warrior to consistently use the kindful options of breathing and writing:

*As a bisexual teenager in 2020, some would think that there would be no trouble at school, and for the most part that is right. Most of the hatred I get is online bullying. Being bullied is very hard on anyone mentally, and I personally started to get very anxious and depressed. One way I would cope through all this is breathing and writing down all my thoughts in a journal. The strategy that helps me the most, I think, is writing down my thoughts so I can really think them all through and realize my self-worth. After writing down all the bad and sad thoughts I am having, I write down any and all positive and happy thoughts I have, for example, things about my friends who support me or productive things that I did that day.*

✦ ✦ ✦

During emotionally challenging times, kindful practices toward ourselves offer significant help. They might not fix our unhappiness, but by helping us be patient and gentle with ourselves, we can soften our pain and reduce confusion, anxiety, and depression.

### EXAMPLE

Jim Doty, a neuroscience professor at Stanford and author of *Into the Magic Shop: A Neurosurgeon's Quest to Discover the Mysteries of the Brain and the Secrets of the Heart*, wrote about a woman who taught him kindful practices he directed toward himself.

Jim grew up in poverty; his father was an alcoholic who would show up from time to time, and his mother was suicidal. As a teenager he learned valuable lessons about mindfulness from a woman who befriended him when he went into a magic shop. The woman was wise and could see Jim needed a friend. Jim tells what he learned from her: She taught him that his negative self-talk was like a radio station. He could use mindfulness to switch to another station, a positive station. He had seen himself as a failure, full of anger at his parents. Using mindfulness to turn to a positive station allowed him to stop blaming his parents and see them as suffering human beings, each struggling with their own demons. He kept listening to his positive radio station. In doing so, over the years he was able to achieve success in his personal life and professional career.

PUT INTO **Practice**

Describe a time when you felt disturbed or in despair from something outside of your control, such as illness, an accident, or loss.

_____

_____

From the viewpoint of the Diligent Detective, describe any coping techniques you read about in this workbook (such as reaching out to others with kindness, the Three-Breath Method, sensing mindfulness, grounding techniques, micropractices, meditation, or skills of action) that might have helped you deal with your feelings:

_____

_____

_____

## PUT INTO **Practice**

If you have a religious/spiritual/cultural practice, describe how it helped you cope with a difficult time in your life.

_____

_____

## PERSONAL **Challenge**

While kindful options can help us in hard times, they can also brighten and enrich our lives during less stressful times. As you read the kindful options in this chapter, identify one you would like to make into a kind habit right away. Near the end of the chapter, there will be a Personal Challenge in which you will be asked to choose one kindful option to turn into a kind habit.

# Kindful Options for Hard Times in Our Physical World

To find kindful options in hard times, we first take on the role of the Diligent Detective to answer this question: What kindful actions can we take in the physical world to reduce our current distress? We will read about four kindful options that might help us cope with our distress:

1. Spend time engaging in pleasant habits and fun activities with those we care about.
2. Engage in pleasant habits and fun activities on our own.
3. Deepen our mindfulness practice.
4. Help others.

## Spend Time with Those We Care About

Making an effort to spend time with those you care about and who care about you: a spouse/partner, friends, family members—especially siblings and parents—and your pet can be very helpful during hard times. Reach out (literally, through physical contact) to people you trust and can be open with. Try to be physically close to those who are protective and caring toward you; for example, share a meal, play games, play sports, dance and sing with others, volunteer, and go to performances, movies, and plays. As much as possible, use the closeness to receive feelings of love, care, and safety. Warm connections are often found within your faith group, spiritual group, tribe, or other type of support group. Warm connections can also be found with close friends or mentors. How do your feelings change when you feel connected to close friends or mentors?

**Religious/Spiritual/Cultural Practices for Hard Times**

For many people, but not all, a source of solace and help during hard times comes from their religious/spiritual/cultural practice. All religions have some form of prayer, guidance for navigating hard times, and access to a faith or cultural leader for worship and counsel (pastor, priest, rabbi, monk, imam, tribal leader, or pujari). In diagnosing our religious/spiritual practice, we might begin in our mental world with prayer and then act in our physical world by following the guidance of our faith and the advice of our faith leader. The Diligent Detective consolidates the information from the guidance and advice of the religion and comes up with a plan of action that the Wise Warrior implements. Guidance and advice can also come from our spiritual or cultural practices. See Appendix B: "Kindness in World Religions" online at https://bit.ly/LH_AppendixB.

*EXAMPLE*

A particularly hard time comes when we grieve over the loss of a loved one, our health, or our mobility. While we will usually not be able to quickly eliminate our grief, kindful options can soften our grief. Sandra, a young woman living away from home for the first time, identified two kindful options she could have used to cope with the passing of her grandmother: meditation and spending time with those she cares about.

*After my grandmother passed away last November, I had a really hard time processing my feelings. She was a hard lady to deal with: stubborn, opinionated, and sometimes not very kind. But I still loved her so much, and she was the first loss I've ever had to deal with. Despite trying to not think about it, I cried a lot. Something that I think would have helped me a lot would have been daily meditation to give myself a time every day where I could let all the conflict in my mind go. I could have also spent more time with those I cared about; talking to the people I trust about what I was dealing with would have been really great.*

 PUT INTO **Practice**

List some people you would be comfortable spending time with during difficult times.

_____

Do you feel you need to have more people who would be available for you to spend time with when times are hard? If your answer is yes, list one or two people you will try to connect with and how you will make that initial contact.

_____

_____

## Engage in Pleasant Habits and Fun Activities on Your Own

While sharing pleasant kind habits and fun activities with those we care about is often the most rewarding, many pleasant kind habits do not require interacting with other people. Drawing, shooting hoops, bicycling, exercising, singing, playing a musical instrument, and spending time in nature are all activities we can enjoy on our own. How do pleasant activities make you feel? How do you feel when there's an absence of pleasure in your life?

To increase the calming effects of these activities and add to your enjoyment, activate your sensing mindfulness and grounding techniques in multiple ways: Tune in to smell and taste by eating foods you enjoy. For visual stimulation, appreciate new spring growth, fall colors, scenic rivers, and mountain landscapes, or wear bright-colored clothing. To engage hearing, listen with your full attention to music or to sounds in a park. Use soft-ears to listen to the hum of multiple conversations. Consider activities that engage multiple senses: watch something upbeat, funny, even inspiring; watch a spotting event; or make a video for friends. How does it feel to be fully attentive and engaged when you use multiple senses?

PUT INTO **Practice**

Read over the lists of pleasant kind habits you were asked to create on pages 70–71 in Chapter 4. Read each one aloud and then write how naming the pleasant kind habit made you feel.

_____

_____

## Deepen Your Mindfulness Practice

When times are really getting us down, we may find it very helpful to focus on intensively engaging activities to get relief from our fears and regrets. For example, if we are walking with constant negative mind-wandering, sensing mindfulness might not sufficiently engage our attention. Instead, we might try listening to music we can lose ourselves in or a very absorbing audiobook, or talking with a close friend.

A time of difficulty is also an opportunity to dig deeper into your mindfulness practice, which can help take your attention off your troubles.

Here are four possibilities to deepen your mindful practice:

### *Intensify Your Three-Breath Practice*

Inhale and exhale very deeply for each breath. Expand your chest to its fullest extension as you inhale, then exhale slowly and completely. If you want, you can simultaneously open your arms and reach outward to further the sense of expansion as you inhale. As you exhale, bring your arms back together in front of you. On the third exhale, form your lips like you are sucking from a straw and keep exhaling until all the air has been pushed out of your lungs.

You might also find useful these four steps of holding your breath as you inhale and exhale:

1. Breathe in as you count to four.

2. Hold your breath as you count to four.

3. Exhale as you count to four.

4. Hold your breath as you count to four.

### Example

Here is how Jason described using breathing to calm himself:

*There have been a lot of times when I'd have a big project due, and I'd be stressing about it on the bus on the way to school. I'd have to just tune everything out and focus on my own breathing for a while. I had already finished [my project], and I froze up the entire night before. I seriously couldn't move over the massive anxiety attack I was having all night. What ended up happening was as soon as our slideshow was over, the teacher complimented me and my partner about how we'd done something different and how he enjoyed how we presented it. From this whole ordeal, I learned that there was nothing to be stressed about and the whole reason I was able to do the slideshow was because of mindful breathing I had done that morning on the bus on my way to school. It's really important to find something that works for each individual that will calm them down in a high-anxiety situation.*

PUT INTO **Practice**

Spend a few minutes going through the four steps to intensify your Three-Breath Practice. Then describe how this intensified breathing made you feel.

## Rotate through Your Grounding Techniques

First, find a comfortable position—you can be upright, sitting, or lying down. Then go through your grounding techniques in any order. Possibly engage soft-touch for several breaths, then shift to soft-ears for several breaths, then sharp-eyes, then soft-eyes. Continue the rotation until you begin to feel relief.

When Jason was riding the bus to school and feeling anxious about the report he had to give, he did more than just the Three-Breath Method. He also rotated through several grounding techniques to ease his worry, beginning with soft-touch: sensing the pressure from sitting on the seat, feeling his hand resting on his leg, and the shifting of his weight as the bus turned. Next, soft-ears: listening to the buzz of conversations, the road noise from the movement of the bus, the sounds of cars driving alongside. Finally, alternating sharp-eyes (focusing on a tear on the seat across) and soft-eyes (widening his peripheral vision to see what was in front and on both sides of him in the bus). Jason reduced his anxiety by rotating through his grounding techniques.

## PUT INTO **Practice**

Spend a few minutes rotating through your grounding techniques. Then describe how rotating through your grounding techniques made you feel.

_____

_____

### Reduce Your Fears about the Future

A third way to deepen your mindfulness practice is to work on reducing your worries about the future. Here we are not referring to the personal fears caused by a frightening medical diagnosis or from grief after losing your pet or a loved one; these fears are instinctual and will take time to process. But when it comes to constant, everyday worries about the future, a mindfulness technique that can bring calm is to tie your breathing to a modification of a line from Rumi's poem "There's Nothing Ahead."[1]

"If you can say 'There's nothing ahead,' there will be nothing there."

As you inhale, say to yourself, "there's no _____" (name the source of the fear that is causing the negative mind-wandering).

As you exhale, say to yourself, "Ahead."

*Example: Pain.* If you are afraid that you will always have the pain that interrupts your sleep at night:

Inhale . . . "There's no pain"

Exhale . . . "Ahead"

*Example: Humiliation.* If you fear humiliation at school or work:

Inhale . . . "There's no humiliation"

Exhale . . . "Ahead"

Repeat this process until you feel your worries begin to release, or you feel you need to try another kindful option.

### Use Visualization

When our mind is consumed with negative self-talk, we can use visualization coordinated with movements of our head to calm our mind. We visualize an image that brings up positive emotions and that involves movement. We link the movement of our head to the motion in our visualization. This visualization with head movement practice is particularly helpful during meditation when the self-talk seems overwhelming. (You can also just visualize without moving your head.) Here are four examples—two are common to most of us, and two not all of us do frequently, if at all.

- Visualize standing at the side of a swing in a playground, watching its back-and-forth motion. As we visualize the swing going to the left, we can move our head up and to the left and then move our head down and then up to the right as the swing moves in that direction.

- Visualize watching a tennis game. During the visualization, we can move our head slightly to the left as one player hits the ball to the left and then to the right as the other player hits the ball back.

- Visualize skiing downhill in powder snow. The powder snow makes skiers feel like they are floating in air. During the visualization we move our head slightly from side to side as we shift our weight from side to side carving into the powder to ski down the mountain.

- Visualize watching a duck feed underwater. First the duck swims down to the bottom of the lake, then the duck swims along the bottom gathering food, then swims back to the top. Finally, it swims on top of the lake back to its starting point. During the visualization we can move our head slightly for each stage: down, across the bottom, up, and across the top back to the original starting point.

PUT INTO PRACTICE **Journal**

For the next 3 days, work on one of the following four ways to deepen your mind-fulness practice: 1) intensify your practice of the Three-Breath Method, 2) rotate through your grounding techniques, 3) reduce your fears about the future, or 4) practice visualization and body movement.

At the end of 3 days, answer the questions on page 292.

## Help Others

Sometimes, when we are in distress, we may find relief by putting in effort to help others in need.

### *Example*

Patrick, a senior at a Jesuit high school, talks about how he was able to soften his grief over the loss of his pet dog, a situation he couldn't alter, by being kind to others who were experiencing their own grief. He did this by volunteering to help others in distress from a huge wildfire that had displaced hundreds of families:

*The year 2020 has been difficult for so many, including my family. Oregon was on fire, and the smoke engulfed the air in the Portland area. But that wasn't the worst part; what really hit me was the loss of my pet Lab of almost 16 years. One day he just wasn't himself, and the next day we took him to the vet, where we learned we needed to put him down that same day. It was one of the hardest decisions collectively we made as a family. I can't remember a memory at the house that he wasn't a part of. That night it was hard to be in the house because it felt quiet and empty. I just needed to get away and figured that I would help those affected by the fires. I headed down to the Oregon State Fairgrounds to volunteer with the American Red Cross to help those displaced by the fires. It was a good release because I was able to throw myself at something else, getting out of my head to help the people who really needed it, because some of them had lost everything.*

# Kindful Options for Hard Times in Our Mental World
## Recognize That Distress Is Not Permanent

When coping with difficult times, we must recognize that our distress is not permanent. When we feel deeply disturbed, we often believe our feeling is a permanent condition when in fact our feelings are constantly changing. Take a moment: How are you feeling right now? Have you felt exactly that same way all day? Did you feel that same way all day yesterday? All week? All year? Of course not; our feelings change. Consequently, even while we are distressed, we can have confidence that relief will arrive, even if at first for only a short time. One way to show how feelings change is to pick a few kind habits—ones that bring enjoyment to you. Do some of them every day and notice how your feelings of enjoyment arise. And if we are stuck in an unhealthy environment for a long period of time, such as a home full of distress, we can soften our negative self-talk by imagining what our life can be like in the future when we will be out of the situation; for example, youth who live in an abusive household and are stuck there until they are 18 can visualize what they will do when they can leave home.

## Ask for Help for Those in Need

Asking for help for others can be a powerful way to draw our attention away from our own disturbed feelings. Pain, worry, and disturbance isolate us. Focusing on the needs of others reminds us that we are not the only ones suffering and can also increase our gratitude and appreciation for the good things we have. Naming individuals also reminds us to be aware of opportunities to act with kindness toward them. All religions include some sort of prayers for help for those in need.

You can ask for help for others by using the Embracing Kindness Meditation described in Chapter 5. Here is a slight variation of that meditation in which you coordinate your breathing with naming people who are having difficulty: As you inhale, say to yourself the name of a person who is suffering, then as you exhale visualize sending peace and ease to that person. For example, say to yourself the person's name as you inhale and then say one of these phrases, or one you create, as you exhale:

> May you be happy and safe.
> May you be healthy, peaceful, and strong.
> May you give and receive appreciation today.
> May you find joy and connection in your day.

You can also send yourself peace and ease. As you inhale, say, "I." Then as you exhale, say an encouraging phrase, for example, "May I be happy and safe." When you say these phrases, what feelings emerge?

**CAUTION**

Skip the following Put into Practice if thinking of the needs of others makes you anxious or makes you feel superior to others whose needs are greater than yours.

PUT INTO **Practice**

Use the Embracing Kindness Meditation coordinating your breathing with naming a person who is having difficulty. Describe how this made you feel.

_____

_____

## Use this New Breathing Exercise

Dealing with hard times is usually stressful. Give yourself a break by trying this new breathing exercise: Inhale through your left nostril and exhale through your right nostril.

Get ready to begin this breathing exercise by exhaling completely.

1. Close your right nostril with a finger on your right hand.
2. Inhale slowly and deeply through your left nostril.
3. Now close your left nostril with a finger on your left hand.
4. Exhale slowly and deeply through your right nostril.

PUT INTO **Practice**

Repeat Steps 1 through 4 ten times. Then describe how the new breathing exercise made you feel.

_____

_____

## Activate Our Gratitude

Experiencing gratitude can bring us relief from our distress. There are many activators for gratitude, such as reflecting in our mind on the importance of the basics: caring relationships, food, shelter, health, and access to education. Going through in our minds all the people we care about and how they care about us can activate gratitude. We can read through our list of pleasant kind habits and reflect on all the other useful things we have learned about mindful kindness. Finally, remembering special times of joy can activate our gratitude; for example, being with close friends and loved ones (including animals), spending time in nature, and being humbled by the kindness of others.

*Experiencing gratitutde can bring us relief from our distress.*

### EXAMPLE FROM AN AUTHOR

When Doug wants to be humbled, he thinks of a woman in his community:

She adopted six severely disabled children from Cambodia and brought them to live with her in her home. He not only appreciates her kindness, but is humbled by her devotion to these children.

✦ ✦ ✦

All kinds of memories of kindness can activate our gratitude. In Chapter 3: "Expand Your Idea of Kindness," we read about two examples of gratitude that resulted from heartfelt kindness: The kindness Honduran Yanelle Cruz received in China and the kindness Latisha and her mother showed to Stephan in high school. Both Yanelle and Stephan could call up these memories to activate their gratitude.

### EXAMPLE

Over the last year, friends had kept moving away, leaving Jacob alone over and over again. Through his ever-shifting seeking of new friends, he learned to be more inclusive toward others, some of whom he had previously ignored. Having made the effort to make friends with those he (and others) had ignored, he had taken the negative situation of losing friends and transformed his loss into a positive change for himself and in the lives of others. Jacob's kindness brought him relief from having lost friends in the past, and thinking of this activates his gratitude for being able to make friends with people who brought new experiences in his life.

✦ ✦ ✦

Another way to activate gratitude for having people who care about us in our lives begins with a smile. We smile and spread the feeling of the smile across our face and imagine it moving down into our chest and abdomen. Then, we visualize someone we care a great deal about. We see their smile. We join our smile to their smile. We do this several times as we feel the gratitude and joy for having that person in our lives. Have you felt joy for having such a person in your life?

## PUT INTO **Practice**

Try one of these three ways to activate your gratitude:

1. Visualize someone you care about as you smile and spread your smile through your body.
2. Think of memories that were joyful, when you were kind to others, or humbled by the kindness of others. Make a list of these memories on a sheet of paper. Keep this list where you can see it daily and practice activating your gratitude by recalling some of these memories.
3. Do a breathing exercise coordinating pleasant memories with your breath: Call a memory to mind as you inhale, and say an inner "thank you" as you exhale. You can repeat this breathing practice for several special memories.

Describe what you did to activate your gratitude and how you felt when you activated your gratitude.

_____

_____

## Turning a Kindful Option into a Kind Habit

Each kindful option gives us a way to respond to disturbing, strong emotions. So think of the kindful options as a kind of insurance that can be called on to help (and even pay benefits) when something goes very wrong. By practicing these kindful options before you are in distress, you will be ready to draw on them when you truly need them. It can be very difficult to learn these kindful options in the midst of a very difficult situation. So, consistently, day after day, employing kindful options not only prepares us for hard times but also turns them into kindful habits that will eventually come to us without effort—improving our relationships, stress management, problem solving, awareness of opportunities to act with kindness, and our ability to experience joy and contentment.

Some people find physical kindness options work better for them, such as spending time with those they care about and engaging in pleasant activities and environments. For others, mental kindness options such as mentally asking for help for others and calling up positive memories are more effective.

## PUT INTO PRACTICE **Journal**

Pick one of the kindful options you want to turn into a habit and, for 3 days, work on making it a kind habit (or better yet a pleasant kind habit!). Write about that experience on page 292.

# Learning from Hard Times

While we will probably never be grateful for feeling disturbed or distressed, we can be grateful for what we learn from those difficult times. As one spiritual teacher (the Dalai Lama) said, "If you lose, do not lose the lesson."

Going through a time of extreme difficulty can increase our empathy and compassion for others, as well as give us greater trust in our practice of mindful kindness and make us more willing to forgive ourselves and others.

### FROM THE OTHER SIDE

Cody, one of Roy's students, suffers from multiple health issues as well as chronic pain. Here, he describes how he took on the mind of the Wise Warrior and was able to continue his practice of mindful kindness in prison:

*The emotions I'm having are anger, depression. The pain and suffering. The long nights lying awake in bed. Can't sleep till I been up so long that my body shuts down, only to wake right back up to pain. The tears. The feel of neglect. I could tell that it was taking me way off my practice. A practice that has made me a strong person. Only just a few weeks ago, I realize this can make me a stronger person. Stop crying. Take a few deep breaths and bring good out of it cause bad ain't getting me nowhere. Yeah. It hurts. But I got to suck it up. I got myself here. Nobody else. So I started being even more kind to all the medical staff and thinking about others [prisoners]. How to help them in any way I can and in doing this, seeing and hearing joy. . . . I have went over some names of people in my life that have tried to help me and that have help me and how they help me. I send them my best and good health be with them. Then I thought about the ones that have just treated me like I was scum on their shoes . . . . I smiled and wished their family wishes of good health and strength. Then I will take me a few deep breaths.*

✦ ✦ ✦

It can be more difficult to feel gratitude for hard times that were caused by another person, such as Roy being abused by his father. As the Catholic Saint Mother Teresa said, "Some people come in our life as blessings. Some come in our life as lessons."

What about forgiving the person who harmed us? Forgiveness means to stop feeling angry or resentful toward (someone) for an offense, flaw, or mistake. So if you don't forgive, that means you will continue feeling angry or resentful toward the person who harmed you. Feeling angry and resentful is negative mind-wandering that can be agitating or even deeply distressing. By forgiving, we eliminate the negative mind-wandering, which improves our mental health and happiness. Forgiveness does not excuse a person's harmful behavior, but allows us to leave the activating memory behind and move on with a healthier mindset.

Sometimes, difficulties open a door to a new opportunity.

### EXAMPLE

Jody Bothe, a counselor, remembers helping a student process disappointment:

*A young man I work with was telling me that he worked for a painting company and recently his boss fired him for reasons that were not clearly explained. The young man was furious, but after sitting a bit and processing together, we came to the realization that it was a gift in disguise. He was better off starting his own business as a young house painter with his own ideas of how to run a business. He now has his own small business and might even add on a few employees over the summer to expand. I personally wonder if the original boss fired him to force him to branch out on his own!*

✦ ✦ ✦

Sometimes difficulties teach us to be gentle and humble with ourselves. When we are not making the progress we would like to make with a problem, there is no point in being angry at ourselves for not making enough progress. We can be grateful we are making progress even if the progress seems slow. Being humble, we realize that working through distress is not easy. It is OK to take a break from trying to work on kindful options to deal with our stress. Later, we can return to our kindful options when we feel better prepared to deal with our difficult situation. If deep distress is relentlessly tightening its grip on our mind and body, we need to seek guidance or treatment from a counselor, therapist, peer, healer, spiritual advisor, or trusted friend.

## EXAMPLE

A famous actor and former WWE wrestler talks about the importance of being able to ask for help:

Dwyane Johnson, The Rock, was entering the University of Miami with great hopes of becoming a star football player. After tearing ligaments in his shoulder during practice, Johnson was benched for an entire season. The injury subsequently sent Johnson into a deep depression that lasted for months. However, while he was working out with his father, his dad told him that he couldn't give up and he had to keep fighting: "You can't dwell on your injury. If you let yourself get stuck there, you're gonna stay stuck there. That thing, that voice in your head, that's fear. It's trying to make you doubt yourself, trying to steal your confidence. But you can't let it. You got to tune it out and keep going." Johnson, speaking of his father's advice to an audience of youth, said, "My dad was just letting me know that I wasn't alone, and that's what I want to share is that you're not alone. If you're going through it and you're struggling and you're depressed, you're not alone, and it's OK to ask for help. Asking for help isn't a weakness. Asking for help is actually our superpower."[2]

## PUT INTO **Practice**

Write about something you learned from a hard time in your life.

_____

_____

How does it feel to know you've had a life lesson and can move on?

_____

_____

# Wrapping Up

This chapter discussed how kindful options can help us cope with difficult times that bring deep distress. Here are options we can take when we're facing hard times:

- Take the perspective of the Diligent Detective to look for ways to actually change our situation and the role of the Wise Warrior to take action in spite of our deep distress.

- Rely on our religious/cultural/spiritual practices and beliefs.

- Be with those we care about and who care about us

- Spend time in positive, engaging, enjoyable activities.

- Deepen our mindfulness practices by intensifying the Three-Breath Method, rotating through our senses, reciting "no _____ ahead," and using visualization and body movement.

- Recognize that distress is not permanent

- Ask for help for those in need.

- Activate our gratitude.

We also can learn from hard times. And if we are proactive, we can try to practice our chosen kindful options before we need them so they will be ready when the hard times come.

PUT INTO **Practice**

Write about how you might respond kindly, and how you might respond unkindly, when you are waiting in a store line that is moving very slowly because the customer in front of you and the clerk are having a long conversation. Or write about how you might respond kindly and how you might respond unkindly when you speak on the phone to a company representative who is not able to help you sufficiently. Think about your responses in both your mental and physical worlds.

Waiting in a store line that is moving slowly

- Kind response _____

  _____

- Unkind response _____

  _____

Speaking on the phone with a customer representative not able to help you

- Kind response _____

  _____

- Unkind response _____

  _____

## ✓ Checking In

Review what you wrote at the end of Chapter 2 for your Kindful Vow and ask yourself how you are following through on each part:

I will be more kindful to myself by . . .

I will be more kindful in all my relationships . . .

I will extend the reach of my kindfulness by . . .

# Time for Reflection

Take a few moments to reflect on the degree to which these practices are benefiting you. On a scale of 0 through 4, how are you feeling about these practices? 0 = Haven't tried it yet; 1 = Hasn't helped yet; 2 = Often doesn't help; 3 = Sometimes helps; 4 = Usually helps

\_\_\_\_\_   Mindful micropractices

\_\_\_\_\_   Building a kind habit

\_\_\_\_\_   Breaking an unkind habit

\_\_\_\_\_   Meditating on a regular basis

\_\_\_\_\_   Sensing mindfulness

\_\_\_\_\_   Grounding techniques

\_\_\_\_\_   Using the kind conversation skills

\_\_\_\_\_   Performing at least one act of kindness by showing appreciation, offering to help, being friendly, or reaching out to those in need

• • •

What are you grateful for today? Think about each statement and then circle Yes or No.

| | | |
|---|---|---|
| I feel grateful for people and pets I care about. | Yes | No |
| I feel grateful for something that went well today. | Yes | No |
| I feel grateful for what I can do with my body and mind. | Yes | No |
| I feel grateful for people who help me and others. | Yes | No |
| I feel grateful for my beliefs that give me purpose and meaning. | Yes | No |
| I feel grateful for having fun and laughter. | Yes | No |
| I feel grateful for the earth and universe. | Yes | No |

• • •

Write about how you have been kind in one of these ways:

- Be friendly
- Show appreciation
- Offer help
- Reach out to those in need

_____

_____

Chapter 12

# Extend the Reach of Your Kindfulness

*Life's most urgent and persistent question is:*
*"What are you doing for others?"*

Dr. Martin Luther King, Jr.

**Before beginning this chapter, for one minute meditate in the way that works best for you.**

A typical self-help book is about helping ourselves, not other people. *Lasting Happiness* is not just a self-help workbook; it is also an "us-help" workbook. We cannot be truly kindful to ourselves without being kind to others because our lasting happiness depends on close, caring relationships with others in and outside of our communities. Being kind to others is easiest with people we know and with people who have a clear need for our kindness. But we also benefit from extending the reach of our kindfulness beyond those close to us.

## EXAMPLE

Angela was a single mom with two young children who relocated to the Austin, Texas area. She was studying to be a nurse online at night while working as a medical assistant at a doctor's office. Her children were enrolled in an elementary school nearby, which worked well for her except on Wednesdays, when the school had early release. Being new to the area, Angela didn't have anyone to babysit her children until she got off work, which put her in a tough situation. She couldn't take time off work because she needed to provide for her family, but no one was able to watch her kids while she was at work. Dr. Ingram heard of Angela's issues finding child care. Dr. Ingram, who had been raised by a single mom herself and had to support herself in medical school, understood how difficult and challenging it can be to raise children on your own. She told Angela to bring her kids to work on Wednesdays, where they could hang out in the staff lounge. Dr. Ingram provided toys, arts and crafts materials, and books to occupy the kids while their mom worked. Angela could check in on her kids and no longer had to take time off work. Dr. Ingram's similar upbringing made it easy for her to empathize with Angela's struggles and extend her kindness to a new employee.

✦ ✦ ✦

With strangers we have little in common with, reaching out with kindness is more challenging. We generally are inclined to reach out to strangers whose background is similar to ours. We have common understandings and experiences that link us together, making it easier to extend our kindness to those who are similar to us.

## EXAMPLE

Think back to Tasha, who had the unkind habit of using her cell phone to withdraw from people because of her feelings of inadequacy. After studying mindfulness, when her feelings of inadequacy in a social setting triggered anxiety, Tasha was able to replace her unkind habit of reaching for her phone with the new kind habit of reaching out in conversation with those nearby. She did this at work, at her church, and at social gatherings. Reaching out was doable because the strangers were all people similar to her, and the kind communication habits described in Chapter 4 gave her the skills to interact. However, in social situations around strangers who were very different, she was too reluctant to reach out; instead, she hid behind her cell phone.

# Extending Kindness to Strangers with Different Backgrounds

Extending kindness to strangers with different backgrounds, beliefs, behaviors, or life experiences is more challenging, as Tasha found. We may not share the same experiences and be less able to empathize with those who differ from us or who treat us poorly. Therefore, it is often difficult to connect with them. Ask yourself: When was the last time I acted with true kindness to a person outside of my community, belief system, or social circle?

 PUT INTO **Practice**

Identify someone with a different background who you have minimal contact with and who you would like to reach out to with kindness. Explain why you think you have not reached out to establish a relationship with them before.

_____

_____

# Steps in Reaching out with Kindness

## — *Key Idea* —

In this chapter, we will focus on reaching out with kindness to persons with significantly different backgrounds and viewpoints than ours, especially those commonly discriminated against in our community

## Obstacles to Developing Empathy and Compassion

So how do we reach out with kindness to people we do not usually have contact with, people with different backgrounds or experiences? We activate our Diligent Detective to help us secure the knowledge to understand and share the feelings of another person (empathy) and to care about their well-being (compassion).

Unfortunately, stress makes us less likely to experience empathy and compassion for others, especially those with different backgrounds and who are discriminated against in our society.* Without compassion and empathy, we are also less likely to look at things from another person's point of view; in other words, we cannot see a situation from their perspective. So the increasing stress youth are experiencing tends to reduce their empathy and compassion for those with different backgrounds and reduce their ability to take the perspective of individuals who are different.

---

* There is evidence that due to greater stress, empathy and compassion among youth have been decreasing. A University of Michigan study, which analyzed data on empathy from almost 14,000 college students gathered between 1979 and 2009, found a 48% decrease in empathy concerns and a 34% decrease in perspective taking, which is the ability to look at things from another person's point of view. Konrath, S. H., O'Brien, E. H., & Hsing, C. (2011). Change in dispositional empathy in American college students over time: A Meta-analysis. *Personality and Social Psychology Review, 15*(2), 180–98. Retrieved from https://pubmed.ncbi.nlm.nih.gov/20688954/

Today's pressures also force many people to live in a bubble of like-minded people. Social media exacerbates these bubbles, forcing us to see messages that reinforce our point of view rather than opening us up to the viewpoints of others. These bubbles can lead to an empathy deficit, which is the root of many of our society's biggest problems.

There is something we can do about it, though. Researchers have shown that a lack of empathy is not an unchangeable trait. Empathy can be developed and strengthened.* In fact, the exercises in this workbook, especially those in this chapter, can help us develop or harness our empathy and compassion for those who are different than us.

## Bias

Bias, which results from a lack of empathy and compassion, causes harm and is a major obstacle to kindness.

> **bias**
>
> Being in favor of or against one thing, person, or group compared with another, usually in an unfair way.

Researchers at the Pew Research Center say that "most humans display a bias against out-groups—people who are different from them."[1] For example, the out-group for Democrats are Republicans. And the out-group for Republicans are Democrats.

In-groups and out-groups can be based on many different factors besides political parties: religion, ethnicity, race, gender, education level, and even the sports teams people favor. If we are to be kind, we must be aware of our biases and work to weaken them. Bias is a major barrier to extending the reach of our kindness to members of our out-groups.

Below are key findings in a study by the Robert Wood Johnson Foundation[2] of discrimination:

- Nearly half (45%) of African Americans experienced racial discrimination when trying to rent an apartment or buy a home.

- 18% of Asian Americans say they have experienced discrimination when interacting with police. Indigenous Americans are much more likely than Chinese Americans to report unfair police stops or treatment.

- Nearly 1 in 5 Latinos have avoided medical care due to concern of being discriminated against or treated poorly.

---

* A *New York Times* article describes an increasing lack of contact among people who have different beliefs and backgrounds. "More and more, we live in bubbles. Most of us are surrounded by people who look like us, vote like us, earn like us, spend money like us, have educations like us and worship like us. The result is an empathy deficit, and it's at the root of many of our biggest problems. There are steps people can take to acknowledge their biases and to move beyond their own worldviews to try to understand those held by other people." The *Times* article makes a very important statement: "Researchers have discovered that far from being an immutable trait, empathy can be developed." Miller, C. C. (n.d.). How to be more empathetic. *The New York Times*. Retrieved from https://www.nytimes.com/guides/year-of-living-better/how-to-be-more-empathetic

- 34% of LGBTQ Americans say that they or a friend has been verbally harassed while using the restroom.

- 41% of women report being discriminated against in equal pay and promotion opportunities.

In earlier chapters, we discussed how to be empathetic to those close to us and, most importantly, to use kindfulness to build kind habits and break unkind habits we direct toward them. In this chapter, we first describe how we can develop empathy and compassion toward people who are different from us, especially those who are subject to our bias. Later in this chapter, we present three steps to weaken our biases.

# Developing Empathy and Compassion for Persons with Different Backgrounds

It can be challenging to show empathy and compassion toward people with different backgrounds when we really know little about them. An important way to develop empathy and compassion toward people with different backgrounds is to take on the role of the Diligent Detective to learn about their experiences, viewpoints, challenges, childhood, and generational traumas. The goal is to develop an understanding of how people's current and past different experiences and challenges can affect their views and behaviors. For example, while watching a favorite television show, compare and contrast the views of the characters with your own views and behaviors. Or while on a bus or train, consider the reactions and behaviors of others compared with your own. We can also learn a great deal from written material, social media, and movies about people who are very different from us.[†]

Below are several examples of what we can learn about people.

## EXAMPLES

### Addiction

Janine had just finished a sociology course during which she saw videos of several former drug users trying to survive in the streets. Addiction was something that had brought great grief to several of her cousins. She wanted to help them, but realized she had mixed feelings towards drug users and did not have much empathy toward them. She wanted to learn more. She found a book that Nicholas Kristof, a reporter for *The New York Times*, wrote about what happened in a small, virtually all-white Oregon community of about 1,200 people when factories shut down

---

[†] Books can be a powerful source of knowledge. Reading fiction can actually increase our empathy (Mar, R. A., Oatley, K., Hirsh, J., dela Paz, J., & Peterson, J. B. [2006]. Bookworms versus nerds: Exposure to fiction versus non-fiction, divergent associations with social ability, and the simulation of fictional social worlds. *Journal of Research in Personality, 40*(2006), 694–712. Retrieved from http://capricorn.bc.edu/moralitylab/wp-content/uploads/2011/11/Mar-et-al-2006_bookworms-versus-nerds.pdf).

New studies show that when people read fiction, their brains really feel like they're entering a new world. The research showed that people are able to identify with people and groups that are actually outside of themselves. It shows that people can relate to people who live lives that are entirely different than their own (Paul, A. M. [2012, March 17]. Your brain on fiction. *The New York Times.* Retrieved from http://capricorn.bc.edu/moralitylab/wp-content/uploads/2011/11/Mar-et-al-2006_bookworms-versus-nerds.pdf).

When reading literature, we are able to understand characters' actions from their interior point of view by entering into their situations and minds. In other words, where we would ordinarily not have access to another person's thoughts, literature gives us a window into the inner thinking of other people. One source of finding books that deal with discrimination or bias is the Good Reads web site: https://www.goodreads/com/list/show/21184.Best_Novels_on_Racism_and_Discrimination

and most good blue-collar jobs disappeared. Kristof described how a toxic combination of drugs and alcohol, domestic violence, school dropout, and unexpected children led to numerous family tragedies. Addictions were common. In one section of the book, the author described a young woman who seemed poised for success. She was the first in her family to graduate from high school, and then she took a job at a telecommunications company, managing databases and training staff. She married and had three children, and for a time was thriving. When her father and sister died, her grief overwhelmed her. A doctor prescribed medications like Xanax, and she became dependent on them. After running out of the prescription drugs, she began smoking meth for the first time when she was 32."I was dead set against it my whole life," she remembered. "I hated it. I'd seen what it did to everybody. My dad was a junkie who cooked meth and lost everything. You would think that was enough." It wasn't. She bounced in and out of jail and lost her kids. Reading the book, titled *Tightrope* (2020, Knopf), gave Janine a much deeper understanding of why so many people in that community had difficulties with drug addiction and other unkind habits. Reading this book was an important step in Janine's development of empathy for people with addictions.

## Refugees

Devin had heard members of his family talking about their resentment about the money the government was spending on foreigners, saying how the foreigners were ruining America. His father believed that the foreigners were taking advantage of the American system by receiving government welfare and did not contribute to the society.

Several members of his soccer team were asylum seekers. Though not very talkative, they seemed to be nice kids, but Devin stayed away from them because of what his family said about immigrants.

One day in a social studies class, the teacher showed a video of a talk given by Ahmed, a refugee who had been a professor of engineering in Syria. His life had almost been destroyed by the civil war in that country. When the war started, Ahmed's family was forced to flee their country and ended up in a refugee camp. After years of waiting in the refugee camp, he and his family were given permission to enter the United States and moved to Arkansas to start a new life. Unfortunately, his engineering credentials were not transferable and he could not work as an engineer. Getting a license to be an engineer would require years of study at an American university, an impossibility because he knew little English and had to earn money to support his family. To provide for his family's needs and save money for his children's education, Ahmed spent years doing two jobs, working nights as a janitor and driving a taxi during the day. Few people appreciated the extraordinary effort and sacrifices he was making for his family. A neighbor of Ahmed's spoke of the number of times he had seen Ahmed treated with disrespect as people assumed he was poorly educated. Ahmed spoke of his gratitude to his new country where his children were thriving in school and would hopefully be professionals who would contribute to their adopted country.

Devin's awareness of the challenges faced by Ahmed increased his empathy. After viewing Ahmed's talk, Devin began to realize the difficulties his teammates and their parents may have experienced. Ahmed's talk help Devin realize he needed to learn more about his teammates' lives.

### Houselessness

During a discussion with some people interested in helping the homeless, Jerry talked about how he developed empathy for a homeless man. Jerry, when he was in college, spent the summers working as a waiter in a resort hotel about 70 miles from New York City. Each summer, the kitchen manager went to a homeless shelter and hired several homeless men to assist in the kitchen. One of the men, Raymond, was assigned to work with Jerry preparing the tables before each meal. After working together for about a month, Jerry noted that Raymond always had books about science with him. Raymond rarely talked with anyone so Jerry asked the manager if he knew anything about Raymond. The manager said that Raymond used to work in a chemistry laboratory, but lost his job after he began drinking too much. Raymond had turned to drinking to deal with his grief after one of his sons had been killed in an auto accident. The drinking led to him losing his job, then his license to drive, and finally to divorce and the streets.

### Body Image

Caitlin writes about the painful life of her obese grandmother who did not meet the norms of a typical grandmother: *Every restaurant I walk into, I am looking to see where she could sit and feel all right. She struggled so much with her size, and she was so ashamed of that, and her deep fear was to be embarrassed in public, to break a chair, or for someone to not understand her accent, or her not be able to read a certain English word. Her shame was her sorrow and her sorrow was her shame. And I was her protector, bearing that for her, concealing it for her, eating it for her, and holding it in my organs. Her secret keeper and her ever-vigilant bodyguard. And now, loyal to a fault, I still look out for her in every seating arrangement, see her hands with the gold rings grip the side of the table as she goes to sit down, the look of pain deeply carved in her face, the swelling and flaking of the flesh on her feet—the hour before we go out, her voice asking me to comb her thin hair and clean it a bit, help her force her feet into shoes.*

Caitlin witnessed how people treated her grandmother, so she saw the impact these judgments made. She showed compassion by helping her grandmother and vowed never to ridicule other obese people. Now she works to show more empathy and compassion to others who are discriminated against.[3]

## PUT INTO **Practice**

Describe a time you felt empathy for a person who is a member of a group you rarely have contact with.

_____

_____

_____

# Ways to Reduce Our Bias: Connect with, Learn from,

# and Extend Kindness

One of the most powerful ways to reduce our bias is to be in contact with members of groups subject to our bias and prejudice.* We will cover three ways to reduce our biases: 1) establish relationships, 2) develop respect, and 3) activate our kindness.

## Step 1: Connect by Establishing Relationships

There are a number of ways we can begin relationships with members of groups who differ from people we regularly have contact with: volunteering, joining activities that bring us in contact with members of these groups, joining diverse groups on social media, and engaging in one-on-one conversations.

### *Volunteering Gives Us an Opportunity to Develop Relationships with People Subject to Bias*

Volunteering is a powerful way to increase empathy, and by helping others we can reduce our own biases. When volunteering, it is important to know that it's a two-way street: It can benefit you as much as the people you are helping.

Volunteering is a great way to make new friends, extend your social networks, and boost your social skills. It can give you, as a young adult, valuable insight into your own strengths and preferences for a future career.

Here are some examples of how volunteering helped reduce bias:

- **Lower-income families**

    Janice, an African American high school senior, heard from a classmate who had just served as a volunteer with Habitat for Humanity that a multi-racial team of Habitat for Humanity volunteers was going to help a Latinx low-income family construct a house. Janice's friend encouraged her to volunteer, but Janice was initially reluctant to join because she had no experience building things and had never worked with a multiracial group. Using her Wise Warrior, she signed up. When she arrived at the site where the house was being built, the father of the family began to teach her how to use a hammer. Over the next months, Janice learned a great deal about building things, but

> Habitat for Humanity is an international organization that gathers volunteers and materials to help low-income families build or renovate a home. Habitat's homeowner families buy the houses that Habitat builds and renovates. Habitat homeowners also invest hundreds of hours of their own labor working alongside volunteers. As a result, Habitat for Humanity houses are affordable to low-income families around the world.

---

* A technical review of over 500 studies with over 250,000 participants interacting with members of another group found a reduction in prejudice and basic in an amazing 94% of the cases. See Pettigrew, T. F., Tropp, L. R., Wagner, U., and Christ, O. (2011). recent advances in intergroup contact theory. *International Journal of Intercultural Relations, 35*(3), 271–280. However, a more recent study did not find the same level of power in reducing racial and ethnic discrimination. Paluck, E., Green, S., & Green, D. (2019). The contact hypothesis re-evaluated. *Behavioral Public Policy, 3*(2), 129–158. doi:10.1017/bpp.2018.25

more importantly developed a strong relationship and respect for the family and the other volunteers, all of whom worked very hard and were extremely cordial and helpful. Her empathy for the family increased as she learned how the family had overcome many obstacles, including a severe injury to the dad that caused him to lose a good job and a fire that destroyed their previous residence.

- **Intellectual and developmental disabilities**

  Adyson became a volunteer with Best Buddies International, an organization dedicated to establishing a global volunteer movement that creates opportunities for one-to-one friendships with individuals with intellectual and developmental disabilities. Here is Adyson talking about her experience: *My life has taken a turn for the better since joining Best Buddies. I have a better understanding that people have differences, but that doesn't mean that they shouldn't be included. I have also grown as a person being more accepting and understanding of others' special abilities. My best buddy, Katie, also says that Best Buddies has changed her life.*

- **Elderly**

  Avon had loved his grandfather, but had not liked visiting him in the nursing home where he lived during the last years of his life. A year after his granddad died, Avon's mom told him that the nursing home was looking for volunteers to keep the old men there company. Avon did not really want to do it, but thought about how his granddad would be proud of him. Using his Wise Warrior to overcome his reluctance, Avon agreed to volunteer. He spoke with the nursing home director, who arranged a schedule for Avon to come and visit with the men during the afternoons when several of them watched baseball together. Over the weeks, Aaron learned about the men's courage in how they had dealt with the deaths of their spouses and old friends. He watched them deal with disabilities without complaining. He became particularly friendly with a man who spoke with him about the mistakes he had made in his life and how his children almost never visited him. His mom was surprised that her son had developed such a high degree of empathy and compassion for his new friends.

 PUT INTO PRACTICE **Journal**

Find volunteering opportunities that may bring you into contact with people of different backgrounds. Pick the possibility that most appeals to you. This is a good opportunity to ask friends or teachers if they can help you find volunteering opportunities. If you are unable to volunteer, try joining a Facebook group where diverse groups of people gather, such as your local homeless support group.

On page 292, write about how you will take advantage of this volunteer opportunity.

## Five Suggestions for Having a Conversation with Someone from a Different Background

When working to establish a relationship with a person from a different background, be sure to be respectful, communicating your genuine interest in what the person has to say. Chapter 4 described kind communication habits and guidelines for having a caring conversation (and unkind conversation habits to avoid). Here are several additional suggestions:*

- **Be curious.** The less you talk, the more opportunities you have to listen. Asking a lot of good questions increases the chance that you'll understand the other person's views and communicates respect to the speaker.

- **Learn to use the phrase, "Can you please tell me more about . . ."** You don't even need to formulate a question—just invite the other person to tell you more about the topic that you would like to better understand.

- **Learn to withhold judgment.** Empathetic listening means learning what it's like to walk in someone's shoes before you *form an opinion about their beliefs*. This doesn't mean you can never assess the merits of a viewpoint. Rather, it means listening with a genuine desire to understand.

- **Learn to stop your mind from pre-generating responses or rebuttals.** When having a conversation, we may invest more mental energy on what we're going to say rather than on what we're hearing. Empathetic listening means turning off or turning down the part of the brain that pre-generates responses as the other person is sharing. Instead, focus on listening and understanding well.

- **Converse with respect.** Remember the basic kind conversation skills. Do not interrupt. Use appropriate body language. Maintain eye contact if it is culturally appropriate.

## — Role-Play —

With a partner, one of you take the role of a person from a different background who you are meeting for the first time. Role-play having a caring conversation. Describe how it went when you did the role-play.

_____

_____

_____

_____

---

* Here are links to two articles that contain more in-depth information about conversation skills:
  http://mem.intervarsity.org/blog/secret-connecting-people-different-us
  https://www.lifehack.org/906008/how-to-improve-listening-skills

*Engaging in Activities and Online Content That Bring You in Contact with People of Different Backgrounds*

Consider participating with organizations or in activities that will bring you into contact with people from different backgrounds. As noted earlier, connecting with members of groups subject to our bias is possibly the best way to reduce our bias. For most of us, this will involve activating our Wise Warrior to fight our excuses for not engaging in these types of activities. Here are a few possibilities:

- Join a gym that has a diverse group of members.
- Join a recreational sports team. Most park departments have leagues for those of us who are not good athletes as well as for the physically talented.
- Take a fun class that attracts a diverse group of students; e.g., salsa dancing.
- Attend music or art events that will attract a diverse audience.
- Get involved in a campaign on an issue important to a diverse population.
- Attend a cultural event such as an Indigenous event that is open to the public.
- Join a civic or church club that attracts a diverse group of participants.

You can also look at websites that provide listings of different activities and events. Be a Warrior to fight your discomfort to engage in a new activity, but do not be a foolish Warrior. If you are nervous about attending something, or should be nervous about attending, consider asking a few friends to come along with you. You can also start online by joining groups, looking for virtual cultural events, or watching live streams of people with different backgrounds and views from you.

# Step 2: Develop Respect

One of the most powerful ways to honor a member of a group different from us is to show respect for the person or group. Respect undermines bias. It is possible, but difficult, to feel bias against a person you respect. Sometimes. Respect is developed through contact with members of a different group.

## *EXAMPLE*

About 40 years ago, when he was young, Jerry was doing a social justice volunteer project, but needed to earn some money. He got a job in a large department store, on the crew of 20 whose job it was to mop the floors. All the workers besides Jerry were African American, and almost all of them also worked the night shift in a nearby car factory. Many were earning money to pay college tuition for their children.

The first few days Jerry was mopping, he could barely move his arms after working for just two hours. Despite their differences, his coworkers saw his suffering and came to his aid, patiently showing him over several days how to swing the wet mop efficiently. Even though he was leading a much different life from these men, after a while they treated him as part of their team. Jerry developed a lifelong respect for these men, the challenges they faced, and the kindness they showed him.

### EXAMPLE FROM AN AUTHOR

Doug learned respect for an unhoused woman picking up litter along the street:

*One day I was walking home and noticed an unhoused woman picking up litter on the street. "Wow! Thanks for helping pick up trash. Do you do this often?" I asked. She replied, "Whenever I see trash on the street, I try to pick it up. I can't contribute much to the community, so this is one thing that I try to do in order to give back." Her response lingered with me. I realized that she is an active member of the community. She takes pride in her city and was doing her part to help out. I grew to respect her and realize that she is a proud community member like me.*

### EXAMPLE

During the summer of 2020, people of many backgrounds demonstrated, protesting the murder of George Floyd and violence experienced by other Black Americans due to police brutality. Anza, a White teen, attended these demonstrations after hearing an African American classmate speak about the effects of intentional and unintentional acts of racism. Her classmate explained that being Black is like being in a chess game where you're the pawn that will be sacrificed because your life doesn't really matter at all to the game. Anza said she had never thought in those terms before and that hearing the speeches helped her understand the challenges faced by African Americans and other minorities impacted by the policing system. She respected how her schoolmate was dealing with those challenges.

### EXAMPLE FROM AN AUTHOR

Doug learned respect for his incarcerated friends:

*Throughout this workbook, we've been reading about the experiences of Roy, Tad, Cody, and John, in their own words. By now, perhaps, like me, you can see them as human beings who were abused over and over as children and became abusers themselves as adults. Yet they've learned to transform themselves into kinder, more mindful, and compassionate men, despite the fact that three of the four will never leave prison. I now respect these men because of the ways they have transformed themselves from being abusers to being kindful practitioners.*

### FROM THE OTHER SIDE

Tad, Roy, and others in our partnership expanded their circle of kindfulness to include prison staff, which seemed to benefit the staff in an unexpected way. As the guards and nurses experienced kind treatment from these prisoners, it became easier for the prison staff to be less aggressive and to respond with prosocial emotions like kindness, compassion, and gratitude to the prisoners.

I witnessed this firsthand when my wife Linda and I flew from Oregon to Arkansas to visit Roy, who was suffering from health problems. While we were talking to Roy in the visiting area through 4-inch-thick bulletproof glass, a burly, tough-looking sergeant poked his head into the room. He politely interrupted our conversation to ask if we could please encourage Roy to eat more so he would stop losing weight.

The kindness shown by the prison staff benefited not only the prisoners but also the staff themselves, whose health is harmed by the stress of working in a prison. The suicide rate for prison guards is nearly 40% higher than the average for all other professions. Longtime prison guards have an average life expectancy about 20 years less than the general public. Acting with kindness can build resilience in powerful ways. That's why cultivating kindness and compassion among prison workers is vital for the well-being not only of the prisoners, but also the staff.

✦ ✦ ✦

Once you have started connecting with members of groups who are different than you, you will start to develop new ways of thinking about them. You will no longer be reliant on stereotypes and the media's portrayal of people. You are breaking down your bias and developing a new healthy and respectful belief system.

## PUT INTO PRACTICE **Journal**

Earlier in this chapter you read about developing empathy, which is also a way in which we can develop respect for members of groups we are biased against. Here are some of the different ways you can learn about a group you are biased against: read a book, watch videos, read magazine articles, listen to talks, have personal contact. Identify a group you are biased against and use one of these ways to learn more about them.

A week from now on page 293, name the book, article, talk or other activity you will be learning from, and tell why you selected this way to learn.

## Step 3: Activate Your Kindness

Listening to stories of kindness can teach and inspire us to extend the reach of our kindness to those in serious need, especially those who are subject to bias.

### EXAMPLE

A stranger is kind to a young transgender youth:

*I knew at an early age that I was different. Being poor was one thing; being transgender was a layer deeper. Rural Texas didn't create much space for a kid like me, and because I had lost my mother in a tragic car accident at a young age, most people just thought I hadn't been taught how to be a proper woman.*

*I found myself, at 16, standing in an orchestra audition room. The flute I'd borrowed from my high school was resting inside my sweaty palms. My band director had told me that my talent and skill were enough that I could potentially win a scholarship to a large public university in our state, and he sat with me as I wrote an email requesting information about scholarship auditions. I took one breath in before striking my first note in front of a panel of professors. I let my final note echo in the room before I exited to the waiting area.*

*"Are you here alone?" a woman said, peering at me kindly. She had short red hair and a gentle smile.*

*I replied that I was. She asked me how I thought I did, where I was from, how old I was. Rather than seeing me as a transgender youth, she saw how I was similar to her own children—a high schooler who loved band and the joy of music.*

*Long story short, I got the scholarship, and she offered to take me into her home like one of her own kids. I lived with her and her family for close to a year, and during that time she helped me fill out my FAFSA and drove me back and forth to community college so I could take prerequisite courses. Moments and connections like these are what changed my life—adults who gave me opportunities, who sat with me and listened, who helped in the small ways they could.*

### EXAMPLE

If you're homeless, getting to school can be challenging, especially if you need to take public transportation. Most homeless students cannot afford a bus pass A high school student took action by setting up a donation box to purchase bus passes for students who could not afford them. Many teachers and students donated money. The money was distributed to homeless students in a very private way so that no one felt uncomfortable. It was a win-win in the end for both the givers and receivers. One senior wrote a note to those who donated, letting them know how what they had done had not only helped her to get to school, but more importantly, had given her a signal that she was not alone in the world and there were people who could help her.

### EXAMPLE

Celebrities being kind to low-paid workers who lost their jobs due to the COVID-19 pandemic:

NBA stars Giannis Antetokounmpo from the Milwaukee Bucks, Blake Griffin from the Detroit Pistons, and Kevin Love from the Cleveland Cavaliers each pledged $100,000 to aid employees at their local arenas.[4] New Orleans Pelicans player Zion Williamson is paying employee salaries for 30 days.[5] Golden State Warriors owners, players, and coaches committed $1 million to a disaster relief fund for employees.[6]

✦ ✦ ✦

While most of us do not have millions of dollars to donate, we can find opportunities to help with acts of kindness. For example, in South Dakota, two teens washed and detailed cars in a parking lot over the summer to raise over $3,500—every cent of which they donated to a nonprofit organization that seeks to improve the quality of reservation life through education and engagement with the Lakota people. During the pandemic, many people in New York City were highlighted in the media when they donated time to shop for the elderly who could no longer safely go to the grocery store.

When we are reaching out with kindfulness to others, it can be easy to be overwhelmed by their suffering. When we learn about how COVID-19 killed disproportionate numbers of poor people or about the hardships of being unhoused, we might experience guilt and shame. The guilt and shame might make us so uncomfortable that we switch our main goal from helping the poor get vaccinated or securing shelter for the unhoused to getting rid of our uncomfortable feeling of shame. The following example reminds us to keep our focus on being kind to others rather than worrying about getting rid of our shame.

*EXAMPLE*

In her 20s, Berkley Carnine's social justice organizing focused on supporting Navajo elders being forced to relocate from their tribal lands. One of Berkley's activities was to bring non-Indigenous volunteers to help the elders continue their traditional way of life. Here is what Jordan Flaherty said about his interview with Berkley in his book *No More Heroes: Grassroots Challenges to the Savior Mentality*:

*Berkley Carnine often sees a pattern among non-Indigenous volunteers. They are confronted with the deep injustice of Native American genocide and the lasting impacts of the generational trauma, and don't know how to deal with those feelings. That produces guilt and shame, which then trigger another set of emotions. "I'm feeling bad, and I want to be able to take some action and alleviate that bad feeling." So then the goal becomes not alleviating the suffering of others but alleviating one's own suffering.*[7]

Instead of dwelling on our own suffering, we need to be kind to others and do so with respect and kindness.

PUT INTO PRACTICE **Journal**

You can activate your kindness by acting in these ways to members of groups you are biased against: be friendly, show appreciation, or give help. A week from now be prepared to describe how you are going to activate your kindness towards members of a group you are biased against by doing one or more of the following: be friendly, show appreciation, give help.

Write what you will do on page 293.

# Understanding Explicit and Implicit Bias

Let's look at bias in more detail. There are two recognized types of bias, explicit bias and implicit bias.

### explicit bias

A person with **explicit** bias is very clear and conscious about their negative feelings and attitudes toward members of a particular group.

### implicit or unconscious bias

A person with **implicit** or **unconscious bias** does not realize that they have negative attitudes toward a particular group, but at times acts negatively and in a discriminatory manner toward that group.

## Explicit Bias

Explicit (or conscious) negative bias can occur when a person has no or almost no empathy for members of a group and can lead to harmful thoughts and actions directed at members of that group. Extreme examples of explicit bias include verbally and physically attacking people because of the color of their skin, their sexual orientation, their language, their nationality, or their religious and political beliefs. Extending the reach of our kindness to include active racists and other members of hate groups is too difficult a challenge to address in this workbook. However, we do encourage those who feel comfortable to use the tools in this workbook with extremists in their lives.

Less extreme but still very damaging are times when a person actively supports policies that discriminate against members of the targeted group, denying them equal opportunity and a positive and safe environment. While this type of explicit bias does not involve physical violence, the effects are still damaging. It is important to examine the laws, people, and policies we support through a kindness lens. Our support of policies is also an extension of our kindness to others, especially marginalized people.

Racial bias is particularly widespread. In a survey, Non-Hispanic Black (84%) and Hispanic (72%) and Non-Hispanic Whites (59%) said racism is widespread in the United States. Fortunately, some measures of explicit bias show large decreases, for example, in 1958 only 4% of White Americans approved of Black-White marriages; today 87% of White Americans do. Another example is that in 1937 only 33% of Americans believed that a qualified woman could be president; in 2015, 92% endorsed the possibility.[8]

### EXAMPLE

Kindness and mindfulness can help some people in dealing with explicit bias directed toward them. A young indigenous leader who read *Lasting Happiness* commented:

*In my experience, these techniques have been the only things that allow me to cope with bias and prejudice against myself or marginalized groups: Viewing people participating in racism with kindness is difficult, but it can preserve your own ability to cope with these issues. Most of the time I am able to look at the generational history, trauma, education, etc., of people involved in racism and hate groups and find*

*some understanding as to why they do what they do. "It is not their fault" in a way. Me being angry with*
*them does not solve their racism; being kind preserves the chance for connection with them, and in turn*
*the chance for storytelling and communication that may reduce their bias.*

## Implicit Bias

Implicit (unconscious) bias refers to situations in which a person, while saying they are supportive of a particular group, takes actions that are harmful to members of that group. The harm of implicit bias occurs in all aspects of our life, including hiring, promotions, career options, on social media, and in the workplace.*

While outwardly we may say and even believe that we feel positive toward a group, our actions at times indicate we have negative feelings and beliefs about that group. Most of the time we are not aware of how often what we say we believe does not fit with what we actually do. For example, many White people believe they are not biased toward people of color because they have acquaintances who are people of color and they support many initiatives that try to help people of color. But if they carefully examine their actions on a personal level, they will find they have implicit biases.

### EXAMPLE

Bridget's family prided itself as being antiracist. Bridget went to a special public school in New York City with kids from all races and backgrounds. Bridget's mother bragged to her friends about the antiracism policy of the school. However, her mother did something that really troubled Bridget. When Bridget brought over friends to visit who were African-American, her mother acted much differently than when she brought over White friends. When Bridget confronted her mother about this, her mother explained that she was worried that because of their poverty these friends might steal something from the house if they had an opportunity. Bridget's mother had assumed the kids were poor, which was wrong—their parents were professionals. Bridget's mother assumed that because of their race, the children were poor. Her mom's actions showed implicit bias.

✦ ✦ ✦

Finding out that we have implicit (unconscious) biases against certain groups of people can make us feel many things, from denial to shame, but acknowledging our bias is an important first step on the road to kindness to all. Fortunately, implicit anti-gay, anti-black, and anti-dark-skin attitudes have all shifted toward neutrality (in other words, less bias). In contrast, negativity toward the elderly and people with disabilities has changed very little.[9]

---

* According to an American Bar Association article, "In a workplace environment, unconscious biases can affect hiring and promotion decisions, work assignments, and career tracks, and unfortunately can result in hostile work environments and discrimination. These biases can also cause problems and damage relationships, as well as affect the reputations of businesses. In addition, these implicit biases have deadly consequences when they affect such individuals as police officers, who must assess situations quickly and make life-and-death decisions—decisions that may be the result of an implicit bias." Steinhauser, S. (2020, March 16). *Everyone is a little bit biased.* American Bar Association. Retrieved from https://www.americanbar.org/groups/business_law/publications/blt/2020/04/everyone-is-biased/

## PUT INTO **Practice**

Do you have an implicit bias? To what group is it directed toward?

---

# Beginning to Address Our Implicit Biases

Understanding our implicit biases and the damage they cause, and having developed some empathy and compassion for those subject to our biases, we will be more able to reduce the harm we cause because of our biases. Confronting our implicit biases will take a major effort. Fortunately, there are a number of ways we can begin to address our implicit biases today: training programs, online learning materials or activities, talking to peers and trusted adults about bias, mindfulness, and embracing mindful meditation.

## Training Programs

Over the past decades, a number of programs have been developed to help people become aware of and confront their biases. If you enter "learning not to be biased" or "training programs for bias" into a search engine, you will find many resources to help you begin your journey to confront your biases and increase kindness to all. For example, the website wikiHow presents an overview of steps you can take as you begin to confront your biases.*

One book dealing with the pain of racial bias, written for both White and Black populations, comes from Resmaa Menakem, an African American therapist, who has focused on the distress that systematic racism has caused Whites as well as African Americans. His book, *My Grandmother's Hands—Racialized Trauma and the Pathway to Mending Our Hearts and Bodies*, works to aid the reader in understanding the effects of racial bias on both groups. It contains a number of exercises for White Americans designed to make them aware of their unconscious bias toward African Americans. Here is one exercise:

> You are invited to an African-American coworker's wedding reception. When you arrive—a bit late—you discover that you are one of over 300 guests. As you stand in the doorway, you scan the room. You are the only non-Black person in the hall. Even the servers are all Black. You feel a hand touch your shoulder. You turn and see an unfamiliar face, a smiling, middle-aged Black man. He says, laughing a bit, "Go on in. We don't bite."
>
> Pause. What do you notice in your body right now?[10]

When doing this exercise, Doug reported, "I experienced a tightening of my chest, suggesting that I have an unconscious bias toward Black Americans, which surprised me given my close working relationship with Black educational leaders around the country early in my career. My reaction is probably the result of my unconscious bias, which may have stemmed from my childhood in an area of Southern Illinois that had a good deal of racial prejudice."

---

* See https://www.wikihow.com/Overcome-Unconscious-and-Hidden-Biases

A primary purpose of *My Grandmother's Hands* is to provide exercises to make Whites aware of their biases and to increase their willingness and likelihood to make efforts to reduce those biases. By reducing their biases, they can better act with genuine respect and kindness.†

# Mindfulness

Mindfulness can help us become aware of our implicit biases. Throughout each day, we come in contact with many people. Often, we have a split-second reaction toward a person that arises and quickly disappears, all in a fraction of a second. Our reaction may be positive: friendly person, important person, good-looking person, safe person. Or it may be negative: dangerous person, weird person, lazy person, racist person. Using mindfulness, we can become aware of what goes through our mind during these split-second reactions. These reactions can be indicators of our implicit bias. Using mindfulness, we can become conscious of these split-second reactions, which may help us identify our implicit or unconscious biases and begin to work on them. For example, as we walk down the street, sit on a bus, or stand in line at a store, our biases can quickly arise based on a person's appearance or actions. Usually these thoughts last for less than a second and then we move on to other thoughts. But these reactions can help us to identify our biases, which are likely to be many: biases based on attractiveness (pretty or ugly), skin color (not my skin color), type of clothing (worn out), facial expressions (anger), and grammar (ignorant).

We have to be very mindful to notice these split-second biased reactions because they are usually unconscious. We must actively attend to our internal feelings to be able to identify these biased reactions.

### EXAMPLE

When Larry explained to his friend Jackson that we often have biased thoughts we are not aware of, Jackson disagreed; he insisted that he did not have biased thoughts based on people's race, appearance, etc. About six months later, when the friends met again, Jackson said he had been more mindful of his reaction and thoughts and was surprised to realize that in fact, biased thoughts often came into his mind. Larry said that mindfulness did not stop his biased thoughts from arising, but mindfulness did in fact start him on the path to being aware and kept him from adding negative thoughts on to his initial reaction and from acting in an unkind way because of his thoughts.

 PUT INTO PRACTICE **Journal**

For the next 3 days, try to notice when you are having any biased reactions. Make a note on your phone or on a piece of paper when you have a split-second biased reaction.

On page 293, describe a few of the biased thoughts and write about whether you think those are implicit biases you have. Tell if you added negative thoughts to feed the bias or acted in an unkind way because of the bias.

---

† This discussion does not address how to deal with racial bias. For a detailed example of how individuals can work to unlearn racial biases, read Chapter Eight in *My Grandmother's Hands*.

## Embracing Kindness Meditation

If we realize we have biases toward a group and are ready to begin work to change those biases, one action we can do is to use Embracing Kindness Meditation (introduced in Chapter 5). During the meditation, we can extend our positive thoughts to include targets of our bias. Here's how: After focusing our Embracing Kindness Meditation on yourself, loved ones, and friends, shift your focus to those against whom you are biased. Visualize a member of the group you are biased against. Send thoughts of kindness to them as you breathe in and then breathe out any unhappiness they may have. Here are some phrases you might use to send kindness as you inhale. Say them with feeling.

- May you be happy and safe.
- May you be healthy, peaceful, and strong.
- May you find healing from your challenges and trauma.
- May you give and receive appreciation today.

Inhale kindness and exhale unkindness for the person until you have a warm or at least neutral feeling toward that person. Then bring them into your awareness, envisioning them with perfect wellness and inner peace.

 PUT INTO PRACTICE **Journal**

Pick a group toward which you have implicit bias. Identify an individual in that group and include that person in your positive thoughts through several Embracing Kindness Meditation sessions. What phrases did you use in your meditation? How did it feel to include that person in your meditation?

After 3 sessions, write about what happened on page 293.

# Wrapping Up

Our world is filled with people of different backgrounds, interests, viewpoints, history, and races. But most of us are reluctant to try to reach out with kindness to them because they are so different or because we were taught they were different. The greatest challenge is reaching out to those who are subject to our bias. In this chapter, we learned the importance of and ways to develop empathy for those who differ from us, especially those subject to our bias. Next came three steps: connect, develop respect, and activate kindness. Two types of bias were described (explicit and implicit), followed by suggestions for beginning to deal with implicit bias.

# ✔️ *Checking In: Revisiting Your Plan to Break an Unkind Habit*

At the same time as we are extending the reach of our kindfulness, we must not forget to continue to weaken our unkind habits. Turn to pages 290–291 and read your in-depth plan for weakening an unkind habit. Then come back here and answer these questions.

How have you progressed in implementing the plan? What's worked and what hasn't?

_____

Has anyone noticed that you are weakening your unkind habit?

_____

Do you need to make any changes to the plan after reading this chapter? If so, what will you do differently in the future?

_____

_____

Did you display your plan so you can easily see it?

_____

Have you thought about adding reminders on your phone or on sticky notes, such as using three breaths or sensing mindfulness?

_____

If you don't see progress yet, don't worry about it. Weakening unkind habits takes time. If you need to, put your plan away and take a break from working on it. If after taking a break, you still feel your plan is not going well, you might review the section titled "Four Steps for Making Habits Stick" in Chapter 6. If you try those steps with the mindset of the Wise Warrior and still feel frustrated, you might want to abandon your plan and create a new plan.

## Time for Reflection

How would you rate your comfort zone on a scale of 1–4 (1 being least comfortable and 4 most comfortable) when:

   a.  You see someone on a corner holding a sign saying "I'm hungry"?  1, 2, 3, 4
   b.  You pass by a group of loud teenagers of a different race on the street walking toward you and don't know any of them?  1, 2, 3, 4
   c.  You need to walk through a wooded path alone to get to your destination?  1, 2, 3, 4
   d.  You see a line of people waiting in line for a meal at a shelter?  1, 2, 3, 4
   e.  You see a gathering of LGBTQ youth?  1, 2, 3, 4

    f.   You see a political rally of a candidate you do not support?  1, 2, 3, 4

    g.   You see someone in a wheelchair who seems to need help opening a store door?  1, 2, 3, 4

    h.   You see someone hitchhiking?  1, 2, 3, 4

    i.   You see a dog that seems to be lost?  1, 2, 3, 4

    j.   You see an Indigenous person on a reservation drinking and making a scene?  1, 2, 3, 4

Which of your uncomfortable responses would you like to change? How might you do that?

## ☑ *Checking In: Useful Kindful Practices*

Look at the list below of some of the kindful practices you've learned. Put a checkmark by the kindful practices that are most useful in your life.

_____ Meditation

_____ The Three-Breath Method

_____ Sensing mindfulness

_____ Engaging in kindful conversations

_____ Grounding techniques

_____ Mindful micropractices such as leaving an orderly space, cleaning up after eating, and taking out the garbage

_____ Asking for help for those in need

_____ Calling up memories of joy and gratitude

_____ Taking on the role of a Diligent Detective

_____ Taking on the role of a Wise Warrior

_____ Taking on the role of a Kindful Practitioner

_____ Getting together more frequently with someone you care about who needs your attention

_____ Remembering to refer to your pleasant kind habits list for ideas on how to be engaged/have fun

_____ Using kind conversation skills

_____ Performing at least one act of kindness by showing appreciation, offering to help, being friendly, or reaching out to those in need

Give an example of how you have recently applied one of these kindness skills:

- Be friendly
- Offer help

- Show appreciation
- Reach out to those with serious needs

_____

_____

Chapter 13

# "Right Now" Is All We Have— Make the Present Moment Kindful

*Stop acting as if life is a rehearsal. Live this day as if it were your last. The past is over and gone. The future is not guaranteed.*

Wayne Dyer

**Before beginning this chapter, for one minute meditate in the way that works best for you.**

Imagine you are on a train leaving one station and traveling to the next. Many of us think of our lives as being on a train: The previous station is our past, and the train we are on is moving to the next station, our future.

But our past exists only in the present moment. Think about it. Our past, which contains all that has happened to us, is what makes us who we are right now and is there for part of the present moment. Similarly, everything we expect, anticipate, hope for, or dread about the future is also part of who we are right now, and so it is also part of the present moment. We live **our lives in current moments that are strung together to create our entire life.** To put it another way, **the present moment is all we have. Because this is all we physically have, it is important to find and practice the thoughts, actions, and words we want to bring into these present moments to make them healthy for ourselves and others.** We are not guaranteed more time than this present moment. So let's make the best of the present moments **and fill them with kindness.** For example, eating mindfully allows us to fully appreciate the tastes and textures of a ripe, juicy orange. And being kind in the present moment releases those feel-good chemicals.

## "In a Moment, Life is Gone"

Doug was writing at a table overlooking the McKenzie River when he heard a loud splash. He looked up and saw an osprey (a large hawk-like bird) lifting skyward, holding a fish in its talons. Watching the osprey carrying away the fish reminded him of this teaching: "In a moment, life is gone." That moment had come for the fish, as it will for all of us. He never felt more keenly that our entire life exists in the present moment.

### — Key Idea —

The previous chapters provided practices to allow us to be kindful in the more challenging moments of our life. The purpose of this chapter is to shine a spotlight on the idea that each moment of our life is of great importance—there is physically nothing more than this present moment for each of us. So, in each moment, our decision to be kindful or not is how we are living our entire life. And living a kindful life is what brings us close, caring relationships and lasting happiness.

What we can do is frequently ask ourselves this question: "How can I be kindful right now?" The answer is not in the form of spoken words, but in our actions, beliefs, and thoughts. Are we coping as best we can with an upsetting situation? Are we enjoying this moment to the fullest? Are we doing what needs to be done in this moment? Are we honoring our families, communities, and ancestors with what we are doing in this present moment?

The opportunity to be mindful in the present moment arises within every moment, including moments of unhappiness. For example, we have chores we prefer not doing, such as cleaning the toilet. When cleaning the toilet, we can let negative mind-wandering dominate our thoughts—thinking about who should actually be cleaning the toilet (or about how we don't have time to waste doing this). Or we can choose to be a kindful practitioner by making toilet cleaning a mindful micropractice, attending to the feel of the toilet brush as we clean the toilet and thereby giving our mind a rest. Through our actions and thoughts, we answer this question every moment: "How can I be kindful right now?"

*FROM THE OTHER SIDE*

Tad wrote about the present moment, using his painting of a rose with thorns as a metaphor:

*I started out using Skittles and M&Ms for the colors in the paintings because I was limited in art supplies. But later I saw a teaching in using candy as paint: "Utilizing what is available around us at all times." What the present moment gives us—be mindful and utilize it, even if it's candy or a small prick from the thorn of a beautiful rose that draws blood. The thorns are there to remind us not to grasp just for the beauty in life, but to be mindful of all that is around us. Don't just desire instant gratification in life, but be mindful of every opportunity we encounter or create.*

 PUT INTO **Practice**

### A New Breathing Exercise

Mindful breathing exercises are excellent ways to fully experience the present moment. This breathing exercise is very similar to the one you practiced in Chapter 11. The title of this exercise is: Inhale through your right nostril and exhale through your left nostril.

To begin this exercise, exhale completely.

1. Close your left nostril with the thumb of your left hand.
2. Inhale slowly and deeply through your right nostril.
3. Now close your right nostril with a finger on your right hand.
4. Exhale slowly and deeply through your left nostril.

Repeat Steps 1 through 4 ten times.

# Find Your Purpose

**sense of purpose**

> The reason for why we act and think the way we do.

Having a sense of purpose helps us identify things that are important to us. It serves as an internal guide for how we want to live our life. A number of international studies report that youth who have a positive sense of purpose have greater satisfaction in life, better health, and a longer life.[1] Unfortunately, most youth report that they don't have a sense of purpose. One study found that only 70 of 270 youth aged 12 to 20 reported having a purpose.[2] According to Bill Damon, author of *The Path to Purpose: How Young People Find Their Calling in Life*, "The biggest problem growing up today is not actually stress, it's meaninglessness."[3] The implication is clear for youth: There is great value in having a clear, positive, and healthy purpose. We can choose to make our purpose being a Kindful Practitioner throughout the day.

# Let Mindful Kindness Drive Your Life

A way to understand the central role that mindful kindness can play in living a life with purpose is to think of how the parts of a car and our roadways help us to get to where we desire to go.

Our purpose—living a life of mindful kindness—is a roadmap for the car and driver. Our kindful practices include the steering wheel that allows us to move toward kind habits and the brakes that stop us as we approach unkind habits. Health is our engine. It allows us to speed up in building kind habits and keep going when times get hard. Forming caring relationships requires many parts: headlights to clearly see where we are going and to allow others to see us clearly, an exhaust system to let off unkind, unhealthy emotions and thoughts, lubrication to smooth out differences that are causing friction, and the cooling system that brings the temperature down when we are overheated. The benefit of our kindfulness is the fuel that gives us energy to keep moving forward. Recreation is the stereo system that can lighten our mood and energize us. The community is the system of streets and highways that allow our car to travel from place to place.

*A way to understand the central role that mindful kindness can play in living a life with purpose is to think of how the parts of a car and our roadways help us to get to where we desire to go.*

What happens when we lack purpose and don't have a roadmap for where we are going? Potentially, the driver never starts the car or drives around aimlessly. What if we are driven by anger? An angry driver races the engine, brakes abruptly, honks the horn at other drivers, and may be under the influence of alcohol or drugs. The potholes aren't visible until it is too late.

### EXAMPLE

Alicia was a 16-year-old who lived on the streets and didn't attend school anymore. But her life changed and gained purpose when she entered a residential program sponsored by the local St. Vincent de Paul Society, Rotary, and various other organizations. Alicia and other unhoused teens found themselves in a safe place to live for up to 24 months while they stayed in school and worked with mentors and peers toward rebuilding their lives.

One of the Rotarians gave free ukulele lessons to any of the girls who were interested, which included Alicia. She became quite skilled and loved playing it. She even began helping other girls learn to play the ukulele. While living at this new home, she went back to school with lots of courses to retake, but still she made time to go out and help her friends master playing the ukulele. Alicia developed a sense of purpose; she finished school and discovered her ability to help others. Having kindfulness as part of her purpose as she reached out to others greatly increased her happiness and other positive outcomes in her life.

## PUT INTO **Practice**

Think about times you felt you had no purpose, did not do anything, and did not think you had anything worth doing. How did you feel during those times?

_____

Now think of a time when you were working to take care of yourself or working to help another person. How did you feel during those times?

_____

# The Kindful Practitioner Recharges and Gives Kindfully

Part of our purpose in life can be to live as a Kindful Practitioner.

A Kindful Practitioner lives by giving kindfully and recharging by making efforts many times every day to act with mindful kindness toward self, the earth, and others.

What exactly does it mean to give kindfully and recharge ourselves?

*Recharge ourselves.* We recharge ourselves by engaging in mindfulness practices, meditation, and pleasant kind habits that energize and refresh us, give us joy, and make us more willing and able to give kindfully to others. Self-care is an essential aspect of recharging: Managing our stress; obtaining the education and skills needed for our work; getting a good amount of sleep, water, exercise, and healthy food; and weakening the unkind habits we direct at ourselves are all part of our self-care and love.

*Give kindfully.* We give kindfully when we act with mindful kindness toward others, our ancestors, and the earth. The benefits to us of giving kindfully to others include feelings of well-being, gratitude, and calm that provide the energy and desire to be kind. Our ability to give kindfully depends on how well our meditation and mindfulness practices are helping us weaken our unkind habits and build kind habits. A Kindful Practitioner must be present in the moment in order to fulfill their purpose of being kindful. There are times in which it becomes hard to be present in the moment. When we keep losing our focus on our intention, we recognize that we need to take the time to recharge ourselves and then we can refocus on giving kindfully. Recharging is essential; it is impossible to stay in a state of continual giving. The cycle of giving kindfully and then recharging helps maintain a balance of kindness toward others and kindness toward ourselves.

### EXAMPLE

Jordan Taylor, a 20-year-old, was stocking shelves in a Baton Rouge, Louisiana, grocery store when he noticed a young man had been watching him for several minutes. Jordan recognized that the young man was autistic and asked him if he would like to help place the drinks on the shelves. The autistic boy's father was touched. "To me, when you go to a grocery store with an autistic kid, especially when they're young, people don't understand, they're not very accepting. Somehow this young man reached my son . . . he went into my son's world."[4]

PUT INTO **Practice**

When we ask ourselves the question "How can I be kindful right now?" we have two positive answers: We can recharge ourselves or we can give kindfully. Think about your mindfulness and meditation practices and your pleasant kind habits.

List two ways you have recharged yourself.

1. _____

2. _____

Then list two ways you have given kindfully to others.

1. _____

2. _____

Giving kindfully—physically, mentally, and spiritually—can be gratifying but tiring, even if we are not giving kindfully by doing physical work. Although the brain is only 2% of our body weight, it uses about 20% of our energy. So giving kindfully engages our brain and uses about 20% of our energy. On the other hand, when recharging with meditation, mindfulness, micropractices, and grounding techniques, we are mostly taking in sensations of speech, sight, touch, hearing, taste, and thought. Receiving sensations requires less physical effort and less energy for the brain than giving kindfully requires, so receiving sensations when recharging rests the mind and is calming rather than tiring. The calming is often accompanied by increased energy and joy.

## Challenges That Keep Us from Recharging and Giving Kindfully in the Present Moment

Many challenges can keep us from recharging ourselves and giving kindfully in the present moment. Here are a few of the more common challenges to living as a Kindful Practitioner:

- An unhealthy focus on the past and/or future
- Strong negative emotional habits
- Self-criticism
- Inaction (not taking action for long periods of time)
- Boredom and restlessness

Being aware of these challenges will enable us to work on them or at least notice them more quickly so that we can be kind regardless of the challenges that arise.

# Getting Stuck by Thinking About the Past Too Often

We cannot undo the past. Dwelling on past negative or traumatic moments takes us away from our intention in the present moment. Dwelling on the past reduces our ability to be mindfully kind in the present. Perhaps, in the past, in a moment of anger, we said something hurtful that ended a friendship. We can take responsibility for what we did by apologizing and trying to make amends. However, it is helpful to tell ourselves that being consumed by regret and guilt over what happened will likely never make it right. It is not healthy to let our regrets and guilt continue to consume us to the point of making it nearly impossible to act with kindfulness in the present moment. Remember, we can't change what happened in the past; we can only learn from it to help us be kind in the present moment.

*EXAMPLE*

A high school football quarterback, Denzel, hoped to receive a scholarship to play football in college. Denzel was playing quarterback in the quarterfinals during his senior year in high school.

*I saw the clock was winding down and the team was counting on me for the win. The ball was snapped and I was hit head-on by the linebacker. I took the full force in my thigh, snapping the bone in half. I ended up with a gnarly compound fracture. Not only was the game over, but I thought my football career was over too.*

It took months for Denzel's injuries to heal, but even longer for his mind to begin the process of healing.

*After months of me being stuck thinking about my injury, my coach pulled me aside and pointed out that my leg had now healed. I had the opportunity to get back out on the field so I could make my college dreams a reality.*

Denzel followed his coach's advice. After working hard on strengthening his leg, he was able to compete in track that spring (another sport in which he had always excelled). Not only did his leg hold up, but he earned a full-ride track scholarship to one of his first-choice schools. By moving beyond his past pain, Denzel was able to renew his purpose and accomplish his goal of securing a scholarship to college.

*EXAMPLE*

An Indigenous young person often found herself feeling anger and grief for the genocide that had been inflicted on her ancestors. When she felt this anger arise, it prevented her from being kind in the moment, especially to White people. As she learned the lasting effects of trauma passed down through generations, she often thought her family would be better off, her mental health would be better, or her future would be brighter if her people did not go through genocide.

In her culture she was always taught to honor her ancestors, to make them proud. Embracing her culture and desire to make her ancestors proud helped her reduce her anger toward her ancestors' history. She realized her state of anger or resentment in the present moment would never take away the history and lasting effects of trauma in her tribe. Learning to be kind, live with purpose, and pass on culture and abundance to her children would make her ancestors proud and, in a way, help her heal from the traumatic ancestral history.

# Getting Stuck by Overthinking about the Future

There are two ways to get stuck in the future: anticipating something positive and dreading something negative. It's natural to think about the nice things in store for us. When a pleasant thought about something we expect to happen enters our mind, we can choose to acknowledge the feeling of anticipation or hope, enjoy the feeling, and then return to our present activity. The anticipation can become problematic, however, when we hold on too long and too intensely to the point of distraction or inactivity over long periods of time.

Imagine a friend is trying to talk to you, but instead of truly listening, you are thinking about what you plan to do on a date that evening. You're missing the opportunity to fully listen and enjoy time with your friend, who is right in front of you.

The flip side of anticipating something positive is worrying about something negative that may occur. When worries about the future arise over and over again, and not only distract us from the present but also cause unhappiness, we can use our skills of action (Kindful Practitioner, Diligent Detective, or Wise Warrior) to help remain focused on our present activity with a healthy mindset.

## EXAMPLE

Brandon, a person-of-color college student, describes how anxiety kept him from being aware of positive, life-affirming aspects of the present:

*I spent the first six to seven months of 2020 in bed unable to move. I was horribly sick, going back and forth to the hospital to run tests and figure out what was wrong with me. It turned out I had a tumor and abnormal tissue growth in my reproductive organs. Faced with my health progressively getting worse, I made the tough decision to remove my reproductive organs. The entire time I was making this choice, I felt this sense of loss and dread because I always wanted to be a dad and that choice was no longer available to me. I became hyper-fixated on worrying about never being able to have a family. However, one day I stumbled across a section in a medical journal that described research where blood cells and stem cells were being used to create gametes for those struggling with infertility. Somehow this research gave me a bit of hope that I could father a child and raise a family, and I realized that I had spent most of the lockdown time worrying about a future that was yet to come rather than focusing on the present. I have friends and family who care about me, and I'm close to finishing my degrees. There was so much positive around me, but I was too caught up in my worry that I failed to recognize it.*

✦ ✦ ✦

When we feel ourselves becoming consumed with worry about a problem that may or may not occur in the future, we can take action right away, before the worry becomes a negative mind-wandering habit. We can use our Diligent Detective to reduce the likelihood of the problem occurring in the future. For example, Brandon could have begun searching medical articles soon after he received the diagnosis of his medical problem. He could have then used the Wise Warrior to focus on those things within his control (finding where he could go to receive this new treatment) and not worry about what was not under his control.

To prevent worry and regret or anticipation and dread from becoming strong habits, we need to start weakening or addressing these thoughts as soon as we notice them. At the same time though, it's important to be gentle with ourselves and not expect that we can instantly stop these habits or thoughts.

Note that planning for the future is actually necessary. For example, a youth with a rough home life can find it extra hard to be kind. Making plans and thinking positively about the future can help people find hope and kindness while living in unhealthy environments as a teen or adult.

 PUT INTO **Practice**

Think about something that is causing you to regret the past or worry about the future. Maybe you regret a cruel social media comment or you are anxious about seeing a friend you had a fight with.

Write about how regretting the past or worrying about the future is affecting your mindfulness practice as a Kindful Practitioner.

_____

_____

Write about how you could deal with the regret or worry.

_____

_____

## Getting Stuck By Strong Negative Emotional Habits

Many strong emotions come from traumatic events, such as loss of a loved one, serious injury in accidents, abusive relationships, or public humiliation. These strong emotions can be with us for some time. Unfortunately, these events can contribute to negative mental habits throughout our lives, such as being anxious and disturbed.

The list of unkind habits that can produce strong negative emotions include those that we direct at ourselves (e.g., negative self-talk, substance abuse, self-harm, procrastination, being a doormat) and those we direct at others (e.g., frequent criticism, contempt, defensiveness, stonewalling, anger, aggression, rudeness, arrogance, dishonesty, and being uninterested in the needs of others). Many biases can also lead to strong negative emotions. Much of this workbook is devoted to steps we can take to break (or at least weaken) our unkind habits and reduce our biases in order to be more kind and happy.

In terms of instincts, fear can trigger our survival instinct and wipe out any thought of either giving kindfully or recharging ourselves. For example, in an intense emotional argument, the survival instincts of fight, flight, or freeze are hardwired in our genetic makeup to activate. Our goal should not be to never let these emotions occur, because they are natural. We can, however, focus on recovering from these overwhelming emotions more quickly, before they continue as negative mind-wandering or accelerate and turn into unhealthy actions or violence. Fortunately, mindfulness allows us to develop the skills to rebound faster when overwhelming emotions occur. We see that the inability to quickly recover from overwhelming emotions such as anger can have fatal consequences in the most extreme of cases. Over 40% of the murders in the United States occur from uncontrolled anger during arguments.[5]

### EXAMPLE

Jesse was walking in the woods when a cyclist came speeding over the top of a hill. Jesse heard him coming and was able to leap out of the way just in time to not be injured. Scared and upset, Jesse felt the fight, flight, or freeze response arise as a feeling of tightness across his chest. A moment later, a second cyclist came along at a more reasonable pace. This time Jesse didn't get out of the way but stood in the middle of the trail to stop him and ask if he knew the cyclist who just passed. After the cyclist said yes, Jesse unleashed his anger, fueled by adrenaline. Jesse demanded that he tell his friend to be more careful. But after he departed, Jesse couldn't stop thinking about it. He was still angry, but now Jesse was also worried that the first guy would come back to confront him. At first Jesse could not let go of those thoughts and feelings of anger and fear. But after a couple of minutes, as he walked farther along the trail, he used the Three-Breath Method and began noticing the many shades of green foliage and feeling each step as his foot made contact with the ground. His agitation softened. Jesse's mind took a rest by halting the unmindful-unkind cycle of anger and fear—and Jesse was able to enjoy the remainder of his walk.

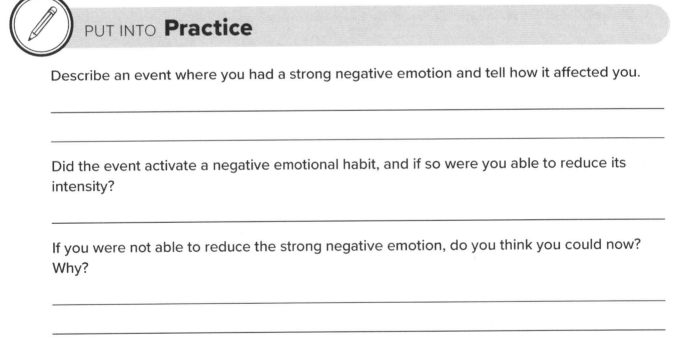

PUT INTO **Practice**

Describe an event where you had a strong negative emotion and tell how it affected you.

_____

_____

Did the event activate a negative emotional habit, and if so were you able to reduce its intensity?

_____

If you were not able to reduce the strong negative emotion, do you think you could now? Why?

_____

_____

## Getting Stuck by Self-Criticism

Most of us frequently criticize ourselves because of an unfulfilling job, resentment toward where we live, unattractiveness, or having too little money or too few friends. Looking more closely at our journey toward kindfulness, we experience high moments and low moments. As we move along this path, it will help to not become too critical of our progress.

It's not unusual to get down on ourselves, criticizing our progress in becoming a Kindful Practitioner by thinking, for example, "This is too hard" or "This mindfulness practice is a waste of time" or "I messed up, what's the point?"

One way to reduce self-criticism is to set realistic goals or expectations. Setting unrealistic goals can lead to frustration, for example, expecting that you will see a quick end to an upsetting unkind habit, like interrupting others and talking too much. Set a realistic goal for the next week, such as not talking two times each day when you have the urge to talk. Progress will come if you persist.

### EXAMPLE

The COVID-19 pandemic led to frustration for most of us. Here's one person's realization about the need to adapt her expectations rather than be self-critical:

*I realized that this virus had me feeling sad—yes—but it also sent me into a tailspin and everything about my schedule, my hours of sleep, and my regular routine was completely out of control. Taking a deep breath, I reminded myself that I have tools to use. I wrapped up my crying and began to feel like the clouds had parted. I could see clearly, and I knew what I needed to do: Rewrite a new Self-Care Plan. The world had changed in a matter of days but my formalized plan had not—and so it was clear to me that, just as I needed to be adaptable, the plan needed to be, too.*[6]

✦ ✦ ✦

We must realize that negative thoughts will arise from time to time. Even the most successful Kindful Practitioners will experience negative emotions, often arising from our instincts of survival, success, and reproduction. What matters is to **not** act on those emotions/thoughts. For example, our survival instinct could trigger anger when the driver behind us is following too closely. What matters is to not add anything extra. Examples of adding something extra might be driving super slowly to force the driver who is following too close to slow down or allowing that driver to pass us and then following them very closely.

In this example, the driver might think she hasn't made progress because she was angered, but by not acting on her anger, thoughts, or emotional impulses toward the driver behind her, she is showing progress. She might have improved more than she realized. In fact, the conscious mind is often not aware of the progress we are making.

One way to determine if you are making progress is to look over some exercises you did in the earlier chapters in this workbook. Notice if you are experiencing less negative mind-wandering now than you were back then. Ask yourself, Do I direct fewer unkind actions toward myself and others? Am I kinder more often? Or you might ask someone close to you if they have noticed any changes in terms of the habits you have been working on.

Keep these points in mind to help reduce self-criticism:

- The quest for kindness is not a competition.
- Avoid comparing your kind practice to that of others.
- Focus on doing what you can. And don't forget to celebrate your successes.
- Focusing on your accomplishments will fuel your optimism.

- Realistic goals will help you see the progress you are making.
- Forgive yourself for making mistakes

## PUT INTO **Practice**

Respond to the following questions.

What are your biggest self-criticisms about your mindfulness or meditation practice?

_____

_____

How do these self-criticisms make you feel?

_____

How are you dealing with these self-criticisms?

_____

_____

## Getting Stuck By Inaction

Many times we have ideas about what we want to do, but we find ourselves stuck by inaction and do very little. For example, we learn more to improve ourselves by reading and talking about our problems and what we plan to do about them. However, making plans accomplishes little unless we actually put what we have learned into practice. We move from learning (the Diligent Detective) to taking action (the Wise Warrior).

Imagine reading about how to ski, but never putting on skis and actually trying to ski. Obviously, studying about something is different than doing something. In the same way, reading, discussing, and thinking about mindfulness and kindness cannot give you the same experiences and understanding as actually being kindful. It would be like talking and reading about dieting without changing what you ate, or reading a book about fitness and never actually doing any exercise.

Reading and talking about new ideas can motivate us to stick with our kindfulness practice and give us solace, hope, and guidance in difficult times. Study can stimulate ideas about how to strengthen our practice and remind us to be humble from the perspective of how much there is to learn, grow, and understand. However, action is required to give kindfully. Taking action when we learn something new applies to all aspects of our lives. One of our character skills is being responsible for getting the job done. Think of the Nike trademark: "Just do it!"

✏️  PUT INTO **Practice**

Reflect on the reading, thinking, and discussions you have done recently on kindness.

1.  Identify an area of kindness you have read about or discussed and then put into practice:

    _____

2.  Describe how you felt after putting this kindful action into practice:

    _____

3.  Identify another area of kindness you have learned about and tell when you hope to put it into practice:

    _____

    _____

## Getting Stuck by Boredom and Restlessness

Sometimes, we may feel an activity is boring and unimportant. Our restlessness causes us to forget about this moment being an opportunity to give kindfully to ourselves or others in the present moment.

### EXAMPLE

Every day, boring tasks can open up opportunities for meaningful acts of kindness. Olivia had a younger brother who was 18 months old:

*I had to watch him for an hour after school. I initially found this to be boring and spent as much time as I could on my cell phone. After taking a kindness class, I realized that I could make this an opportunity to give. I read several articles about child development and activities that can stimulate toddlers. Each day, I tried some of these activities, which became more fun as my brother learned new words and skills. During my brother's nap times, I sent pictures and updates about the toddler to my aunts and grandparents.*

◆ ◆ ◆

Olivia transformed a seemingly unimportant time into a kindful time. When we feel bored, we can engage in practices described earlier in the workbook. We can use sensing mindfulness, micropractices, or grounding techniques such as soft-ears, soft-eyes, sharp-eyes, soft-touch, and soft-contact to transform an unpleasant feeling such as boredom into a positive experience. Using kindful practices during a time of boredom also teaches us that we do not have to be stimulated all the time. Then we can appreciate spending time with ourselves in a low-key situation.

## PUT INTO **Practice**

Describe something you find boring in your life.

_____

_____

Describe how you could engage in kindful activities in that situation.

_____

_____

# Returning to Balance

These challenges to being mindful in the present moment can interfere with our intentions and efforts to give kindfully and recharge ourselves. We can think of shifting out of a kindfulness challenge as returning to a balance of giving kindfully and recharging. The founder of the martial art Aikido, when speaking about balance, said his goal was not about always keeping his balance, because that is impossible. Instead his goal is to quickly return to balance.

Scientists analyzing human movement have determined that people don't actually keep their balance as they walk, but go through a cycle of falling forward and rebalancing with every step. Similarly, our mind frequently falls into mind-wandering about the past or future—sometimes negative and sometimes low-key. The challenge is to return to kindfulness quickly, just as we return to balance when we are walking. We quickly shift to our intention in the present moment and shift our attention away from these challenges:

- A focus on the past and/or future

- Strong, negative emotional habits

- Self-criticism

- Inaction

- Boredom and restlessness

Repeated practice is essential in learning to return more quickly to balance in both our mental and physical world. We can use sensing mindfulness, grounding techniques, and daily activities that are micro-practices, for example, walking, driving, cleaning the toilet, dressing, showering, and brushing our teeth. Other excellent ways to return to balance are to frequently take three deep, slow breaths and to ask ourselves, "How can I be kindful right now, by recharging or giving kindfully?"

As you turn some of the practices in this workbook into habits, you will find yourself able to maintain your balance for increasingly longer periods of time and to rebalance yourself to kindfulness more quickly when you do make a mistake. Learning to make frequent, quick transitions back to kindfulness is a secret of success for being a kindful practitioner.

## Mindful Walking

A way to practice returning to balance (mentally and physically) is slow walking with sensing mindfulness. In this activity, you walk for a minute, slowly extending one foot after the other, heel down first with each step. You focus your attention on the movement and sensation of rebalancing from one foot to the other. After a minute, walk even slower for another minute. When you step forward, first feel your heel coming in contact with the ground, next the bottom of your foot, then the front of your foot, and finally the front of your foot propelling you forward.

Once we become skilled at slow walking with sensing mindfulness, we can use this sensing mindfulness skill any time we are walking. For example, if we are walking with negative mind-wandering and three mindful breaths does not free our mind, add in mindful walking (sensing mindfulness directed to our feet as we walk slowly). Attending to the sensations coming from our feet and from our breathing will help us shift out of negative mind-wandering.

 PUT INTO PRACTICE **Journal**

Practice slow walking with sensing mindfulness several times, then try to use it at times when you feel agitated over the next week. On page 294, write about or reflect on what happened (including your feelings) with both your mental and physical balance as you did the mindful walking.

## Understanding How Kindful Practitioner Challenges Keep Us from Giving Kindfully and Recharging Ourselves

Science and religion both see kindness as a driving force in humanity. And yet, Kindful Practitioner challenges can steer us away from our intention to give kindfully and recharge. To better understand what this interference looks like, we're going to imagine ourselves in a glass-bottom boat looking down through its glass floor at the beautiful ocean landscape below. The glass is like mindfulness—mindfulness does not create the colorful scene in the sea below. It just gives us access to see with clarity the beauty that is there all along, In the same way that the glass allows us to see the rich and important ocean life, our mindful kindness allows us to see the deeper parts of ourselves, including our deep willingness to give kindfully and take care of ourselves by recharging. In addition, seeing the beauty within us energizes and brings joy followed by calmness.

Sadly, these Kindful Practitioner challenges are like heavy boots spreading mud over the glass floor, which can make seeing the beautiful ocean floor almost impossible. If we add mud from our Kindful Practitioner challenges day after day, the glass will be really hard to clean. Just as the mud keeps us from seeing the beautiful ocean below, our challenges keep us from recharging ourselves and deplete us of the energy and purpose we need to be kind to ourselves and to give kindfully.

Eventually, we get fed up with adding more mud day after day and are now ready to face our unkind habits, which might come, for example, from our biases and instincts. We face these unkind habits with mindfulness practices: the Three-Breath Method, sensing mindfulness, grounding techniques such as soft-eyes, micropractices, and other calming practices such as tai chi or yoga. Still, life's events and unkind people will continue to catch us off guard and throw piles of mud on our glass. Our lifetime job as a Kindful Practitioner is to clean off the mud so that we can continue to give kindfully and recharge ourselves.

The lives of Doug's prisoner friends, Roy and Tad, have been filled with trauma. During their childhoods, they grew up with other people spreading mud all over their glass, making it very difficult for them to see the beauty within themselves. As adults, they suffered from all the Kindful Practitioner challenges described earlier. Before they could take on the third part of the Kindful Vow—extending the reach of their kindfulness—they needed to focus their mindful kindness on themselves. Being mindfully kind did not immediately rid them of these challenges, but it reduced the time they spent being controlled by them, which meant less mud to clean off the glass. After Roy and Tad had sufficiently recharged themselves, they were able to give kindfully to those close to them and later reach out further to gang members, bullies, those who were socially withdrawn, and even prison staff.

## PUT INTO **Practice**

Describe how you felt at a time you were deeply distressed. During that time, were you able to think about how to be more kind to others around you?

_____

_____

_____

Now describe a time where things were doing well and you were feeling good. Did you have more feelings of kindness toward others?

_____

_____

_____

## PERSONAL **Challenge**

Write about what you want your purpose in life to be. Will the Kindful Practitioner, who gives kindfully and recharges, be part of your purpose?

_____

_____

_____

_____

# ━━━━━ Wrapping Up ━━━━━

Having purpose helps guide us as we live each moment of our life. At any moment, we can ask ourselves, "How can I be kindful now?" We try to avoid Kindful Practitioner challenges that keep us from giving kindfully and recharging, such as:

- A focus on the past and/or future

- Strong negative emotional habits

- Self-criticism

- Inaction

- Boredom and restlessness

Minimizing the moments we spend in being controlled by these challenges increases the moments we can give kindfully and recharge ourselves as a Kindful Practitioner. In addition, free of these challenges, we are more aware of the consequences of our kind and unkind habits. Then by recharging and giving kindfully to others, we begin to enjoy lasting happiness.

 PUT INTO PRACTICE **Journal**

Imagine that something is going to happen in the next moment that would dramatically change your life. Describe an important problem with a relationship that you have left undone.

_____

_____

Write about how you might take action right now to solve the relationship problem.

_____

_____

If you can, actually do that activity later, on page 294, write about what you actually did and how taking that action made you feel.

 *Checking In*

Turn back to your responses on page 154 in Chapter 8: "Face Up To Your Unkind Habits." You designated some habits as hard to break and some as easier to break. Read over the list. Write the names of any habits that you no longer feel would be hard to break. Also describe any unkind habits you have worked on weakening.

# Time for Reflection

How are your practices going? Take a few moments to reflect on the practices below. Which ones have proven most helpful for resting your mind? Use the scale 0–4, with 0 = Haven't tried it yet, 1 = Least helpful, and 4 = Most helpful.

_____ Micropractices

_____ Pleasant kind habits

_____ Sensing mindfulness

_____ Grounding techniques such as soft contact

_____ Meditation

_____ Kind conversation skills

_____ Performing at least one act of kindness by showing appreciation, offering to help, being friendly, or reaching out to those in need.

• • •

What are you grateful for today? Circle yes or no. Do you feel grateful for:

| | | |
|---|---|---|
| People and pets I care about | Yes | No |
| Something that went well today | Yes | No |
| What I can do with my body and mind | Yes | No |
| People who help me and others | Yes | No |
| My beliefs that give me purpose and meaning | Yes | No |
| Having fun and laughter | Yes | No |

• • •

Give an example of how you have recently applied one of these kindness skills.

- Be friendly
- Show appreciation
- Offer help
- Reach out to those with serious needs

_____

_____

## Chapter 14

# Do You Want to Be a Kindfulness Ambassador?

*I've been searching for ways to heal myself, and I've found that kindness is the best way.*

Lady Gaga

**Before beginning this chapter, for one minute meditate in the way that works best for you.**

There are times when we all crave distraction. In fact, researchers at the University of Virginia found that when left alone in an empty room for just 15 minutes with nothing to do, 12 out of 18 young adult men and 6 out of 24 young adult women would voluntarily give themselves a painful electric shock rather than simply sit quietly with their thoughts.[1]

Think about what your life was like when you first made the decision to pick up this book. Maybe you were someone who spent long periods dwelling on your worries or resentments, who focused on yourself so much you were blind to the needs or feelings of others, or who expressed your negative thoughts by lashing out with unkindness toward the people closest to you. Maybe you were even someone who would give yourself an electric shock just for a distraction from your own thoughts.

But now you're able to calm yourself during difficult times and find more moments of joy and gratitude, increase your kind habits, and weaken some of your unkind habits. You've come a long way by adding a number of tools to your toolbox, such as sensing mindfulness, the Three-Breath Method, grounding techniques, and micropractices. Take a moment to acknowledge the progress you've made.

Now we are ready to begin a new stage in our development, taking on the role of Kindfulness Ambassador.

## Kindfulness Ambassador

A person who not only acts kindfully, but also teaches others to be more kindful.

### EXAMPLE

A young worker in recovery encounters a Kindfulness Ambassador:

*I was helping a regular customer today. He's always very kind and has some of the best vibrations that a person can give off. He mentioned how he just got back from California. I asked if he had fun. His response was that his mother passed away and he had to settle the affairs and put her to rest. Despite this, he was in good spirits and seemed just as kind as ever. He tipped me more than I would have expected and said not to worry about it and that "good things happen to good people, and good people are what make good things happen."*

◆ ◆ ◆

The customer's larger-than-expected tip was an act of kindness. In this statement, "good things happen to good people, and good people are what make good things happen," the customer is acting as a Kindfulness Ambassador.

You may not be comfortable or ready to use the techniques in this chapter to become a Kindfulness Ambassador. Also, as a Kindfulness Ambassador, it may be hard to find the right time to talk to others about them becoming Kindfulness Ambassadors. However, encouraging others to be Kindfulness Ambassadors can be as simple as telling others about the value of mindfulness, such as the Three-Breath Method, and about the value of kindness and stopping unkind habits, such as gossiping and negative thinking.

*EXAMPLE*

A 16-year-old high school student acts as a Kindfulness Ambassador:

I've definitely found myself encouraging others to be more kind and mindful since I began reading this book! I've suggested three mindful breaths when family members are stressed, and I've discouraged my friends when I find them gossiping or thinking negatively.

◆ ◆ ◆

In recommending three mindful breaths, the student teaches about the mindfulness aspect of kindfulness. In discouraging gossiping and thinking negatively, she teaches about the kindness/unkindness aspect of kindfulness.

# Ways To Be a Kindfulness Ambassador

Following are some ways to teach others to be more kindful.

## Talk to Your Friends: "Each One Teach One"

In the Southern United States before the Civil War, many slaveholders forbid their slaves to learn how to read. In spite of the danger, African American slaves often shared the skill of reading with each other through a system called "Each One Teach One." When one slave learned to read, they gave kindfully by teaching another slave to read in spite of the danger of doing so. Teaching a slave to read is an act of kindness. Encouraging the slave being taught to read to teach others was the act of a Kindfulness Ambassador.

Doug's incarcerated friends have become experts in "Each One Teach One." As prisoners, they first learned about mindful kindness and then acted with mindful kindness to other prisoners. But they also were Kindfulness Ambassadors by teaching other prisoners to be more kindful. One of these men, John Bruno, has kindfully helped so many other prisoners with mindful kindness that one of the mental health counselors in the prison calls him "Doc." John is also a Kindfulness Ambassador because he taught many of them to be more kindful in how they treat themselves and others. Since Doug began corresponding 11 years ago with prisoners Roy Tester, John Bruno, and Tad, they have continued "Each One Teach One" with kindfulness. They have taught dozens of other prisoners to be Kindfulness Ambassadors. In turn, this second generation of Kindfulness Ambassadors (young and old) continues to teach other prisoners to practice kindfulness. While these Kindfulness Ambassadors continue to confront problems—Tad, for example, has been diagnosed with PTSD, bipolar, and schizophrenia—they continue to experience moments of peace and contentment.

*FROM THE OTHER SIDE*

As Tad approached the end of his 15-year sentence, he prepared to leave his student Chris behind. Tad realized the importance of teaching Chris to extend his kindful practice to others in Tucker Max, where Chris will spend the rest of his life.

*Chris and I were having a discussion on friendship and the responsibilities it holds. I tried to get him to understand, if him and I are friends then it's BOTH of our responsibilities to conduct ourselves in an honorable virtuous manner to produce a real mindful friendship. We must also be mindful of others that claim or state they're our friends.*

*Leadership is the most characteristic quality I tried to build in Chris in the short time we spent together. His willingness to sacrifice and act kindfully (be humble) will make him into a great leader. But with leadership comes great responsibility. "Be wise as a serpent, but kind as a dove."*

◆ ◆ ◆

When you show appreciation to someone, you are acting with kindness. When you explain to a friend the value of showing appreciation, you are using "Each One Teach One" as a kindfulness ambassador. For example, here is what you might say to your friend: "A teacher (or boss) went out of their way to give me extra time to explain in more detail my assignment. To show appreciation, I put in more time and effort to do an excellent job on my assignment. Also, I told my boss (or teacher) that I was able to do such a good job because of the explanation they gave me." This example shows your friend how and why to be a kindfulness ambassador: You ended up benefiting by performing better on the assignment and by being able to act with kindness. Your teacher (or boss) benefited from your expressions of appreciation.

## Be Ready To Answer Common Questions about Kindfulness

We need to be prepared for the questions we may run into when people ask us to explain what it means to be a Kindfulness Ambassador. Or we may be asked these questions because we have encouraged someone to learn more about mindful kindness. We may also be asked these questions as people notice our use of mindfulness and kindness. We want to be ready when people ask us why we seem more positive and relaxed.

Below are six commonly asked questions and suggestions for how to respond. Please feel free to use these ideas and put them into your own words so that your responses are more authentic.

Q: What are the benefits of kindness?
A: Having mostly kind habits contributes to close, caring relationships that in turn contribute to a longer, healthier, more loving, and happier life. Also, those receiving your kindness benefit from the ways you have treated them with kindness.

Q: What does mindfulness mean?
A: Mindfulness means paying attention to what we are intending to do in the present moment, not being distracted by thoughts or emotions, and not being judgmental of ourselves or others.

Q: Why is mindfulness important?
A: Mindfulness keeps our focus on our intention in the present moment (rather than rehashing the past or worrying about the future) and makes us more aware of how our actions are affecting our relationships (especially our close ones). Mindfulness can bring us contentment, decrease our unhappiness, enable us to weaken unkind habits, and help us be more genuinely kind to ourselves and others.

Q: Why might I want kindfulness to be a primary purpose in my life?

A:  Kindfulness is a combination of kindness and mindfulness. Having kindfulness as a primary purpose of your life is a powerful way to foster your well-being and the well-being of everyone touched by your kindness. Your kindness will especially benefit those you are close to, but also will benefit other relationships at home, work, and throughout your social world, as well as your relationship with the earth itself.

Q:  Where can I get some ideas about how I can be more kindful?

A:  There are an increasing number of sources to learn about how to be more kindful. Below are organizations that provide lots of information and opportunities to give kindfully.

- **The Choose Kindness Foundation** (choosekindnessfoundation.info) offers grants to increase kindness across entire organizations, such as schools and the workplace, which appear at the top of the Foundation's logo.

  The Foundation also offers grants to support youth to go through this workbook in facilitated group settings. Similarly, grants are provided to support incarcerated adults in learning to be mindfully kind by working through the Foundation's book, *How Love Wins*. This intensive work at the individual level appears at the bottom of the logo. Finally, community engagement (at the center of the logo) occurs with the Foundation's funding of organizational and group work in the same community.

- **The Random Acts of Kindness Foundation** (randomactsofkindness.org) has created a platform with tools, resources, and a large support network to help people take action, get involved, and share the benefits of kind actions in their daily lives at school, at home, at work and in their community.

- **Lady Gaga's Born This Way Foundation** (https://bornthisway.foundation) also has many resources for young people to increase their kindness. The foundation's mission is to look "forward, toward a future that supports the wellness of young people through an evidence-based approach that is fiercely kind, compassionate, accepting, and inclusive . . . Together, we're building a community that provides approachable resources, fosters genuine connection, and drives action."

- **DoSomething.org** (dosomething.org/us) is the largest not-for-profit organization devoted exclusively to young people working for social change. DoSomething's members represent every U.S. area code and 131 countries. Using its digital platform, DoSomething members can join or volunteer with social change and civic action campaigns to make real-world impact on causes they care about.

Q:  How has kindfulness changed your life?

A:  You might respond to questions about the value of kindfulness by describing how you've increased your kindness and how components of mindfulness have enabled you to become happier. You can describe how kindfulness has benefited you in terms of the five elements of happiness listed on the next page.

## PUT INTO **Practice**

Identify a friend who is already kind and will probably react positively to the idea of becoming a Kindfulness Ambassador. What would you say to your friend to explain the importance of kindfulness?

_____

_____

_____

## PERSONAL CHALLENGE **Journal**

Actually meet with your friend and explain the importance of kindfulness. On page 294, write about how your friend responded to your explanation. Then write about how you felt about the conversation after you finished talking to your friend.

## How Kindfulness Contributes to the Five Elements of Happiness

The following list shows how kindness links to the five elements of happiness:

1. **Positive emotions** come from the feel-good chemicals released in our body when we are kind, receive kindness, or observe kindness. Close, caring relationships are a reliable source of positive constructive emotions.

2. **Engagement** is feeling absorbed in what we're doing. Engagement comes when mindfulness allows us to focus on what we're doing.

3. **Relationships** refer to having close and caring relations that occur when we are kind to others and thereby create a caring connection with them.

4. **Meaning** is believing in and acting on our purpose in life, for example, one of our purposes can be living our life as a Kindful Practitioner.

5. **Achievement** occurs when we feel competent in things we feel are important. Utilizing mindfulness helps us to gain competence that leads to achievement.[2]

Having sufficient amounts of all five of these elements contributes to us having deep and consistent happiness. Our happiness is decreased when any of these five elements is insufficient in our lives. Consider the effect on your life from: failure (the opposite of achievement), aimlessness (opposite of meaning), loneliness (too few caring relationships), indifference (in contrast to engagement), and too many negative emotions (too few positive emotions).

## PUT INTO **Practice**

For each of the five elements of happiness in the table below, circle where you were before you started reading this workbook and where you are now on a scale of 1–4, with 4 = Achieved most of the time, 3 = Achieved some of the time, 2 = Achieved occasionally, and 1 = Almost never achieved.

| When You Started Book | | Right Now | |
|---|---|---|---|
| Positive Emotion | 1  2  3  4 | Positive Emotion | 1  2  3  4 |
| Engagement | 1  2  3  4 | Engagement | 1  2  3  4 |
| Relationships | 1  2  3  4 | Relationships | 1  2  3  4 |
| Meaning | 1  2  3  4 | Meaning | 1  2  3  4 |
| Achievement | 1  2  3  4 | Achievement | 1  2  3  4 |

Describe how you would explain to a friend interested in kindness what has been responsible for the changes in your life. Be sure to explain how kindfulness has contributed to those changes.

_____

_____

## Motivating Groups of People and Communities To Be More Kindful

You can find several examples of how to motivate groups of people and communities to be more kindful by going to https://bit.ly/LH_Ch14_Bonus on the internet.

## Boost Interest in Giving Kindfully

To recruit Kindfulness Ambassadors, we might be able to increase our friends' interest in kindness through discussing one of these two options:

- Kindness appears in surprising places
- Kindfulness is relevant to global survival

### Kindness Appears in Surprising Places

We know humans and other animal species practice kindness by taking care of their young and helping others in their in-group. The book *Random Acts of Kindness by Animals* by Stephanie LaLand (2nd ed., 2008, Conari Press) describes many instances of different species committing acts of kindness.

It will probably surprise your friends to learn that kindness also occurs in the plant world; trees also give kindfully to their young and help others in their in-group.[3] Scientists have been learning a great deal about the kindness of trees.

***Taking care of their young.*** In some trees, such as the Douglas fir, a "family" relationship among trees growing near each other is maintained by an interconnected system of roots and fungi ,which allows the trees to share information, nutrients, and water. A mature "mother" Douglas fir will take care of its "children" (trees growing from its seeds) by making more space for them to grow new roots and by sharing nutrients. When children Douglas firs are in distress, they signal their distress through the release of chemicals to their mother Douglas fir, which in turn sends help in various forms back to its offspring. The mother Douglas fir nurtures her own children.

***Taking care of the elderly.*** Some types of trees send nutrients to stumps to keep them alive; a stump has no leaves and cannot create its own nutrients. Scientists do not yet know why trees would use their nutrients to keep a stump alive.

***Friendships.*** Contrary to what many think, some fungi on a tree are not harmful but actually help to facilitate the uptake of nutrients that are not typically easily accessible to the tree. In turn, some trees give about 30% of the food they produce (sugar) to fungi. When dying, a tree can pass along some of its carbon to nearby friendly trees.

***In-group support.*** Some trees maintain relationships by communicating through the air. When a giraffe starts chewing acacia leaves, the tree notices the injury and emits a distress signal in the form of ethylene gas. Upon detecting this gas, neighboring acacias start pumping the chemical tannins into their leaves in large enough quantities to sicken or even kill giraffes.

***In-group versus out-group.*** Interestingly, some trees will form supportive relationships with some other types of trees. Cedar and maple trees communicate with each other. Douglas firs communicate only with hemlock. So cedar trees treat maple as part of their in-group but treat Douglas fir and hemlock as members of an out-group. However, trees do not intentionally harm members of their out-groups the way humans do.[4]

Although there are many examples of how trees give kindfully to one another, the question is: Why do trees help each other? "Actually, it makes evolutionary sense for trees to be communal and not behave like resource-grabbing individualists," Professor Suzanne Simard says about trees, "They live longest and reproduce most often in a healthy, stable forest. That's why they've evolved to help their neighbors."[5] The same goes for humans. We live longest and happiest when we have close, caring relationships and live in healthy communities.

To fully appreciate the power of these findings about trees, watch the documentary *Intelligent Trees* (intelligent-trees.com).

PUT INTO **Practice**

Think of a friend who is curious about kindness. Describe what you would say to them about the ways trees are kind to each other.

_____

_____

_____

## *Kindfulness Is Relevant to Social Problems*

Our society faces many challenges, and some of these challenges, such as climate change, threaten the entire world. For example, forests produce about 20% of the oxygen we breathe while sea plants create between 50% and 80% of the rest. Eighty percent of the world's forests have been destroyed or badly damaged. Gradually warming ocean temperatures have killed off 40% of the sea plants since 1950. People born in 2020 will be 80 in 2100. If humans continue killing off too many trees and sea plants, we could bring on earth-wide suffocation. We need kindness to the earth for our survival. Youths are increasingly taking leadership in calling for kindness to our environment.

Although no one of us can solve the climate crisis, for our own mental health and to decrease the harm to the planet we can join with millions of people around the globe in taking small positive steps to limit climate change. For example, one small step Doug takes is to reduce his use of electricity by turning off unneeded lights, which also provides many opportunities each day to practice mindfulness. Doug's wife, Linda, reduces the use of fossil fuels by driving an electric car. Maybe Doug and Linda's greatest act of environmental kindness has been planting about 80,000 trees. Trees play an important role in our environment, absorbing carbon dioxide as they grow, slowing the rate of global warming. Trees also reduce wind speeds and cool the air as they lose moisture and reflect heat upwards from their leaves.

Doug and Linda created a wildlife preserve and protected it with a conservation easement that provides habitat for both plants and animals.*

While individuals cannot by themselves change the way governments and corporations treat our natural world, we can let them know our concerns by supporting organizations and advocating for policies that support responsible use of natural resources. On a personal level, we can reduce our consumption of fossil fuels, meat, and other resources.† We can bike or take the bus; hang our clothes out to dry in the air rather than using the clothes dryer; replace lawns that require frequent watering with gardens, rocks, and spaced plants; and not immediately buy the newest version of a computer, phone, watch, and TV when the ones we have still work. We can also practice the three Rs: reduce, reuse, and recycle. For example, we can reduce plastic use by carrying groceries in paper bags and paper containers. We can recycle plastic by turning it into building materials. We can reuse plastic bags by washing and air drying them or donating them to be repurposed as sleeping mats for the homeless.[6]

 PUT INTO **Practice**

Write about what you would say to a friend about showing kindness to the earth by improving the environment in your community. For example, recycle glass bottles, shower for a shorter period of time to save water, pick up litter, or bike or take the bus instead of driving.

_____

_____

* Read more at www.mckenzieriver.org/2015/12/its-the-trees/ and www.mckenzieriver.org/protected-lands/conservation-eastments/native-oaks-ridge/

† To take on the role of the Diligent Detective and learn more about kindness to the earth, go to: http://www.spreadingkindnesscampaign.org/spread-kindness/kindness-to-the-earth/

# Wrapping Up

The foundation skills you read about in Chapter 2—skills of action, skills of character, and the skill of diagnosis—and the sections that followed—build kind habits, train your mind, and deal with unkind habits—have hopefully benefited your physical, behavioral, and mental health and increased your feelings of happiness and well-being for you and those you come in contact with. This chapter recommends that we become Kindfulness Ambassadors to encourage others to bring more kindness into their lives. We can do this by acting on some of the suggestions described in this chapter:

1. Talk to your friends using "Each One Teach One."

2. Be ready to answer common questions about kindfulness.

3. Explain how kindfulness contributes to the five elements of happiness.

4. Motivate groups of people to be kindful.

5. Boost interest in giving kindfully.

    • Kindness arises in surprising places.

    • Kindfulness is relevant to social problems.

## Time for Reflection

Describe how you will give kindfully.

_____

_____

Describe how you will recharge.

_____

_____

Give an example of how you have recently applied one of these kindness skills.

   • Be friendly

   • Offer help

   • Show appreciation

   • Reach out to those with serious needs

_____

_____

# Chapter 15

# Make Kindfulness a Permanent Part of Your Life

*At least for me, a form of therapy or feeling better is just practicing acts of kindness.*

Kevin Love, NBA star

**Before beginning this chapter, for one minute meditate in the way that works best for you.**

Your next step is a big one: the rest of your life. This is where the real work comes in. It's one thing to learn new ideas about kindfulness. It's another to try them out once or twice, and it's yet another to apply them—day after day, week after week, month after month—until you've formed habits defining who you are as a Kindful Practitioner. Don't expect an overnight change in how you feel and act; it is a lifelong journey. The steady progress is what matters as you work to become kindful.

> *Don't expect an overnight change in how you feel and act; it is a lifelong journey. The steady progress is what matters as you work to become kindful.*

### FROM THE OTHER SIDE

Ernesto Rodriguez, arrested as a teenager, now mentors other inmates by guiding them through Doug's mindful kindness book for adults: *How Love Wins* (2017, Mindful Kindness Project). The day before Ernesto was transferred to another prison, he wrote the following note while "in the hole" (solitary confinement) for his own protection. The note shows how, through steady progress, he has transformed himself and is reaching out with kindness to a stranger.

*I do not know how we will be remembered, Doug. But I do know that it is not about remembrance. It is about the prisoners, the youth, the parents, the officers, anyone we touch with our kindness to improve their lives with our service—that is How Love Wins.*

*I am leaving these things on the bunk of my cell for the next inmate to be in this cell: a hearty meal, toothpaste, deodorant, soap, coffee, writing paper, and some sweets. I am going to also place a Bible and a copy of* How Love Wins *on my bunk. I wrote a note inside of* How Love Wins *that says, "I hope you enjoyed your meal. My wishes are that you have all you need to wash yourself. I do not know who you are, or what you have been through. But if you are in this cell and have opened this book, you may wonder or ask yourself, How does love win? I've been in prison for 22 years. And one day I realized that I didn't love anyone but myself. Since that day, I worked hard to change. Sought my education. Began to be kind to others. And was blessed by a beautiful family. Strangely enough, I began to be kind to myself. Only when I was able to love myself was I able to love others—and that is How Love Wins. If you are tired of being in the hole, and maybe you can't sleep at night because you miss your family, take a chance and write me. I'll serve you so that you can start that process and one day, you'll also say—that's How Love Wins."*

# Reflection

To help you decide if you want to make kindfulness a permanent part of your life, think about how much you have changed as you have gone through this workbook. You began this workbook by answering questions about how you want to live your life. In Table 15.1 is a copy of the same set of questions. Respond to the questions "How I Want to Live My Live" again and then answer the Put into Practice questions that come after the Personal Challenge.

**TABLE 15.1**  *Personal Challenge: How I Want to Live My Life*

Next to each statement, put a check in the box under the number that applies to you.

| | Strongly Disagree 1 | Disagree 2 | Agree 3 | Strongly Agree 4 |
|---|---|---|---|---|
| **Relationships** | | | | |
| After reading this workbook, I have more close relationships with people who really care about me. | ☐ | ☐ | ☐ | ☐ |
| After reading this workbook, I am more comfortable meeting friends in person. | ☐ | ☐ | ☐ | ☐ |
| After reading this workbook, I am less anxious when I'm in a group with other people my age. | ☐ | ☐ | ☐ | ☐ |
| **Mental Well-Being** | | | | |
| After reading this workbook, I feel calmer. | ☐ | ☐ | ☐ | ☐ |
| After reading this workbook, I feel less distracted. | ☐ | ☐ | ☐ | ☐ |
| After reading this workbook, I feel less anxious and worried less about the future. | ☐ | ☐ | ☐ | ☐ |
| After reading this workbook, I feel less regret for the mistakes I've made. | ☐ | ☐ | ☐ | ☐ |
| After reading this workbook, I am more able to forgive people for how they have treated me in the past. | ☐ | ☐ | ☐ | ☐ |
| After reading this workbook, I am more able to control my anger. | ☐ | ☐ | ☐ | ☐ |
| **Mindfulness** | | | | |
| After reading this workbook, I now use mindfulness, meditation, and other techniques to calm my mind. | ☐ | ☐ | ☐ | ☐ |
| After reading this workbook, I have a healthier balance between work or school and the rest of my life. | ☐ | ☐ | ☐ | ☐ |
| After reading this workbook, I am more able to be present and listen carefully when others speak. | ☐ | ☐ | ☐ | ☐ |
| **Kindness** | | | | |
| After reading this workbook, I have more kind habits. | ☐ | ☐ | ☐ | ☐ |
| After reading this workbook, I show more appreciation toward others. | ☐ | ☐ | ☐ | ☐ |

| | Strongly Disagree 1 | Disagree 2 | Agree 3 | Strongly Agree 4 |
|---|---|---|---|---|
| After reading this workbook, I help my family and friends more. | ☐ | ☐ | ☐ | ☐ |
| After reading this workbook, I am more friendly to family and friends by showing that I am interested in what they care about. | ☐ | ☐ | ☐ | ☐ |
| After reading this workbook, I interrupt other people less during conversations and meetings. | ☐ | ☐ | ☐ | ☐ |
| After reading this workbook, I am more patient. | ☐ | ☐ | ☐ | ☐ |
| After reading this workbook, I feel more appreciated and respected. | ☐ | ☐ | ☐ | ☐ |
| *Reaching Out* | | | | |
| After reading this workbook, I am more kind to those in serious need. | ☐ | ☐ | ☐ | ☐ |
| After reading this workbook, I am more respectful to those I disagree with. | ☐ | ☐ | ☐ | ☐ |
| After reading this workbook, I am more respectful and protective of the natural world, including plants and animals. | ☐ | ☐ | ☐ | ☐ |
| After reading this workbook, I make more effort to be kind to those who are ignored or not treated fairly by others. | ☐ | ☐ | ☐ | ☐ |
| After reading this workbook, I am volunteering more often to help others facing difficult situations. | ☐ | ☐ | ☐ | ☐ |
| After reading this workbook, I move out of my comfort zone more often so I can help others. | ☐ | ☐ | ☐ | ☐ |
| *Encouraging Others to Be Kind* | | | | |
| After reading this workbook, I am helping others understand that close caring relationships make you happy and kindness is essential for close caring relationships. | ☐ | ☐ | ☐ | ☐ |
| After reading this workbook, I am more comfortable talking about kindness with others. | ☐ | ☐ | ☐ | ☐ |
| After reading this workbook, I am sharing more with others about ways to be kind and ways to meditate. | ☐ | ☐ | ☐ | ☐ |

🖊 PUT INTO **Practice**

Compare the responses you just made with your responses to the Self-Assessment in Chapter 1, which starts on page 17. Then answer these questions:

1. Were there any surprising changes you feel good about?

_____

_____

_____

_____

2. Which of the changes you made are most important to you?

_____

_____

_____

3. Do you have less negative mind-wandering, especially less negative self-talk?

_____

4. Do you feel better about your relationships?

_____

5. Are you experiencing more happiness in your life?

_____

After you answer these five questions, pick one or both of the paths described in the next section of this chapter. Both paths will help you make kindfulness a permanent part of your life.

## Two Paths to Make Kindfulness Permanent

We have created two paths designed to help you begin your journey to make kindfulness a permanent part of your life. These two paths are guides to take you deeper into kindfulness, including increasing kind habits and weakening unkind habits. If you like variety and enjoy trying something new, encourage yourself to be more kindful by taking the 31 Days of Kindfulness in Path 1. If you're someone who likes to work from a routine, Path 2 is the way to engage yourself in being more kindful. If you really want to take your practice deeper and go much faster, try both!

# Path 1: 31 Days of Kindfulness Calendar

### *Personal Challenge: 31 Days of Kindfulness*

You can find the 31 days of kindfulness challenges on the internet at https://bit.ly/LH_Ch15_Bonus.

Thirty-one days may seem like a long time to carry out an act of kindfulness every day. Go to https://bit.ly/LH_Ch15_Bonus and try a few days to see how it feels. For each day, several kindful actions are suggested; some recharge you, and for others you give kindfully. Begin by selecting the actions you are confident of carrying out. *For every one of the 31 days, you can select more than one item to work on.* If you want, make up your own act of kindness. Also, you can repeat an act of kindness over several days. Remember to make a checkmark in front of the kindful actions you select. Make a copy of the pages showing the actions for the 31 days. Make a checkmark in front of the kindful actions you do each day. You might make several checkmarks in front of some items.

# Path 2: Daily Kindfulness Schedule

For Path 2, you'll make a daily plan to take yourself deeper into kindfulness, including increasing kind habits and weakening unkind habits. When you begin carrying out your plan, you'll use your phone, computer, or paper and pencil to answer questions about how well things went during the day.

### *Steps in Making Your Daily Schedule*

1.  **Spend 10 to 20 minutes in quiet meditation and mindfulness at the beginning of the day:**

    A.  I will not look at my phone, watch TV, read or listen to the news, or have conversations until I have meditated and done my micropractice. Circle one.   Yes   No

    B.  I will meditate for 5 to 10 minutes in (select a place) _____

    C.  I will use treat many of my morning activities as micropractices, such as dressing, cleaning up, making my bed, and eating breakfast. Circle one:   Yes   No

2.  **Plan for during the day and evening:**

    A.  I will invigorate my Kindful Vow, saying it aloud or to myself. Complete each statement:

    *I intend to be mindfully kind to myself by* _____

    *I intend to be mindfully kind in all my relationships by* _____

    *I intend to extend the reach of my kindfulness by* _____

    B.  I will meditate for ____ minutes before going to bed (at least 5–10 minutes, 20 minutes if you can).

C. I will be kind to myself, the earth, and others. I will recharge and give kindfully by working on strengthening a kind habit or weakening an unkind habit.

*The habit I will work on is* _____

D. In addition, I will do one of the following activities to help me recharge. Make an **X** in front the activity below you will use to help you recharge.

☐ Shift into sensing mindfulness, either one sense at a time or rotating through several, one after another.

☐ Practice and deepen the Three-Breath Method—or if you don't have much time, just take one deep mindful breath.

☐ Call up memories of joy and appreciation that activate your gratitude.

☐ Ask for help from others.

☐ Engage in a pleasant kind habit.

3. **Questions I will answer each night about how kindful I was during the day.**

A. How kind was I to others? What went well when I tried to be kind? Why? What did not go well? Why? What might I do differently in the future?

B. How kind was I to myself today? For example, was I strengthening a pleasant kind habit or weakening an unkind habit?

C. Did I meditate in the morning and before going to bed?

D. What is one thing I am grateful for today?

E. What is one thing I did well today?

F. At the end of each week answer this question: How can I extend the reach of my kindness to someone who is subject to bias, or who can I recruit as a Kindfulness Ambassador?

 PERSONAL CHALLENGE **Journal for Path 2**

Carry out your plan for Path 2 daily. Turn to page 295 in your journal to answer the questions about how the day went.

**Option: Use Technology to Prompt Your Kindfulness**

Your phone offers many apps and other handy tools you can use to prompt yourself to be mindful and kind. You can set notifications for 31 Days of Kindfulness or any of the activities from Path 2. For example, try setting a reminder for a time to meditate in the morning or to make brushing your teeth a mindful micropractice. Or create an alert to prompt you to take a break and stretch 3 times during the day.

# Wrapping Up

You have read about two paths designed to help you make kindfulness permanent in your life. Hopefully, you have done some of the activities from one or both of these two paths as well as activities you have created on your own. Engaging in those activities gives you a sense of the work it will take to stay on the course to lasting happiness. Over the next days and weeks and years that follow, what you say, feel, and do will let you know if you are on course, living a life of lasting happiness.

If you feel you get off track on your journey, you can always return to this workbook. Let's say your habit of anger keeps returning. You can go back and read the three chapters that deal with your unkind habits. Be sure to read how you responded to the exercises when you first went through those chapters. This reflection will show you that you are much more on track than you were the first time you went through those chapters. As you reread Chapter 9, "Get Your Unkind Habits Out of the Way," you will be reminded of ways to weaken your habit. You can also look at the table of contents to see if there are other chapters you might want to reread.

 PUT INTO **Practice**

Think about how what you do, say, or think has changed since you began working through this workbook. If you have decided to make kindfulness one of your purposes in life, write why you have made that decision.

_____

_____

_____

Make a list of the practices that you will focus on. Think about the practices that, at different times, have given you more calmness, less negative self-talk, richer relationships, and greater happiness.

_____

_____

_____

Also write what you might do if you feel out of balance and want to give your kindfulness a boost.

_____

_____

_____

_____

**Doug's Closing Comment**

Reading *Lasting Happiness* and completing the exercises provides an opportunity for making great changes in our lives. But the changes do not come quickly or easily. If they did, there would be no need for this workbook.

### Comments by two college students dealing with mental and behavioral health challenges:

Person of color: *I do think being calmer has allowed me to be more kind. It allows me to walk away from stressful situations and approach them with a clearer mind later. For example, recently one of my very close friends (call her friend A) got punched in the face at her own birthday party by another friend (call her friend B), and in the moment I was very upset and frustrated that B would do that to A. Instead of yelling at B, I comforted A with her partner and refused to speak to B until I was calmer. This took 2 weeks since we were all very upset that she refused to acknowledge her alcohol issues as being the root of her violence that night. I spoke to B with A once I was calmer, and we told her we thought she needed to seek help because what she did was wrong and hurtful. Instead of allowing my anger to take over and yell at B on the spot, I concentrated on my breathing and calmed down enough to realize that what A needed in that moment was her friends to get her ice and remove her from the room B was in, and what B needed was friends who cared about her to stage an intervention. If that makes sense.*

*While actively participating in therapy has done wonders for me over the years, I think the mindfulness approach has never been explained better to me than in* **Lasting Happiness.** *One of the methods from the workbook that I've found extremely useful in my everyday life has been counting breaths/the Three-Breath Method. I focus on my breathing more now, especially when I'm in the gym or frustrated. It has helped to keep me grounded and calm when I'm feeling overwhelmed. I've also been more of a Wise Warrior, learning to walk away more often from unkind situations so that I can address the issue respectfully at a later time. I also think that implementing meditation before bed has eased my mind a bit more.*

*Overall, what I learned about mindfulness was useful for me in particular aspects of my life. As someone who has OCD, intrusive and harmful thoughts are often never ending; however, more than actively being kind to myself and others, learning how to calm down and fight intrusive thoughts with a calmer mind has allowed me to grow a bit more as a person. In the past I've given in and acted on intrusive thoughts and behaviors, but I've found myself doing this less and less, which has allowed me to analyze and address my concerning intrusive thoughts with mental health professionals more.*

White female: *The book was helpful to me in two matters. The first matter was that it helped me to remember to practice deep breathing when I was stressed, which was valuable during COVID and especially when I returned to work in the height of the COVID era. The second matter was that it was very helpful in remembering that it's human to fail and it's human to get back up. I am not perfect and I still have areas of growth that I need to work on, but the book helped me remember that's OK, and the only thing I need to focus on is growing as a person.*

### Comments from two students of color attending an alternative high school:

*This book has helped me become a better version of myself. It helped me fix my mistakes and become a kinder person to people every day. It also helped me decrease my anxiety and stress and understand myself better through meditation.*

*I would tell anyone that if they get in a group to study* Lasting Happiness, *their life will change. This book has really helped me to be kinder and more respectful to others and to focus on not being selfish. Practicing the breath counting and meditation exercises helped me to think about my actions.*

**Comments by a young Indigenous leader:**

*Indigenous people have long believed and practiced that everything in the universe is connected in all ways, in each moment. In every moment we are one. In these moments that make up our lives, to choose to be kind to the earth, other humans, animals, and ourselves is powerful. Even if your kindness feels small, know that your moment of kindness has changed the trajectory of a moment that could have been negative, damaging to the future. With moments full of kindness comes growth, comes more kindness. Every day, every moment, you have the power to be mindful, to be and give kindness, to connect, to tune in. In each moment you have the power to honor your ancestors, your past, to shape the present, to enrich the future, to change the world.*

*These deeply rooted beliefs in Indigenous cultures can help us understand and know that every moment matters for us, for the world, and for our future generations. Bringing mindfulness and kindness to as many of our moments as we can is healthy, will bring healing to ourselves and others, and can most certainly change the future for our children.*

# END NOTES

## CHAPTER 1

1.  Murthy, V. H. (2020). *Together: The healing power of human connection in a sometimes lonely world.* Harper Wave.

2.  Aknin, L. B., Hamlin, J. K., & Dunn, E. W. (2012). Giving leads to happiness in young children. *PLoS ONE, 7*(6): e39211.

3.  Seppala, E. (2013, July 24). Compassionate mind, healthy body. *Greater Good Magazine.* Retrieved from https://greatergood.berkeley.edu/article/item/compassionate_mind_healthy_body

4.  Layous, K., Nelson, S. K., Oberle, E., Schonert-Reichl, K. A., & Lyobomirsky, S. (2012). Kindness counts: Prompting prosocial behavior in preadolescents boosts peer acceptance and well-being. *PLoS ONE, 7*(12): e51380. Retrieved from https://journals.plos.org/plosone/article?id=10.1371/journal.pone.0051380

5.  Lyobomirsky, S. (2007). *The how of happiness: A scientific approach to getting the life you want.* Penguin Press.

6.  Nelson, S. K., Layous, K., Cole, S. W., & Lyubomirsky, S. (2016). Do unto others or treat yourself? The effects of prosocial and self-focused behavior on psychological flourishing. *Emotion, 16*(6), 850–61.

## CHAPTER 2

1.  Craig, S. (2020, April 16). The Virus Diaries: Teen offers a 'list of instructions for not giving up.' *Portland Press Herald.* Retrieved from https://www.pressherald.com/2020/04/16/the-virus-diaries-teen-offers-a-list-of-instructions-for-not-giving-up/

2.  Gilbert, A. (2019, April 29). How to help teens develop patience. *Center for Parent and Teen Communication.* https://parentandteen.com/help-teens-develop-patience/

## CHAPTER 3

1.  Keltner, D. (2009). *Born to be good: The science of a meaningful life.* W. W. Norton. Learn more here: https://wwnorton.com/books/Born-to-Be-Good/

2.  Longboat, D. M. (2002). *Indigenous perspectives on death and dying, end of life care* (Module 10). University of Toronto.

3.  Bartlett, M. Y., & DeSteno, D. (2006). Gratitude and prosocial behavior: Helping when it costs you. *Psychological Science, 17*(4), 319–25

4.  Karns, C. M., Moore, W. E., & Mayr, U. (2017). The cultivation of pure altruism via gratitude: A functional MRI study of change with gratitude practice. *Frontiers of Human Neuroscience,* 12 December 2017.

5.  Emmons, R. A., & Stern. R. (2013). Gratitude as a psychotherapeutic intervention. *Journal of Clinical Psychology, 69*(8), 846–55.

6.  Zickl, D. (2019, December 9). Yes, practicing gratitude comes with legit health benefits. *Bicycling.* Retrieved from https://www.bicycling.com/news/a30083046/practicing-gratitude-boosts-physical-health/

7.  Cruz, Y. (2018, April 5). Kindness is a universal language. *Channel Kindness.* Retrieved from https://www.channelkindness.org/kindness-is-a-universal-language/

8.  Venegas, A. (2015, December 22). These Mexican women should teach a course on kindness. *Mitu.* https://wearemitu.com/mituworld/last-patronas-women-who-give-food-and-hope-to-central-american-migrants/

9.  Schreier, H. M. C., Schonert-Reichl, K. A., Chen, E. Effect of volunteering on risk factors for cardiovascular disease in adolescents: A randomized controlled trial. *JAMA Pediatrics, 167*(4), 327–332. Retrieved from https://jamanetwork.com/journals/jamapediatrics/fullarticle/1655500

10.  Konrath, S., Fuhrel-Forbis, A. R., Lou, A., & Brown, S. N. (2012). Motives for volunteering are associated with mortality risk in older adults. *Health Psychology: Official Journal of the Division of Health Psychology, American Psychological Association, 31*(1), 87–96.

**CHAPTER 4**

1. Benson, K. (2017, October 4). The magic relationship ratio, according to science. *Gottman Institute.* Retrieved from https://www.gottman.com/blog/the-magic-relationship-ratio-according-science/

2. Lyubomirsky, S., & Layous, K. (2013). *How do simple positive activities increase well-being?* 22(1), 57–62. Retrieved from https://journals.sagepub.com/doi/10.1177/0963721412469809

3. Hartig, T., Mitchell, R., de Vries, S., & Frumkin, H. (2014). Nature and health. *Annual Review of Public Health, 35*(1), 207–228. Retrieved from https://www.annualreviews.org/doi/10.1146/annurev-publhealth-032013-182443

4. Yeager, R., Riggs, D. W., DeJarnett, N., Tollerud, D. J., Wilson, J., Conklin, D. J., O'Toole, T. E., McCracken, J., Lorkiewicz, P. K., Xie, Z., Zafar, N., Krishnasamy, S. S., Srivastava, S. K., Finch, J., Keith, R. J., DeFilippis, A. P., Rai, S. N., Liu, G., & Bhatnagar, A. (2018). Association between residential greenness and cardiovascular disease risk. *Journal of the American Heart Association, 7*, e009117.

5. Williams, F. (2017). *The nature fix: Why nature makes us happier, healthier, and more creative.* W. W. Norton and Company.

6. Goldstein, P., Weissman-Fogel, I., & Shamay-Tsoory, S. G. (2017). The role of touch in regulating inter-partner physiological coupling during empathy for pain. *Scientific Reports, 7*, 3252.

**CHAPTER 5**

1. Tigar, L. (n.d.). 10 People on how they finally got into meditation, *Aaptiv.* Retrieved from https://aaptiv.com/magazine/meditation-stories

2. Gray, E. (2013, April 26). What I know about stress now that I'm in my twenties, *Huffington Post.* Retrieved from https://www.huffpost.com/entry/what-i-know-about-stress-in-my-20s_b_3165582

**CHAPTER 6**

1. Posada, T. (2018, April 27). How mindfulness changed my life: A law student's story. *Georgia State News Hub.* Retrieved from https://news.gsu.edu/2018/04/27/how-mindfulness-changed-my-life-a-law-students-story

2. Taylor, J. B. (2009). *My stroke of insight: A brain scientist's personal journey.* Penguin Books.

3. Fogg, B. J. (2021). *Tiny habits: The small changes that change everything.* Harvest.

4. Clear, J. (2018). *Atomic habits: An easy and proven way to build good habits and break bad ones.* Avery.

**CHAPTER 8**

1. Gottman, J. M., & Silver, N. (1999). *The seven principles for making marriage work.* Harmony.

2. Grant A., & Grant, A. S. (2019). Stop trying to raise successful kids. *The Atlantic,* December 2019. Retrieved from https://www.theatlantic.com/magazine/archive/2019/12/stop-trying-to-raise-successful-kids/600751/

3. Menakem, R. (2017). My grandmother's hands: Racialized trauma and the pathway to mending our hearts and bodies. *Central Recovery Press.* https://centralrecoverypress.com/product/y-grandmothers-hands-racialized-trauma-and-the-pathway-to-mending-our-hearts-and-bodies-paperback

4. Twenge, J. M. (2020, March 27). Increases in depression, self-harm, and suicide among U.S. adolescents after 2012 and links to technology use: Possible mechanisms. *Psychiatric Research and Clinical Practice.* Retrieved from https://prcp.psychiatryonline.org/doi/full/10.1176/appi.prcp.20190015

5. Haidt, J., & Twenge, J. M. (2021, July 31). This is our chance to pull teenagers out of the smartphone trap. *The New York Times.* Retrieved from https://www.nytimes.com/2021/07/31/opinion/smartphone-iphone-social-media-isolation.html/

6. MacMillan, A. (2017, May 25). Why Instagram is the worst social media for mental health. *Time.* Retrieved from https://time.com/4793331/instagram-social-media-mental-health/

7. Haidt, J., & Twenge, J. M. (2021, July 31). This is our chance to pull teenagers out of the smartphone trap. *The New York Times.* Retrieved from https://www.nytimes.com/2021/07/31/opinion/smartphone-iphone-social-media-isolation.html

8. Harrison, G. (1968). While my guitar gently weeps [Song]. Recorded by the Beatles. On *The Beatles* (the White album). Apple Records.

## CHAPTER 9

1. Su, A. J. (2015). If mindfulness makes you uncomfortable, it's working. *Harvard Business Review.* Retrieved from https://hbr.org/2015/12/if-mindfulness-makes-you-uncomfortable-its-working

2. Himelstein, S. (2016, February 22). Why mindfulness is a good skill for teens to learn. *Center for Adolescent Studies.* Retrieved from https://centerforadolescentstudies.com/why-mindfulness-is-a-good-skill-for-teens-to-learn/

3. Carnine, D. (2017). *Saint Badass: Personal transcendence in Tucker Max hell.* Mindful Kindness Project.

## CHAPTER 10

1. Rancho Santiago Community College District (n.d.). *Bystander intervention.* Author. Retrieved from https://rsccd.edu/Departments/TitleIX/Pages/Bystander-Intervention.aspx

## CHAPTER 11

1. "There's Nothing Ahead," translated by Coleman Barks in *The Essential Rumi* (2004, HarperOne).

2. Yahoo Entertainment US (2021, March 17). Dwayne Johnson praised for tackling depression and mental health on 'Young Rock.' *MSN.* Retrieved from https://www.msn.com/en-us/health/medical/dwayne-johnson-praised-for-tackling-depression-and-mental-health-on-young-rock/vi-BB1eFCCS

## CHAPTER 12

1. Morin, R. (2015, August 19). Exploring racial bias among biracial and single-race adults: The IAT. *Pew Research Center.* Retrieved from https://www.pewresearch.org/social-trends/2015/08/19/exploring-racial-bias-among-biracial-and-single-race-adults-the-iat/

2. Robert Wood Johnson Foundation. (n.d.). *Discrimination in America.* Author. Retrieved from https://www.rwjf.org/en/library/research/2017/10/discrimination-in-america-experiences-and-views.html

3. Breedlove, C. (2021, March 28). The threshold series: 1. *Medium.* Retrieved from https://caitlinbreedlove.medium.com/the-threshold-series-1-cc9fc9d5849f

4. Garuder, D. (2020, March 13). Detroit Pistons' Blake Griffin confirms $100K donation to aid event workers. *Detroit Free Press.* Retrieved from https://www.freep.com/story/sports/nba/pistons/2020/03/13/detroit-pistons-blake-griffin-donation/5047131002/

5. Williamson, Z. (2020, March 13). The people of New Orleans . . . [Post]. *Instagram.* Retrieved from https://www.instagram.com/p/B9sFV-nFTRG

6. Golden State Warriors (2020, March 13). In an effort to assist those impacted . . . [Tweet]. *Twitter.* Retrieved from https://twitter.com/warriors/status/1238642459141234689

7. Flaherty, J. (2016). *No more heroes: Grassroots challenges to the savior mentality.* AK Press.

8. Charlesworth, T. E. S., & Banaji, M. R. (2019, August 2). Research: How Americans' biases are changing (or not) over time. *Harvard Business Review.* Retrieved from https://hbr.org/2019/08/research-on-many-issues-americans-biases-are-decreasing

9. Charlesworth, T. E. S., & Banaji, M. R. (2019, August 2). Research: How Americans' biases are changing (or not) over time. *Harvard Business Review.* Retrieved from https://hbr.org/2019/08/research-on-many-issues-americans-biases-are-decreasing

10. Menakem, R. (2017). *My grandmother's hands: Racialized trauma and the pathway to mending our hearts and bodies* (p. 93). Central Recovery Press.

**CHAPTER 13**

1. Linver, M. R., Roth, J. L., & Brooks-Gunn, J. (2009). Patterns of adolescents' participation in organized activities: Are sports best when combined with other activities? *Developmental Psychology, 45*(2), 354–367.

2. Moran, S. (2009). Purpose: Giftedness in intrapersonal intelligence. *High Ability Studies, 20*(2), 143–159.

3. Lobdell, T. (2011, November 18). Getting off the treadmill. *Palo Alto Weekly.* Retrieved from https://www.paloaltoonline.com/weekly/morguepdf/2011/2011_11_18.paw.section2.pdf

4. Crespo, G. (2018, August 3). This store employee's simple gesture meant the world to a teen with autism. *CNN.* Retrieved from https://www.cnn.com/2018/07/31/health/autistic-man-stocks-shelves-trnd/index.html

5. U. S. Department of Justice, Federal Bureau of Investigation. (2010). Expanded homicide data. In *Uniform Crime Report: Crime in the United States, 2010.* Author. Retrieved from https://ucr.fbi.gov/crime-in-the-u.s/2010/crime-in-the-u.s.-2010/offenses-known-to-law-enforcement/expanded/expandhomicidemain

6. Tygielski, S. (2020, March 31). Rethinking our self-care during the pandemic. *Mindful.* Retrieved from https://www.mindful.org/rethinking-our-self-care-during-the-pandemic/

**CHAPTER 14**

1. Wilson, T. D., Reinhard, D. A., Westgate, E. C., Gilbert, D. T., Ellerbeck, N. E., Hahn, C., Brown, C. L., & Shaked, A. (2014). Just think: The challenges of the disengaged mind. *Science, 345*, 75–77.

2. Seligman, M. (2011). The original theory: Authentic happiness. *University of Pennsylvania.* Retrieved from https://www.authentichappiness.sas.upenn.edu/learn/wellbeing

3. Jabr, F. (2020, December 2). The social life of forests. *The New York Times.* Retrieved from https://www.nytimes.com/interactive/2020/12/02/magazine/tree-communication-mycorrhiza.html

4. McGowan, K. (2013, December 20). How plants secretly talk to each other. *Wired.* Retrieved from https://www.wired.com/2013/12/secret-language-of-plants

5. Grant, R. (2018, March). Do trees talk to each other? *Smithsonian Magazine.* Retrieved from https://www.smithsonianmag.com/science-nature/the-whispering-trees-180968084/

6. Roethlisberger, C. (2019, January 11). Bags to mats program turns trash into treasure for the homeless community. *Oxford Observer.* Retrieved from https://oxfordobserver.org/783/city/bags-to-mats-program-turns-trash-into-treasure/

# Lasting Happiness
# Journal

In this journal section, you will find copies of the exercises that are worked on over multiple days.

## Chapter 1   Learn About Mindful Kindness: The Key to Lasting Happiness

### Put into Practice: Counting Your Breaths *(from page 15)*

Find a quiet place where you will not be interrupted. As you take deep, slow breaths, start counting each breath silently as you exhale. Count five breaths, then start again at one. Your breaths should be deep and slow, but comfortable.

It sounds easy, but you will likely find that your mind wanders. Perhaps you'll notice that you're feeling a little hungry. You might start thinking about what you'd like to eat and make a mental note to stop for something to eat on the way home. Before you know it, you've lost count of your breaths. If this happens, don't worry! Thoughts arise naturally in the mind. Just go back to one and start counting again.

You can start your practice for 2 to 3 minutes daily then gradually increase how long you count your breaths until you're up to 4 or 5 minutes. Don't get upset if your mind wanders, just bring yourself gently back to focusing on your breathing.

For 2 weeks, write the number of minutes you devote each day to this breathing exercise.

| Start date for each week | Sunday | Monday | Tuesday | Wednesday | Thursday | Friday | Saturday |
|---|---|---|---|---|---|---|---|
| | | | | | | | |
| | | | | | | | |

### Put into Practice: Self-Assessment Goals *(from page 19)*

On pages 17–18, you put stars next to three statements that describe areas in your life that you most want to work on. Write those three statements on the lines below so that they are easy to refer back to. As you work through this workbook, you will come back to these statements and connect what we are learning to the goals that you have identified for yourself.

1. _____
2. _____
3. _____

## Chapter 2   Check Your Foundation

### Put into Practice *(from page 26)*

Continue counting your breaths daily as you did earlier. When a distracting thought arises, notice it, then let it go and return to counting. Do this for 2 to 3 minutes. After 3 days, write about the experience on the lines below. Tell if counting your breaths cut out some of your distracting, possibly unpleasant thoughts?

_____

_____

## Put into Practice

*(from page 30)*

For 3 days make a to-do list of things you need to get done. Include the date by which the activity must be done. Check off things when they are done. Write about how you felt after completing all the activities on your list.

---

---

## Chapter 3    Expand Your Idea of Kindness

## Put into Practice: Mindful Breathing

*(from page 47)*

Continue practicing breathing, but instead of counting your breaths, pay attention to the physical sensations—the movement of your chest and abdomen as you inhale and exhale. We'll call this mindful breathing. Without counting, you may notice more negative thoughts. Don't give in to distractions; just return your attention to the physical sensations of your breathing. If it helps, put a hand on your chest and abdomen so you literally feel the inhaling and exhaling.

Do this new mindful breathing exercise two times a day for 2 to 3 minutes for 5 days, then write about the effect of this breathing exercise on how you feel.

---

---

Continue practicing this mindful breathing exercise daily after those 5 days.

## Chapter 4    Increase Your Kindness

## Personal Challenge

*(from page 72)*

You made a list of habits that are both pleasant and important. For 5 days, every time you engaged in one of those kind habits, you made a tally mark next to it.

Now write about how you feel after engaging in your pleasant and important kind habits for the 5 days. (Continue to review your list even after you stop making tally marks.)

---

---

---

---

## Personal Challenge

(from page 74)

Have a conversation in which you communicate with vulnerability, sharing one of your regrets, worries, or fears. Describe what happened during this conversation. Tell how the other person responded.

_____

_____

_____

How did you feel after sharing?

_____

Explain how being vulnerable and sharing may improve the relationship.

_____

_____

## Kindness Plan

(from page 84)

**Write your kindness plan by answering these questions:**

1.  What is the kind habit you have chosen to develop? _____

    _____

2.  How are you hoping to help others by strengthening this habit (or engaging in this activity)?

    _____

    _____

    _____

3.  Who will you ask for support, if anyone? What kind of support will you ask for? _____

    _____

    _____

    _____

4.  What Diligent Detective work will you need to do, if any? _____

    _____

    _____

5.  How, if at all, will you use the mind of the Wise Warrior? _____

    _____

    _____

6. What Skills of Character (growth, mindset, responsible, patient, and humble) will you need most?

_____

_____

7. What action will you take to build the kind habit in your mental world? _____

_____

_____

8. What action will you take in your physical world? _____

_____

_____

**After working on your plan for several days, look back at it and respond to these follow-up questions:**

1. What happened as you tried to implement your kindness plan?

_____

_____

_____

_____

2. How did you feel as you implemented your kindness plan?

_____

_____

3. What adjustment, if any, did you make?

_____

_____

_____

4. What adjustment will you need to make next?

_____

_____

_____

## Kindness Plan Modifications To Make When You Are Working on Chapter 6

On pages 280–281 is the kindness plan you created when reading Chapter 4. Read over the plan and think about how it is working for you.

If you have made progress with your plan, has strengthening your kind habit benefited you? For example, has it helped strengthen your connection with others or given you a sense of accomplishment? If so, write about those feelings and any other positive feelings you have experienced in acting with more kindness.

_____

_____

_____

If you are having trouble with the plan, be a Diligent Detective: What do you think may be causing the trouble? Is it fear? Frustration? An erratic schedule? Is your goal not small enough? Are you acting in a way that usually keeps you from being successful when you want to learn something new?

_____

_____

_____

If you are having difficulty with your plan, either change the plan, making the plan simpler, or make a new, easier plan by beginning with smaller steps. Below are the questions from Chapter 4 that you used to create your plan. Use them to modify your existing plan or make a new plan.

1. What is the kind habit you have chosen to develop? _____

2. How are you hoping to help others by strengthening this habit (or engaging in this activity)?

   _____

   _____

3. Who will you ask for support, if anyone? What kind of support will you ask for?

   _____

   _____

4. What detective work will you need to do, if any?

   _____

   _____

5. How, if at all, will you use the mind of the Wise Warrior?

   _____

   _____

6. What Skills of Character (growth mindset, responsible, patient, humble) will you need most?

   _____

7. What action will you take to build the kind habit in your mental world?

   _____

   _____

8. What action will you take in your physical world?

   _____

   _____

## Chapter 5    Train Your Mind with Meditation and the Three-Breath Method

## Put into Practice: Mindful Listening                         *(from page 90)*

Find a piece of music you love and listen to it while reading a book and eating at the same time. Next, listen to the same piece of music, but without reading or eating. Close your eyes and focus deeply on the music. Write about how your awareness was affected when you directed all your attention to listening. Did you feel more connected to the music, less distracted by thoughts and emotions unrelated to the music?

_____

_____

_____

## Put into Practice: Embracing Kindness Meditation, Part 1      *(from page 92)*

Practice Embracing Kindness Meditation for several days, then describe what went well and what did not go well. Also, describe your feelings toward yourself and the world around you.

What went well? _____

What did not go well? _____

Describe your feelings: _____

_____

## Put into Practice: Embracing Kindness Meditation, Part 2 *(from page 93)*

After 3 days of practicing Embracing Kindness Meditation for yourself and for those close to you, describe what went well and what did not go well. How did you feel when this practice went well?

Describe what went well and what did not go well. _____

_____

Describe how you felt when it went well. _____

_____

## Put into Practice: Wordless Meditation *(from page 95)*

Once you feel comfortable with your Embracing Kindness Meditation, try Wordless Meditation. Start small—5 minutes is good. Gradually increase the length of your meditation sessions over the coming days.

    After a week, write about what went well with your meditation.

_____

_____

_____

## Put into Practice *(from page 96)*

Choose one of the forms of meditation you have learned (such as Embracing Kindness, guided, or wordless meditation) and continue your practice. Make a schedule for what time and for how long you meditate in the morning (and possibly in the evening as well).

_____

_____

Use an app or paper and pencil to indicate how long you actually sit each time. After 5 days describe what went well and what did not go well. Also, describe how meditating made you feel.

_____

_____

_____

## Put into Practice: The Three-Breath Method During Meditation *(from page 96)*

For the next 3 times that you meditate, notice when you are distracted by self-talk and each time use the Three-Breath Method to regain your focus, taking three deeper, slower breaths. After using the Three-Breath Method for several days, describe how you felt using the Three-Breath Method in your attempt to shift away from your distractions.

_____

_____

**Put into Practice: The Three-Breath Method Outside Meditation**      *(from page 99)*

Set a goal for how often you will use the Three-Breath Method during the day, outside meditation. Write your goal.

_____

Use an app or paper and pencil to count how many times you actually use the Three-Breath Method. At the end of 5 days describe what went well and what did not go well.

_____

_____

_____

_____

Describe how using the Three-Breath Method made you feel.

_____

## Chapter 6    Practicing Mindfulness with Sensations and Emotions

## Put into Practice                                              *(from pages 103–104)*

Practicing sensing mindfulness during times of low stress prepares us to use sensing mindfulness when we are under stress. In this exercise you picked one of these two practices—sensing mindfulness while eating or sensing mindfulness while working out.

   After completing the sensing mindfulness exercise you chose to do, write about your experience.

_____

_____

_____

## Put into Practice                                              *(from page 104)*

You chose something that typically makes you nervous. The next time you were in that situation, you practiced sensing mindfulness (intentional noticing of sensations) just before you did the activity.

   Write about if and how your feelings changed when you shifted your attention to noticing the world around you instead of thinking about the activity that makes you nervous.

_____

_____

## Put into Practice: Soft-eyes

(from page 107)

Practice sensing mindfulness with soft-eyes next time you're taking an easy walk or sitting outdoors. Direct your vision to an object in front of you. Then expand your vision in both directions so you are including your peripheral vision.

Write about the experience (including your feelings). Note if you sense a feeling of being interwoven and connected with everything around you.

_____

_____

## Put into Practice: Sharp-eyes

(from page 108)

You tried engaging sharp-eyes in a variety of places or situations. Write about the experience, including what you focused on and the degree to which you experienced a slight energy boost, quiet joy, and calm. Did a sense of concentration, a feeling of connection, or other feelings arise when you used sharp-eyes? (You can also experiment with alternating sharp-eyes and soft-eyes).

_____

_____

## Put into Practice: Soft-ears

(from page 109)

Experiment with soft-ears in a place where you are on your own, but surrounded by people. Describe what you heard, felt in your body, and any times of contentment. Or make a drawing in the back of the work-book that represents the variations in your experience.

_____

_____

## Put into Practice: Soft-contact

(from page 110)

Try practicing soft-contact during different activities throughout the day. Write about the experience, including your feelings.

_____

_____

## Put into Practice: Soft-taste *(from page 111)*

You selected two foods to eat, focusing completely on chewing your food and then on swallowing—not taking the next bite until you finished swallowing the food in your mouth. After 3 days, write about what you noticed when you intentionally shift your attention from taste, to texture, to chewing, and to swallowing for each of two different foods.

---
---

## Personal Challenge *(from page 112)*

Choose two of the five grounding techniques (soft-eyes, sharp-eyes, soft-ears, soft-contact, and soft-taste) and alternate between them several times in a day. Do this for 3 days, then write about the experience of going back and forth from one technique to the other. Is using sensing mindfulness and grounding techniques calming you and making it easier to be kinder?

---
---

## Put into Practice *(from page 117)*

Think about ways you can take a sensing mindfulness break for one minute or less during the day. Start by taking a short sensing mindfulness break at least once a day. If possible, work up to doing it multiple times a day for 3 days. After 3 days, write about the experiences, including feelings such as connection and/or spaciousness.

---
---

## Put into Practice *(from page 117)*

Choose one of the forms of meditation you learned about in Chapter 5, Embracing Kindness: Guided or Wordless Meditation. Make a schedule for what time and for how long you will meditate in the morning (and possibly in the evening as well). Use an app or paper and pencil to indicate how long you actually sit each time. After 5 days, describe what went well and what did not go well. Also describe how meditating made you feel.

---
---
---

## Micropractice Exercise 1            *(from page 122)*

Use sensing mindfulness (smell, sound, touch, taste, sight) on a specific household chore 3 days in a row. At the end of the 3 days, answer these questions.

1. Did using sensing mindfulness improve how you felt about doing the chore, and were you able to keep focused without being distracted by negative thoughts?

   _____

2. If not, what thoughts/emotions distracted you and how did you get yourself back on track?

   _____

## Micropractice Exercise 2            *(from page 123)*

Use sensing mindfulness when doing a personal hygiene activity. Did using sensing mindfulness during this personal hygiene activity give your mind a rest? Describe your feelings.

_____

_____

## Micropractice Exercise 3            *(from page 123)*

Take a few minutes to look—really look—around where you live or work. Choose something to organize. As in other practices, pay attention to your senses. Describe how you felt once you organized your surroundings.

_____

_____

## Put into Practice            *(from page 124)*

If you are still attending school, consider organizing your schoolwork, electronically or by creating folders with sections for each subject area. Put your notes in order so they become easier to study. Create a task list for all of your assignments so you know when your due dates and tests are.

Describe how you organized your schoolwork.

_____

_____

Does the organization reduce your stress? How does it feel to know when things are due?

_____

Does being organized in advance reduce procrastination and increase your sense of calm?

_____

## Micropractice Exercise 4 *(from page 125)*

You put your weekly activities and appointments on a calendar. The schedule/list included assignments for school or work, meetings to attend, cultural events, gym workouts, self-care, and chores. It could also include reminders to call people you want to keep in touch with.

Post this calendar with dates and times where you can see it each day. Or put the activities on your phone calendar or your reminder app. Crossing off each completed task can be very satisfying.

Describe what happens and how you feel as a consequence of making and following a realistic schedule and to-do list.

_____

_____

_____

## Micropractice Exercise 5 *(from page 126)*

Think about a way you are often noisy and try instead to be as quiet as possible when doing that activity. Practice this quiet activity for 3 days, then write responses to these questions.

How did it feel to be quiet?

_____

Was your quiet noticed or appreciated by others?

_____

Or draw a picture of how it felt to be quiet. Consider colors or symbols that depict your sense of quiet.

**Chapter 10   Responding to the Unkind Habits of Others**

## Creating Your Own In-Depth Plan for Weakening an Unkind Habit   *(from page 190)*

You can revise the plan to weaken an unkind habit you created in Chapter 9, or you can create a new plan. To revise your plan or create a new one to weaken an unkind habit, write your answers to these questions.

**Steps in My Plan to Weaken an Unkind Habit**

1.  Select and describe the unkind habit.

    • What is the unkind habit I chose to work on? _____

    • How do I feel after I carry out the unkind habit? _____

    • Who is harmed by my unkind habit? _____

2.  Decide whether to focus first on your mental world or your physical world.

    • What goes on in my mental world that is linked to this habit?

    _____

    _____

    • How does the habit show itself in the physical world?

    _____

    _____

3.  Describe the activator for the unkind habit. Is it in my mental world or physical world?

    _____

    _____

    _____

4.  Describe how you will prevent the unkind habit by acting early.

    • What Diligent Detective work (gathering of information, research) do I need to do?

    _____

    _____

    • What foundational skills of character (growth mindset, responsible, patient, and humble) will I need most?

    _____

- Who will I ask for support, if anyone? _____
- What action will I take to stop the unkind habit in my mental world?

  _____

  _____

- What action will I take in my physical world?

  _____

  _____

5. If you cannot stop the unkind habit, describe how you will replace it with something neutral or positive.

   _____

   _____

   _____

**Follow-Up on Your Plan: One Week After**
One week after you put your plan into action, answer the questions below.

1. What happened as you tried to implement your plan to break an unkind habit?

   _____

   _____

   _____

2. What adjustment, if any, did you make or will you make in your plan?

   _____

   _____

   _____

3. How did you feel as you implemented your plan?

   _____

   _____

   _____

## Chapter 11   Kindful Options for Hard Times

### Put into Practice

*(from page 203)*

Spend 3 days working on one of the following four ways to deepen your mindfulness practice: 1) intensify your practice of the Three-Breath Method, 2) rotate through your grounding techniques, 3) reduce your fears about the future, or 4) practice visualization and body movement.

At the end of 3 days, answer these questions.

1.  What went well? _____

_____

2.  Were some days better than others? Why do you think that might be? _____

_____

3.  What frustrated you, if anything? _____

_____

### Put into Practice

*(from page 207)*

Pick one of the kindful options you want to turn into a habit and, for 3 days, work on making it a kind habit (or better yet a pleasant kind habit!). Write about that experience.

_____

_____

_____

## Chapter 12   Extend the Reach of Your Kindfulness

### Put into Practice

*(from page 221)*

Find volunteering opportunities that may bring you into contact with people of different backgrounds. Pick the possibility that most appeals to you. Write about why you picked this volunteer possibility.

_____

_____

_____

## Put into Practice
(from page 225)

Within the next week, name the book, article, talk or other activity you will be learning from to develop empathy about a group you are biased against, and tell why you selected this way to learn.

_____

_____

## Put into Practice
(from page 227)

Within the next week, describe how you are going to activate your kindness toward members of a group you are biased against by doing one or more of the following: be friendly, show appreciation, give help.

_____

_____

_____

## Put into Practice
(from page 231)

For the next 3 days, try to notice when you are having any biased reactions. Make a note on your phone or on a piece of paper when you have a split-second biased reaction.

Describe a few of the biased thoughts and write about whether you think those are implicit biases you have.

_____

_____

_____

Indicate if you added negative thoughts to feed the bias or acted in an unkind way because of the bias.

_____

_____

## Put into Practice
from page 232)

Pick a group toward which you have implicit bias. Identify an individual in that group and include that person in your positive thoughts through several Embracing Kindness Meditation sessions. After 3 sessions, answer these questions.

What phrases did you use in your meditation?

_____

_____

How did it feel to include that person in your meditation?

_____

## Chapter 13   "Right Now" Is All We Have: Make the Present Moment Kindful

### Put into Practice
(from page 249)

Practice slow walking with sensing mindfulness several times, then try to use it at times when you feel agitated over the next week. Write about or reflect on what happened (including your feelings) with both your mental and physical balance as you did the mindful walking.

_____

_____

### Put into Practice
(from page 251)

You identified an important problem with a relationship that you have not fixed. You also described the actions you could take to resolve that problem.

 Have you taken action to solve the problem? If so, describe the actions you actually took to solve the problem.

_____

_____

Describe how you felt after taking that action.

_____

## Chapter 14   Do You Want to be a Kindfulness Ambassador?

### Personal Challenge
(from page 258)

Meet with your friend and explain the importance of kindfulness. Write about how your friend responded to your explanation.

_____

Write about how you felt about the conversation with your friend.

_____

### Personal Challenge
(from online bonus content, Chapter 14, page 3)

If you can, host the kindness get-together and write what happened.

_____

_____

## Chapter 15   Make Kindfulness a Permanent Part of Your Life

# Personal Challenge: Path 2 *(from page 269)*

Make at least 10 copies of this page. Answer the questions on the page each day for 2 weeks or longer to tell how kindful you were each day.

Day of week _____   Date _____

A.  Write the answers to these questions.

How kind was I to others?

_____

What went well when I tried to be kind? Why?

_____

_____

What did not go well? Why?

_____

_____

What might I do differently in the future?

_____

B.  How kind was I to myself today?

_____

C.  Did I meditate in the morning and in the evening? How did the meditation sessions make me feel?

_____

D.  What is one thing I am grateful for today?

_____

E.  What is one thing I did well today?

_____

F.  (At the end of each week) How can I extend the reach of my kindness to someone who is subject to bias?

_____

_____

# Professionals who work with youth talk about *Lasting Happiness*

*This book enables teens to 30-year-olds to choose a life of personal responsibility through following practices such as mindfulness and learning how to transform unkindness (anxiety, depression, and anger) to being kind to oneself and others. A step-by-step process will be revealed for discovering and living out a life of compassion and joy, full of meaning and purpose.*

*Whether you are a youth striving to navigate the whitewater of adolescence or a young adult seeking to complete the journey into settled adulthood, this unique and highly practical book has much to offer, providing the understanding and the tools to become a more mindfully and more consistently kind member of our social networks and our larger community by serving others and finding common ground with those we might have previously overlooked or marginalized.*

**Dr. Stan Paine, Former National Distinguished Principal**

*This book is a beautiful and empowering tool to help young people understand and extend compassion, mindfulness, and kindness toward themselves and others. In a time of life where youth are dealing with anxiety, depression, bullying, and stress, this book offers them thoughtful insights and immediately applicable practices to improve their well-being and make a difference in their families, friend groups, and communities.*

**River Aaland, After and Out of School Program Coordinator. Ophelia's Place, "helping girls make healthy life choices through empowerment, education, and support"**

*From my perspective as an addiction counselor, I appreciate the focus on kindness toward self as well as others and its use of mindfulness as a tool to help clients create a state of mind that is conducive to growth.*

**Ira Hausman, Drug and Alcohol Counselor**

*As someone who has worked with adolescents for over 15 years, this book offers a different approach in supporting our youth. Lasting Happiness: A Guide for Teens and Young Adults shares anecdotes that young people can relate to, provides practical steps to becoming more mindful and kinder, and allows the reader the opportunity to self-reflect and self-actualize. From a counseling perspective, this workbook could be utilized in individual or group settings as well as allowing the person to engage in the work on their own. In viewing schools as a community, these lessons have the potential to improve on how we treat each other, promote understanding and acceptance, and build on an interconnectedness among people.*

**Morgan Davis, High School Counselor, Former Field Instructor/Wilderness Therapy Program Activities Coordinator/facility for adjudicated youth**

*This workbook is just the tool needed for this generation to define themselves with positive new habits. The writing style is engaging while meeting the needs of an active and fast-paced teen who is geared to expect a quick result, giving them the ability to amplify satisfaction in their lives by learning and implementing simple techniques.*

**Jody Bothe, College Admission Coach**

## Facilitators who have used the *Lasting Happiness* curriculum to teach kindness groups describe their experiences

*At first, when we were told that we were going to run groups, I was hesitant because I thought it was going to be a waste of time for me and the students. I just thought that students were going to join only for the money. I realized that was not true. The students in my group have benefited from each other. They learned how to respect and listen to each other. They found out that they had many things in common. They took care of each other. I've learned so much from them: how they feel, how they think, and how they have survived. They have taught me how to be more empathetic and stronger. Both the students and I look forward to group meetings each week. Every week is something different and exciting.*

**Michael Rodriguez, MSW, Emotional Wellness Counselor, New Beginnings High School**

*Running the groups has been a blessing. It has helped me to see ways that I was not aware of, how I was being unkind to myself as well as unkind to others. Even as a counselor there are still things that I can learn, and I have been able to put into practice the skills taught in the program. I've learned from my students how we all can do more to be kind to others, and some of them are just simple things. The group has been such an inspiring thing to me, and the takeaway is I'm going to try to be more kind daily. It is something you need to practice each day and then try to teach to others.*

**Lucretia Woods, M.S., Mental Health Counselor**

*As a facilitator, it was definitely an amazing experience engaging the students in discussions with the other students, incorporating some hands-on guided imagery, helping to bring things into perspective for them. The curriculum has allowed them to see the bigger picture and how they can now apply it to their daily lives. The biggest thing I've really benefited from personally are the mindfulness practices. It's so important for us to be aware and present, to be whole and in tune with what's going on around us, and this book really helped me to better understand that. The mindfulness practices are also what's really going to help me as a counselor and educator to continue being happy in doing what I do on a daily basis. The book provides the key lessons and skills that will help us to understand what lasting happiness is and how to achieve it in our lives.*

**Maurice Donaldson, M.S., Mental Health Counselor**

*I think that our students are loving their experience in the kindness curriculum: learning about yourself, learning about the meaning of true happiness and what really makes us happy. I think the students have benefited from it. I see it in their actions, their attitudes, the way they stop and think when they're in the heat of things. I see the skills becoming part of their everyday interactions with each other.*

Kim Cage-Mbuyumba, M.S., Director of Academic Programs, New Beginnings High School

## Youth describe how the book has changed their lives

*This book has helped me become a better version of myself. It helped me fix my mistakes and become a kinder person to people every day. It also helped me decrease my anxiety and stress and understand myself better through meditation.*

Xavier G.

*This book is amazing in general. Coming into my life when it did was a blessing from God. I have been going through a lot lately, and the book has really opened my eyes to see how toxic and selfish I have been towards the people I love, as well as myself. I realize now that to love other people, I have to also love myself. I am truly grateful for all the examples and practice activities that have allowed me to open up about my past and to let go of my anger.*

Joshlyn W.

Lasting Happiness *has taught me the importance of being kind to myself and not allowing others to take advantage of me. I learned breathing and meditation techniques that help me reduce my anxiety and stress levels, and I am able to experience more happiness as a result.*

Taylor B.

*This book was very enlightening. The meditation exercises helped me to get up on the "right side of the bed" every morning. Anyone could benefit from the skills taught in this book.*

Craig C.

## Youth describe their experience participating in study groups reading
### *Lasting Happiness: A Guide for Teens and Young Adults*

*I really enjoy going to the kindness groups because they have made a huge positive impact on my life and I feel like they have shaped me to be a better person. I have actually used a lot of the techniques I learned in the group in many different aspects of my life. For example, the Three-Breath Method . . . . I would get angry a lot, I used to let people affect how I felt, but since being in the group I learned I can just take a step back, take three slow breaths, and then it's OK. I can let it go.*

**Kaylee P.**

*I would tell anyone that if they get in a group to study* Lasting Happiness, *their life will change. This book has really helped me to be kinder and more respectful to others and to focus on not being selfish. Practicing the breath counting and meditation exercises helped me to think about my actions.*

**Rodshaun S.**